BEYOND
THE
CHINDWIN

*Being an Account of the Adventures of
Number Five Column of the Wingate
Expedition into Burma, 1943*

by
BERNARD FERGUSSON

Pen & Sword
MILITARY

First published by William Collins and Sons Ltd. in 1945

Republished in this format in 2009 by
Pen & Sword Military
An imprint of
Pen & Sword Books Ltd
47 Church Street
Barnsley
South Yorkshire
S70 2AS

Copyright © Bernard Fergusson, 1945, 2009

ISBN 978 184884 037 9

A CIP catalogue record for this book is
available from the British Library

Printed and bound in England
By CPI

Pen & Sword Books Ltd incorporates the Imprints of Pen & Sword
Aviation,
Pen & Sword Family History, Pen & Sword Maritime, Pen & Sword
Military, Wharncliffe Local History,
Pen & Sword Select, Pen & Sword Military Classics, Leo Cooper,
Remember When, Seaforth Publishing and Frontline Publishing

For a complete list of Pen & Sword titles please contact
PEN & SWORD BOOKS LIMITED
47 Church Street, Barnsley, South Yorkshire, S70 2AS, England
E-mail: enquiries@pen-and-sword.co.uk
Website: www.pen-and-sword.co.uk

To
DUNCAN CAMBPELL MENZIES, M.C.

Lieutenant, The Black Watch,
Rhodes Scholar of Balliol College, Oxford
Shot by the Japanese
whilst a prisoner in their hands
at Zibyugin, Burma,
4th April, 1943

'More brave for this, that he hath much to love'

CONTENTS

CONTENTS

Part Two

EMERGENCY EXIT

CONTENTS

LIST OF MAPS

FOREWORD

I HAD no small share of responsibility for the adventures of Five Column and the rest of Wingate's Force in 1943, in that the formation of the Force and its dispatch into North Burma depended on my decision; and I feel a certain responsibility also for the military training and career of the author of this narrative. So it is perhaps appropriate that I should write a few words of introduction.

Bernard Fergusson was my first A.D.C. I remember well our earliest meeting when he came over to see me on approval. After an hour or two's acquaintance, we decided to give one another a trial, and our parting sentences were, I recall: "You know, sir, I've never been an A.D.C. before, I may make an awful mess of it."

"Well, I've never had an A.D.C. before, I may make an awful mess of you."

(My next candidate for A.D.C.-ship, a cavalry subaltern, two years later, was less diffident; he merely inquired how many loose-boxes were available for his horses and whether he could hunt three days a week.)

Inevitably, Peter Dorans came with Bernard; I was conscious always of his sedulous care for his own officer, and of his caustic eye towards the rest of my staff. Of one senior member of it—now a high-ranking general—who used in camp to do physical exercises in the morning just outside his tent, next to mine, Dorans was heard to observe sardonically: "See yon feller doing his exercises in front of the general's tent—just sweating on promotion, I call it."

Even in that home of orthodox soldiering, Aldershot, I did something to instil into Bernard notions of unorthodox soldiering. He will remember a guerilla-minded subaltern whom I sent to raid the rear of the opposing force during an exercise, to the confusion both of the enemy and of the umpires (that same subaltern in this war was decorated for leading a Long Range patrol in

North Africa and later lost his life in a similar adventure); and how we often discussed training on Moss-trooper lines.

For a time after this, the wagon of his military career ran on entirely orthodox rails; he was an instructor at Sandhurst, a student at the Staff College, all inside the sealed-pattern box of the Aldershot Command. But I felt that the leaven of unorthodoxy was working still, and that the cross-country jeep (then unknown, of course) was really his vehicle.

We began to serve together again a few years later; he was a junior Intelligence officer in Palestine when I commanded there (Orde Wingate held a senior post in my Intelligence); a liaison officer with the Turks in my Middle East command; my forward observation officer with the Free French during the Syrian campaign in 1941; a regimental officer in Tobruk. He returned to "snob" posts for a while, was my Personal Secretary for a short time when I was Commander-in-Chief in India, and then a Planner at G.H.Q. But when he joined Wingate's Brigade in the autumn of 1942, I felt he had reached his real heart's desire. This book shows it and how he took the opportunity to prove himself a fit leader of cross-border raiders—qualified by reiver tradition and by study. He told me once that Robert the Bruce had practised dispersal of columns on the same lines as Wingate—he had found this in the works of an ancient Scottish poet called Barbour.

He has drawn a parallel in this book between jungle and sea navigation. Bernard was an enthusiastic yachtsman while he was my A.D.C. When he went off for a week-end's yachting—"just a quiet sail and back on Sunday evening, sir"—I wrote him off, after a short experience, till Tuesday afternoon at least, since the sandbanks on the East Coast seemed to be numerous, well camouflaged and tenacious. I was, however, never unduly anxious about his return, since I had early decided that his capacity for nautical survival was great. I think this narrative confirms that his tendency to encounter sandbanks and his survival capacity extended also to the jungle. And surely no one and no book has better illustrated the real basis of the survival capacity of the British—an indomitable sense of humour.

Of the expedition itself, I would say these few words. It was not designed as a mere unsupported foray. When I first sanctioned Wingate's proposals and gave him a brigade to train, we both intended that it should be used as part of a grand design for the recapture of Burma. It soon became obvious that the resources for this would not be available for a long time to come. But early in 1943 there was a project for action in Northern Burma; I decided to employ Wingate's brigade in this and dispatched it to Manipur. Just as the force was on the point of starting into Burma, I became aware that the operations which Wingate's force was intended to assist could not take place. I flew up to Manipur and had a long discussion with Wingate whether in these circumstances the raid should take place at all, since it now served no strategical purpose, and the Japanese would be free to concentrate against it. He convinced me that the chances of getting the brigade through and of extricating it again were good, and that the experience to be gained would be invaluable and well worth the risk. There is no doubt too that cancellation would have been a bitter disappointment to troops keyed up to the pitch of action by months of training.

Of Wingate himself, their great leader, I have written elsewhere. I have better cause than any one to recognise his genius, and to be grateful for it. No really great man is easy to serve and he was a stern task-master, as this book shows. But all those worth their salt would rather attempt hard tasks under a great man than serve at ease under a lesser.

I hope that this book of high endeavour and gallant endurance will be widely read, and that it will be in the minds of the readers, what I know the author has intended it to be, a tribute to the valour, comradeship and good-humoured sufferance of the British soldier; or rather, as here, of the ordinary British citizen serving as a soldier at his country's need. These men of Five Column were not specially picked dare-devils who had volunteered for a hazardous enterprise in the love of fighting or in the hope of glory, but mostly men of an ordinary line battalion, sent originally to India for garrison duty. Yet as a tale of toughness and good comradeship in adversity their story will be hard to beat. And there is in the endurance and fellowship of the British soldier an abiding quality of humour and almost of tenderness that is not found in the fighting men of any other race, and has made that race indestructible.

Be it noted too, that though we had last passed through Northern Burma in defeat, though the land had been under Japanese occupation and propaganda for a year, though our victory was still uncertain, we found more friends and helpers than did our enemies.

WAVELL, F. M.

PROLOGUE

To THOSE who took part in it, the Wingate Expedition was a watershed in their lives. Before it, one's appreciation of values was only half developed. Now we have new standards and new touchstones. In my case, at least, things I had previously taken for granted I can now appraise and value in a truer perspective— diverse things, ranging from the human character to water supply, from a cup of tea to food and shelter. I learned how much of what we think to be necessary is superfluous; I learned how few things are essential, and how essential those things really are. I had never before known hunger or thirst in the sense that I know them now; nor appreciated the vital differences between day and night, moonlight and starlight. I had always before supposed that to be cooped up for a long time with the same people meant to quarrel with them. I had supposed that after a long period of strain one would see people at their worst and best, but I had never guessed how, when all the layers are stripped off one by one, far more people are basically good than bad. I did not know how closely linked food and morale really are. I did not know what it was to be hunted, nor the marvellous relief of deliverance.

All these things I now know, and so do my companions. I hope I shall not forget them. Although it is over a year since the adventure came to its end, I have lived in its atmosphere ever since, and recaptured it (in recollection only) in a subsequent expedition which has just finished, and in which we turned the lessons of the watershed to good account. During that period, in the long marching stages, I often took the weight of my pack from off my mind by planning this book.

Here it begins. It is not a history of the Wingate Expedition, but only of No. 5 Column, which I commanded; with such account of the other columns as was known to us at the time, and in so far as they affected our own adventures. At the end, I shall add things which became known to us afterwards; but I invite the reader to try and reflect in his own mind our situation at each given moment, and, like us, to make these discoveries after he has finished the experience of the campaign. I shall leave to the end, also, my appreciation of Wingate himself, and of all that he meant to us.

I joined the expedition to exorcise the thought that I had spent almost all the war in safe places. The feeling of expiation was present all the time. The experience itself was exhilarating. I do not think anybody guessed, unless it was Wingate himself, that it would ever attract attention in the outside world; and all of us were dismayed (I would again except Wingate, because he saw how it would help him forward his ideas) by the vulgar publicity which rose about it like a stench. I want to rescue my own impressions from the morass of tall stories which have been in circulation.

I was much comforted this year by a letter from a Highland friend* in which he said that he looked upon our expeditions as being in the tradition of Montrose; "and at the end," he added "Inverlochy." Inverlochy is not yet, but it will come; and this expedition was, I like to think, the first tentative, ill-found, rather forlorn, but wholly worthwhile foray.

* In 1944, from Brigadier Ian Stewart of Achnacone.

Part One

GRAND ENTRANCE

CHAPTER ONE

FROM DELHI TO MALTHONE:

April—October, 1942

"But here it dwells, and here must I
With danger seek it forth:
To spend the time luxuriously
Becomes not men of worth."
DANIEL.

THE ROOM where we worked in Delhi was covered in maps of Burma. They papered the walls in untidy tapestry; they filled the drawers so that they would not shut; they littered the tables and gathered dust. The recapture of Burma was the subject which filled our days. Innumerable papers, completed and filed away, or in draft, were our constant companions. Once written, they were submitted to higher authority, cut about, re-written, cut about again, and finally reduced to a state of emasculate acceptability, when they joined their forerunners in the steel cabinets, and were succeeded on the stocks by new ones.

The room was the home of the Joint Planning Staff; we, its inhabitants, were a mixture of soldiers, sailors and airmen, with one lonely civilian. The reconquest of Burma was our invariable study. When I began work there, our army in Burma was still withdrawing towards Kalewa on the long hard trek to Tamu, Imphal and the dubious safety of Assam; for at that time there was no telling how far the Japs were willing or able to follow up. My own regiment, fresh from being relieved in Tobruk, had hurried from Syria to reach Rangoon before it fell; but it had arrived at Bombay too late to do anything but start training in India. I, by virtue of some slight planning experience in the Middle East, had been shanghaied into the new-born J.P.S.

Already General Wavell had ordered us to examine the problem of the reconquest, even though the successful withdrawal of the army from Burma was still somewhat in doubt. Mandalay was in process of being evacuated; army and civilians were pouring through Kalewa, the last recognised route to India, like water out of a bath—but uphill; new or hazily remembered routes, such as Indaw-Homalin, the Hukawng Valley, the Chaukkan Pass, were being spoken of as possible alternatives, since a wedge of Japanese had already driven between Mandalay and the one sure route via Kalewa.

Maurice Wright, the Liaison Officer between G.H.Q. and the Burma Army, appeared now and then, to be assailed with questions as to how things were going. People with knowledge of Upper Burma were being sought for, for advice about alternative routes. Calculations were being made as to when the army would be clear of Kalewa, and how much food must be ferried to Imphal, and how much to Tamu. General Wood was appointed "Admingen" with plenary powers over Assam. On the far bank of the Chindwin, Tyrwhitt Wheeler was throwing valises into the river to reduce transport, and the 7th Hussars were breaking open cases of Scotch whisky with a hatchet, so that whoever went thirsty the Japs should not get a drink. Women and children were hurrying north from aerodrome to aerodrome, a few being evacuated at each before the Japs got too near, and the rest were obliged to renew their flight. General Stilwell and his party were splashing through the Chaunggyi. Up in Myitkyina one Captain John Fraser of the Burma Rifles, suddenly and surprisingly appointed Station Staff Officer, was receiving the first refugees and preparing to evacuate them by air. Somewhere in Central Burma Colonel Wingate was hastily finding out all he could about the country. And in Delhi we were planning the reoccupation.

As the month of May, 1942, wore on, the army reached Kalewa

intact and in good order. Thousands of refugees had reached the Imphal plain, but thousands more were still struggling with dwindling hopes along other routes; and very many died. The Hukawng Valley was the easiest of these, but desperately hard for the hundreds of women and children and old men, straight from easy lives and comfortable homes, whose last hope it was. Aircraft, making many sorties a day, were hauling out hundreds from Myitkyina, and the numbers awaiting evacuation there were fast dwindling. The Japanese pursuit to Tamu had slackened, but their drive north was still swift and relentless. As the entrances to the Hukawng Valley route became closed each in their turn, Fort Hertz, up a long cul-de-sac among the mountains, became the last hope for those who could not reach Myitkyina before the aircraft stopped running.

One more pass was known to exist from the far north into Assam: the Chaukkan. Nobody knew much about it; it had been thrice traversed in history, once in the eighties and twice in recent years, but never in the monsoon. It might, we thought, be worth trying, since there was nothing else; but at that moment came a wire from Admingen, to say that he had made inquiries, and found that the best local opinion considered it certain death. And along that route, in the middle of June, there set out several parties: that of Peter Lindsay; that of Sir John Rowland, sixty year old manager of Burma Railways; and Captain John Fraser and Sergeant Pratt, of the 7th Hussars, escaped from Myitkyina after two days in Jap hands.

I read a report, in an Intelligence Summary some weeks later, of John Fraser's capture, escape and appalling journey of 54 days, in the course of which two of his companions were drowned, and he himself rescued from drowning by the skin of his teeth. I read and marvelled at his story; but never thought that he and I were to be so closely associated in the near future, and to owe each other our two lives.

Many people in those days came into our office with plans for the reconquest. Some of their ideas were useful: these were carefully noted, and filed away for future reference. Some were fantastic and foolish: these we made a pretence of noting, and bowed their originators out of the room as quickly as in all civility we could. And still we went on planning, eagerly collecting all relevant information, working out problems of time and space, supply, communication and so on, but realising soberly that with the African war not yet safe, and the European war not yet begun, there was little prospect of any of our schemes coming to fruition for many a long day.

Only in one direction did there seem any prospect of action in the near future. It lay in the person of a broad-shouldered, uncouth, almost simian officer who used to drift gloomily into the office for two or three days at a time, audibly dream dreams, and drift out again. When in Delhi, he would make his headquarters in the G.H.Q. Library, from which he would borrow a dozen books at a time, to the distress of the librarian, who, although he had personally witnessed his books vanishing in armfuls, knew from experience that he had no hope of ever seeing them back on his shelves. In our frenzy of planning, we used to look on this visitor as one of those to be bowed out, as soon as it was possible to put a term to his ramblings; but as we became aware that he took no notice of us anyway, but that without our patronage he had the ear of the highest, we paid more attention to his schemes. Soon we had fallen under the spell of his almost hypnotic talk; and by and by we—or some of us—had lost the power of distinguishing between the feasible and the fantastic. This was Orde Wingate.

I had met him first in Palestine in the Rebellion, in August, 1937. He was an Intelligence officer in Jerusalem, I an outdoor specimen of the same brotherhood in Southern Palestine. I had only known him slightly; my business did not concern him, but another officer who shared his office. Yet I had often seen him, sitting there, rather morose and moody, and once had incurred his annoyance by a mild prank. The safe custody of arms was a matter of particular moment in those days, and one morning I had found his revolver left unattended in an empty office. I took up a blue pencil, laid the revolver on the red blotting-paper, drew a neat silhouette all round it, and signed and dated it. I thought I was prepared for his anger when he next saw me, but I had not reckoned on the two or three biting words with which he actually greeted me. They made me feel neither clever nor funny.

Then I had seen him again in the Middle East, when he was organising his campaign in Ethiopia. His adventures there had been romanticised, but not, I believe, greatly exaggerated. Now he was here in India, soberly plotting wild adventures in Burma.

His proposals did not vary from principles which he had expounded for many years. Briefly, his point was that the enemy was most vulnerable far behind his lines, where his troops, if he had any at all, were of inferior quality. Here a small force could wreak havoc out of all proportion to its numbers. If it should be surprised, it could disintegrate into smaller pre-arranged parties to baffle pursuit, and meet again at a rendezvous fifteen to twenty miles farther on its route. Supply should be by air, communication by wireless: these two weapons had not yet been properly exploited. His proposal was to cut the enemy's supply line, destroy his dumps, tie up troops unprofitably far behind the line in the endeavour to protect these vulnerable areas, and generally to help the army proper on to its objectives.

At intervals throughout the summer Wingate appeared in Delhi, squabbled with most people there, got what he wanted, and returned to the jungle in the Central Provinces where he was training his brigade. Nobody seriously believed in him except General Wavell, and everybody regarded him as a bit of a nuisance. In G.H.Q. his brigade was irritably known as "the Chief's private army," and himself as "Tarzan" or "Robin Hood." I was almost the only person in J.P.S. with patience to listen to him, and was therefore encouraged to deal with him whenever he showed up; and even I thought the whole thing a bit crazy.

Meanwhile the Japs had halted short of Fort Hertz, and were showing no wish to pursue or press on any farther up the road from Tamu. The Lokchau Bridge, which had been demolished to impede his advance, was rebuilt; the withdrawal halted. There was anxiety about Madras and Colombo; it was thought that

Japan would attack Russia; El Alamein was fought and held; the Caucasus looked precarious. The monsoon broke, and our prickly heat abated. We wrote incessant papers, many of which never reached the eye of the commander-in-chief; the others were philosophic, I more and more discouraged. On the first day of every month I asked (and was refused) permission to go back to my regiment, on the plea that the J.P.S. was now launched, and that what they wanted was someone with a knowledge of Burma rather than a knowledge of planning. Once I arranged to fly over Burma in a bomber, to get some idea of the country we were all thinking about, but which none of us had seen; I was refused on the grounds that this would be "unprofitable joy-riding"— perhaps it would. At the beginning of July I went to Kashmir for a week, idled on a houseboat on the Wular Lake, sailed a sailing boat which was rotten, wrote two bad poems and caught three small fish; and came back to find that a paper I had been really pleased with, on the capture of . . . had been mutilated and then approved in my absence. (I am saying all this, not to claim that I was right, but to show my frame of mind.) On the first of September, my monthly request to return to my regiment was granted, and a successor from home summoned by cable. About the middle of September, Wingate popped in again. I told him that I was off back to my regiment.

"You'd far better come and command one of my columns," he said.

That was in the middle of the morning. I told him I would let him know that night. All the afternoon I asked advice of everybody I saw. It was unanimous—not to touch it with a barge-pole. That afternoon at six Wingate came in for my answer. I remember that an irritating fellow in the Air Force buttonholed him and talked about photography, while I was bursting to get my answer off my chest. At last the airman went, and I said "Yes."

I knew, by virtue of my place among the Planners, that my regiment was not to have a show during the forthcoming season, and it seemed to me that I would be better employed gaining experience, against my eventual return, than sitting about in Bihar on internal security duties, which was then their role. So I stipulated that my engagement would be for one campaign only, and that after that I should be free to return to the regiment. I had then to write and break it to my colonel that I was not coming back after all, but that I should be away a further eight or nine months, on business which I could not describe. This crossed a letter from him telling me to bring all the whisky I could lay hands on when I came. I felt a bigger cad than ever.

My relief arrived at the end of the month, and I was heartily glad to see him. Wingate had told me to join as soon as I could. But I felt badly in need of a last fling before disappearing into jungle, and went and sailed a country boat with John Bankes, who had been my fag at Eton, for a happy week on the coast north of Bombay. At the end of that time, brown, fit and happy, I went off to the jungle of Malthone to see what the future had in store.

CHAPTER TWO

FROM MALTHONE TO SAUGOR:

15th October—4th December, 1942

"And the bush has friends to meet him, and their kindly voices greet
him
In the murmur of the breezes and the rivers on their bars,
And he sees the vision splendid of the sunlit plains extended,
And at night the wondrous glory of the everlasting stars."
PATERSON—*Clancy of the Overflow.*

AT THE junction where I had to change, I met a major who came
up to me and asked if my name was Fergusson. I had never to my
knowledge seen him before, but supposed that he must have been
sent to meet me, which seemed an extraordinary courtesy. But
when I acknowledged it, he said:

"Well, my advice to you is to turn round and go straight back
to Delhi. Wingate's crackers, and I'm off."

I rightly guessed that I was witnessing the results of the
process known as "cutting out the dead wood," and was not
therefore tempted to return to the dusty halls of the Joint
Planning Staff.

Arrived at last at the base camp, I was given breakfast; and
with my servant Peter Dorans was put on the mail truck which
ran daily out to the training area in the jungle, fifty miles to the
north. Beside me sat a captain, aged about thirty, who introduced
himself as Peter Buchanan, Adjutant of the Burma Rifles; and
as we drove north towards the Malthone jungle he told me the
first hard facts about the show I was coming to join.

There were eight columns; four basically British, and four
basically Gurkha. Each had three platoons of infantry, and a
support platoon with Vickers machine-guns and mortars. There
was a Reconnaissance Platoon of two officers and forty-five men

of the Burma Rifles; and a Commando Platoon, for demolition work, of mixed sappers and selected infantry. Only a few mules had so far arrived; most of them were still doing centralised training under Brigade Headquarters. The muleteers were partly drawn from the battalion, British or Gurkha, from which the columns had been formed; but in addition the British columns had some Gurkha muleteers. It was Peter who told me that I was going to No. 5 Column, a British one; the commander had not hit it off with Wingate, and was about to depart.

As we rolled along, I took my first view of Indian jungle. As a boy, I had seen a little of New Zealand bush, and earlier that same year I had visited the forest country of the Equatorial Province of the Sudan: otherwise this was my first experience. As things turned out, the jungle in which we afterwards operated bore no resemblance whatever to that in which we trained, which was nothing more than thick thorny scrub, and most unpleasant; but to my innocent eye it looked impressive and not a little formidable.

We reached Brigade Headquarters about half an hour after noon, and I reported to Wingate, who immediately said, "Come and have a swim." So within five minutes of arriving, I found myself in a huge rockbound shady pool, and the dust of the journey washed away. We sat on a rock in the sun, while Wingate talked of what he wanted done.

After luncheon, Wingate himself took me along to the headquarters of the "British Group," formed from the old battalion headquarters to command the British columns. Here I met Lieut.-Colonel Robinson of the Sherwood Foresters, who had commanded this battalion, the 13th King's, almost since its raising at the beginning of the war. With him were my predecessor, and the other column commanders, whom I now met for the first time.

The commander of No. 6 Column was Gim (Gilmour) Anderson, of the Highland Light Infantry, the original adjutant of the 13th King's. He was a sandy-haired solicitor from Glasgow, of which city he was already a councillor at the age of twenty-seven.

Ken Gilkes, of No. 7, was a merchant who before the war had worked in Paris—big, smiling, with a quiet voice. Walter Scott ("Scotty") of 8 Column was in private life something to do with the Liverpool Corporation, had gone to France as a sapper, got a commission after Dunkirk and was now a major. The adjutant was David Hastings (son of Sir Patrick Hastings, K.C.), who had been a small boy at school when I was a big one—quick-witted and amusing.

They were all very pleasant to the interloper which was myself, and my reception by the officer I had come to displace could not have been kinder. I formed a high opinion of him, and at the end of the week asked him to stay on as my second in command, but he reckoned his position might be difficult, and preferred to go. I am glad that we parted the very best of friends.

I walked with him to the place where the column was encamped. It was well concealed in an entirely featureless piece of jungle; for it was always part of Wingate's teaching to ignore the obvious site when choosing a bivouac. A small sluggish stream circled the bivouac area, and it was obvious that the flow of water would not continue much longer. Column headquarters was under a large tree; and the rest of the column was ensconced under other trees or bushes all around, covering a circle perhaps three hundred yards in diameter. All directions looked the same to me, and I was terrified of getting lost whenever I moved from my tree—not so much for fear of not finding my way back, as for fear of ridicule by my new command.

We were living in semi-peace conditions at the time, with centralised cooking and a small officers' mess, so that the utmost time could be spent in training. The officers messed in a hut skilfully built by Burma riflemen. Here we had supper that first evening; and here for the first time I met my officers. John Fraser, whom I have already mentioned, commanded the Burma Rifle platoon. Dark and spectacled, he showed no sign of the shocking ordeal from which he had emerged only six weeks before. Like all the Burma Rifle officers except their Regular colonel, he was employed in one of the big civilian firms in Burma: he was in the rice department of Steel Brothers; and like most of them he was from Scotland. His second officer was P.A.M. Heald, broad-shouldered, fair and young; he had been a housemaster at Borstal before becoming a Labour Welfare Officer under the Burma Oil people at Chauk.

The officers of the King's were Alec Macdonald, a medical student from Liverpool, whom I afterwards made my administrative officer; Bill Edge, Scholar of History at Balliol; Philippe Stibbé, Scholar in English Literature at Merton; and George Borrow, a schoolmaster. It was quite obvious that first evening that we should get on well.

For the first few days, I read up all the copious notes which Wingate had been pouring forth like a sausage-machine. Like everything he ever wrote or said, they were compelling stuff, and I had been warned that he expected one not only to know every word in them, but also to have given deep thought to them, and mastered every possible interpretation. One day, just after I arrived, a large number of officers of the brigade were driven forty miles in lorries to do a tactical exercise on river-crossing, and I realised how strenuous the training was going to be. Every movement, from stand to stand, was done at the double: it was one of Wingate's fads that British officers thought it undignified to run; and he saw to it that this particular form of false dignity did not obtain in his brigade. When he wished to move to another viewpoint, he ran there, and jolly fast too: arrived at the new spot, he would wheel round, and woe betide any one who was not there to hear the first words that fell from his mouth.

That day, having discussed the various approaches to the river, we arrived on its banks, representing, if I remember rightly, the Reconnaissance Platoon. He then asked us all what, in our opinion, represented a good crossing-place. Several people ventured to guess, but to all their answers he replied, "How do you know?" It became apparent that what he wanted was someone to say that you could not tell without reconnoitring the far bank; so again I found myself swimming. When I got back, with my report that the far bank was muddy, and that mules could not negotiate it (not that I had ever seen a mule try anything like it), he said, "Very good," and set off at the double along the bank with all his flock panting behind him, leaving me and a young Air Force officer, who had come in with me, and whose name I found to be Bobby Thompson, to dress hastily and follow. His tactical exercises were always exhilarating, and when one answered his questions, one always felt one was on very thin ice.

Some of us were bidden that evening to some celebration which the Gurkhas were having. I sat between a Gurkha officer called St. George De la Rue, and a captain in the King's called Jacksie Pickering, in 7 Column. I watched fascinated while the Gurkhas postured and danced and sang incomprehensible songs, and offered round what seemed to be unlimited rum.

I was getting to know people, and becoming a member of a very happy family, pledged to do great things.

I had made my new column demonstrate to me the various drills which they had been taught, and gradually I was getting the hang of the thing. I decided therefore to have a three day march, to try out myself rather than the column. On the map, I saw what looked like a most attractive river about twenty miles away, and decided to hang my exercise on that. I can't remember the details, but I recollect that we were to kidnap a "Japanese" official in the village of Dudhai, and bring him back to our secure bivouac. I arranged to march by night across country to a point on the river, where we would lie up all day, and make our raid at night. John Fraser had some other job to do, so Pam Heald was to command the Recce Platoon, and precede us to the rendezvous on the river the day before, reconnoitring the scene of the raid, and incidentally providing from his platoon the "Japanese" official and his bodyguard. I arranged with Arthur Emmett, a teaplanter from Darjeeling who commanded No. 2 (Gurkha) Column, to produce an "enemy" to intercept me on the way home.

I had not realised, and my officers had not dared tell me, what an ambitious programme this was. Twenty miles across country by night is anything but easy, even with the glorious full moon which we luckily had. We did not reach the rendezvous on the river until the full heat of the day, about eleven o'clock; and there we met Pam, who said he had found a wonderful place for lying up. It was on the far side of the river, which could be crossed at a point where a long shelf of slippery rock ran from bank to bank; and on the far side were tall, shady trees, providing perfect cover from air. By the time we made it, we were nearly dropping.

We slept all that afternoon, and started back in the evening. The raid went off successfully, Po Po Tou, the Karen colour-sergeant, playing the part of the outraged Jap to perfection; but the night march home, the second night running and an even longer distance, was misery. We got into very thick thorn jungle and again it was not till eleven o'clock that we reached our bivouac, too tired even to be triumphant.

The spot by the river where we had spent the day had so seized my imagination that I decided to emigrate there permanently with the complete column. Water was running low in our present camp site, and the area had become too thoroughly known to the troops for useful training to be carried out; columns moreover were thick on the ground, and always treading on each other's toes. So, with the Brigadier's permission, I moved the whole column to the Narain Nullah, in the middle of the best tiger country (so they tell me) in the Central Provinces.

The three weeks we spent there were like a dream. We trained from six in the morning until two in the afternoon. The country was fresh, and had more variety than the old area. We concentrated on the crossing of rivers, and became fairly expert in getting ropes over, and slinging stores across. Most delightful of all was the swimming. I held two bathing parades a day, and succeeded in turning many non-nants into fair nants. I had two particularly good swimmers among the men, "Sailor" Thompson, a Lowestoft fisherman, so called to distinguish him from two namesakes, and a young lad called Berger, always in trouble and always lazy except when it was a question of watermanship training, when he was tireless. These two between them taught over a dozen men to swim who could not previously swim a stroke. There was a third, Lancaster, not in the same class as they, but, as so often happens, an even better teacher.

Best watermen of all, however, were the Karens of the Burma Rifles. These men formed the bulk of their regiment, and my platoon consisted entirely of them. They belong mostly to the Delta, between Rangoon and Bassein, although some live in Tenasserim (the long tail of Burma which droops southwards into Malaya), and others, more wild in appearance and habits, known as "Red Karens," from the Karenni Hills. In the platoon we had one man from Tenasserim, Pa Haw, a little wiry smiling chap who in private life had been an "*oozy*" or elephant driver, and who was now John Fraser's orderly.

Nobody who has served with Karens could fail to like them. Thoroughly biddable, and mostly Christians (to a degree which would put to shame most people who profess and call themselves such), they make admirable soldiers, intelligent, willing, energetic, brave. Many of them have been educated by the American Baptist Mission, and rejoice in incongruous names. Ba Than was their subedar, a rather solemn, conscientious man whose brother Wilson was in one of the other columns. Aung Pe, the jemadar, spoke little English, but, though younger, was as good a man. Po Po Tou was highly educated, and had been at Kitchener College, Nowgong, training for a King's Commission; but on the outbreak of war had sped back to Burma to resume his place in the ranks. He was the best educated of the lot. Billy, the Havildar-Major, was a tiny, wizened man, always smiling and very devout, who never went to sleep without first singing softly to himself all three verses of "Jesus loves me, this I know." He was a particular favourite among the British troops.

Their prowess in the water has to be seen to be believed. I have seen Pa Haw swimming mules almost continuously across a river for three hours, taking only the shortest of occasional rests, sitting naked on a rock looking for all the world like Peter Pan, and laughing at the clumsy efforts of his British comrades, before plunging in again, and half-riding, half-swimming the recalcitrant beasts as he would. It looked as though he were whispering directions in the animal's ear. They would build boats from bamboo and groundsheets in a few minutes. I once saw John get his complete platoon across a seventy-yard river in eighteen minutes from the word "go," with equipment and clothing, including Bren guns and wireless set, bone dry, and four mules and a pony; using nothing but their *dahs* (long knives) and groundsheets in addition to what the Almighty had planted by the stream. Never do I ask to command better or more lovable soldiers than these.

In the evenings, in that camp at the Narain, we used to sit late on the logs around the fire, and talk. Since our arrival, we had been joined by three newcomers—Tommy Roberts, Denny Sharp and John Kerr. These three, all very different in background and character, added new material to our already mixed bag. Tommy was an ex-regular N.C.O. of the King's, and one of the finest regimental officers I have ever met. He still talked the language he had learned as a boy, in the married quarters of the King's Regiment, where his father had served before him, eventually becoming R.S.M. Tall, thin and tougher than he looked, he had the greatest contempt for the new deal in the army, which he thought pampered; and his tongue was as bitter as when he used it against recruits on the square.

Denny Sharp was a Flight-Lieutenant in the Royal Air Force. A native of Dunedin, his father kept a hotel in Nelson, New Zealand; and Denny had come home to join the Air Force just before the war. In manner he was on first acquaintance rather casual and morose, and took a bit of melting; he too had a caustic tongue, and often after listening in silence to our arguments he would throw in two or three blistering words which made everybody laugh, and lose the thread of the talk. He had fought in fighters in Singapore, and had had an exciting escape by way of Sumatra.

John Kerr was a land-agent in South Wales. He was stoutly built and forceful in manner, very outspoken and with obstinately held opinions, on which nothing would induce him to compromise. Newly out from home, he had brought with him ideas of man-management and troops' welfare which to us were new-fangled, and to Tommy Roberts anathema. He had recently done a course in what he called "Unarmed Combat," which seemed to consist of low-life gangster fighting, and to include biting, gouging and unpleasantly directed kicking; and he was exceedingly keen to be allowed to teach it to the men. I called it barbaric, and forbade it; he was genuinely unable to understand my attitude, and this subject often occupied us round the fire at night.

"But what can you possibly have against it?" he would say, indignantly.

"We've only fought decently in the British Army," I would answer, partly from conviction and partly because I knew it would set him off; "and I don't see why we should change now."

"That's the very attitude that's going to lose us the war," he would say. "Have the Germans or the Japs ever fought decently? What are you going to say if the Japs try jiu-jitsu, and our men haven't been taught to defend themselves? It's accepted at home, and it ought to be taught out here"; and he would brandish a particularly nasty little book which was his Bible on the subject, and which had been written by some ex-Shanghai police officers.

John was not the only one to rise to a bait. I had not much experience of wartime soldiers; those in my own regiment seemed to have much the same ideas as the Regulars. One night I got the shock of my life. I forget how the subject cropped up, but we were discussing war aims, or the attitude of the fighting man. One of my "intellectuals" said that he felt no personal allegiance to the King. Tommy Roberts swore a round Liverpool oath, and I asked how he reconciled that with holding the King's Commission. He replied that he thought every one nowadays regarded that point of view as an anachronism. I drove him away from the fire to eat the remains of his supper in cold and outer darkness. He was very young.

Philippe Stibbé and I had in common a voracious taste for

books. In some respects, as was only natural considering a difference in age of ten years, his was more enterprising than mine; but he had while at Oxford sat at the feet of Edmund Blunden, whom I did not—and do not—know, but whose writings had long been my study, and whose *Undertones of War* ranked with *The Secret Battle* and *The Path of Glory* as my favourite books of the last war. Together we read his *Hardy* and *The British Village*, both newly appeared, and discussed not only them but the many bypaths into which they led us. I tried to infect Philippe with my current enthusiasm for Trollope; and we often sat round the fire until we were too weary to go and look for more firewood.

Sometimes several of us strayed into religious discussion, which would not bear reproduction here. I would only say how much I admire the fighting spirit of those who go willingly to war without belief in a future life. The sacrifice of those who believe in Resurrection can surely not be compared with the sacrifice of those who do not; who believe that the bullet which puts an end to their life extinguishes everything. One has an envious admiration for their courage, for which one would barter almost anything, except that one belief.

One day I got news that the mules were arriving next morning. Up till now they had all been concentrated for training under Brigade, except for eight or ten which fetched our daily supplies from the nearest point which lorries could reach, some two miles away across the river. When they came, it was a beautiful sight to see them splashing through the water, headed by a small and eager young officer on a fine mare, who stopped to watch them cross. This was Bill Smyly, my new animal transport officer. Nineteen years old, he had come out from home a year before to join a Gurkha regiment, and having an Irish passion for horses, he had been selected for training as an A.T.O. Desperately keen on many things, it was hard to say which he liked best, his animals or his Gurkhas; he tenderly spared the former, but never the latter. Although easily the youngest officer or man in the column, he had no fear of anybody, and gave Egypt to any officer, however senior, who failed to take due care of his mules. He was always in consequence in a state of feud with someone or other, and I had my work cut out to keep the peace.

We only had three days to get the mules into proper shape, for although they had been kept in work while under Brigade, they had never carried their proper loads; and in three days' time, on the 29th November, we had to march into Saugor, and "capture" it as an exercise. There we were to have five days' rest, and then carry out our final exercise, the "capture" of Jhansi, 120 miles to the north. In addition to the mules, we had been given some bullocks for pack purposes; and I had put these in charge of one Ball, a farmer's boy from Hertfordshire, to whom I gave a lance-stripe for the job.

The march to Saugor was a hard one. We left at six o'clock one evening, and marched till eleven next morning with only the briefest of halts. We rested twelve hours, and moved off again about midnight. It was St. Andrew's night, and we made a half-hearted effort to celebrate it among the Scotsmen of the column, with a bottle of whisky and a few songs; but there was not enough whisky to overcome the shyness, and the effort was a flop. We marched from midnight that night to eight o'clock the following evening with only an hour's break, being obliged to do so by scarcity of water, which we found at last in the well of a forest rest-house.

The day had not been without incident. During one of our brief halts, a party of snake-charmers had suddenly appeared and put on a show for us; while Private Baxter had managed to water his mule in a deep pool, into which the silly animal had fallen. They had got it out only by throwing off its girth, so that the saddle and Bren-gun which it was carrying had fallen into the water. Philippe Stibbé and Bill Smyly had pleasantly spent the heat of the day diving for them, and eventually recovered them; but they never caught us up until after the "battle" was over.

Saugor "fell," after a tiring march and a boring battle, at 3 a.m. on the 3rd of December; and I was so weary that I went to sleep on the ground in the mess-tent, being too tired to seek the tent which had been pitched for me somewhere else. At 9 a.m.

I wearily hove myself to my feet, and walked the half-mile to my mule-lines. The flat plain where they stood was covered with small parties of troops exercising; for there was a school at Saugor, where various people went on courses. As I walked towards my mules, I saw a carrier being driven about fifty yards from me; and as it came nearer I saw that the driver wore a Balmoral with a Red Hackle, the badge of my regiment. I shouted to him, and he drove up. Who I was, he had not the least idea; for I had a five-day beard on my face, and was wearing an Australian type bush-hat; but him I recognised instantly as Duncan Menzies, a young Australian who had been at Oxford as a Rhodes scholar on the outbreak of war, and had joined my regiment.

This chance but fateful meeting was the more extraordinary since I had been racking my brains for a suitable column adjutant, and had decided on Duncan as the best man of my acquaintance for the job. I had been wondering whether I dared write and ask my colonel for his services. I knew that he was already aggrieved at my defection, and that he had lost two other officers to the staff despite his protests; and I had almost decided that I could not ask for Duncan. But here he was! Six hundred miles away from where I thought him to be, crossing the *maidan* in his carrier at the very moment that I was doing so myself. As Duncan said afterwards, it seemed to be the finger of God.

His instructor was waxing impatient, so I invited him to come down and see me that afternoon; he said he would be free till four o'clock. I went on my way wondering how I could get his services, and realising once again how splendidly he would do for the game. I did not know him well; our acquaintance had begun one night in Tobruk when I had taken a patrol out to investigate a report from my listening post, a thousand yards in front of the line, that a German patrol was somewhere near them. I had told my cousin Richard, whose company was on my left, that I should be coming back through the gap in his wire, and asked him to warn his men. I was back sooner than he thought (or so he said: I am plumb sure he had forgotten all about it), and on reaching the wire we were greeted with a burst or two of Bren and some Tommy-gun. The noise they made was nothing to the noise I made, and a mutual cursing match developed between me, with my nose boring into the ground, and an angry Australian voice from the blessed safety beyond the wire. This was my first and somewhat inauspicious meeting with one who was afterwards to become one of my dearest friends.

That afternoon I told him something—a very little—of what we were out to do. I told him that I thought the chances of coming back were about even money. He jumped at it, but I told him that I would not take an answer until the following evening; and we arranged that I should come up and have a bath in his quarters, dine with him and hear his decision then.

I had little doubt of what his answer would be, and before I had begun my soup I had heard his "Yes." After dinner, we withdrew to a private corner of the ante-room. I felt free now to tell him more; and we talked of the venture far into the night.

CHAPTER THREE

FROM SAUGOR TO JHANSI:

5th December—12th January, 1943

"What of the faith and fire within you,
    Men who march away
    Ere the barncock say
    Night is growing grey?"
THOMAS HARDY.

THE SAUGOR EXERCISE had been fairly tough, but the one which followed it was tougher by far. The object was the capture of Jhansi, a cantonment and railway junction some 120 miles to the north, and the exercise had been set largely to test our powers of endurance. The five days in Saugor had been anything but a rest; preparations for the exercise were considerable and elaborate, and the Brigadier was here, there and everywhere, like a gadfly. The only relaxation I remember, except for one evening when I again went out to dinner, was a Sunday luncheon with the Burma Rifles, which, in accordance with custom, consisted of an elaborate curry. My hosts exploited my ignorance to the full, and urged on me all sorts of cool-and-innocent looking vegetables, which inwardly were ravening wolves.

Early on the morning of the 9th December we started off. Duncan's posting had not yet come through; much intrigue was still before us before we could get it blest. Pam had been lent to another column, whose Burma Rifles officers were both sick; John was already twenty-four hours ahead with his platoon.

From my point of view, it was a dull and gruelling exercise. I had no independent role, but was tied to the coat-tails of the new group commander, Sam Cooke. (Colonel Robinson, to his great grief, and in spite of manful exertions to prove how fit he was, had been superseded for age.) The columns were spread wide. The idea was to appear to strike at Jhansi from the east, while actually attacking in strength from the west. Wingate himself, with Scotty's column and some Gurkha columns, was going for the aerodrome from the north-west; Sam, with the rest of the British columns, was to feint towards the north-east, march suddenly west and north, and come in on the railway station by a series of forced marches. Various diversions were arranged for the east side: Lieut.-Colonel Wheeler of the Burma Rifles, dressed in all the panoply of a brigadier, was to show himself in unlikely places, while the famous Mike (" Mad Mike") Calvert, commanding No. 3 (Gurkha) Column, was to hare about east of Jhansi to attract attention and raid traffic.

The details of the plan matter little, but the point, so far as Sam Cooke's army was concerned, was that, instead of marching 120 miles in nine days, we had to cover 180 in the same time, in order to accomplish our switch from one flank to the other, and induce the "enemy" to concentrate on the wrong side. The River Betwa ran aslant our line of approach, and was as easy to watch as it was ill to cross. Our orders were to direct our sudden western move towards a bridge where the railway crossed it, use the bridge for our own crossing, and then blow it.

Two unexpected horrors were added to the march. First, a new type of pack was issued called the Everest pack. This is by no means a bad gadget, but one has to have plenty of careful fitting before using it, or the weight is thrown on to the ball of the foot, with dire results to your feet. Secondly, we were all issued with new boots, of an inferior pattern; and after a week's marching the casualties were innumerable. My recollections of the march are few and dim, but quite horrible; and we were all tired by the third day.

Bill Smyly obliged with some comic relief one moonlight night. He was so weary that he kept falling asleep on his horse as he rode up and down the column to see that all mule loads were riding nicely. Every now and then his horse would arrive at the head of the column, when I would wake him up, reverse him and

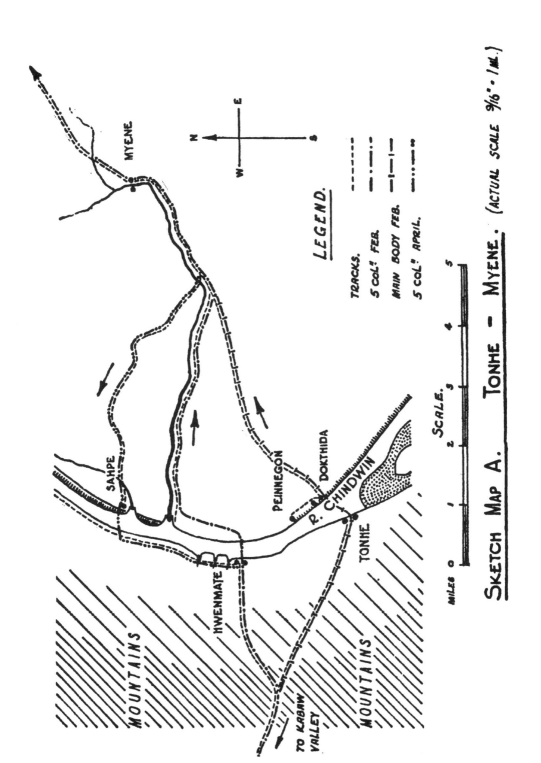

LEGEND.

TRACKS.
5 Col! FEB.
MAIN BODY FEB.
5 Col! APRIL.

N
W — E
S

MYENE.

SAHPE

HWENMATE

PEINNEGON

DOKTHIDA

R. CHINDWIN

TONHE

MOUNTAINS

MOUNTAINS

TO KABAW VALLEY

SCALE.

MILES 0   1   2   3   4   5

SKETCH MAP A.   TONHE — MYENE.   (ACTUAL SCALE 9/16" = 1 ML.)

send him back again. At last I got fed up with this, and for fun let him carry straight on. Gradually his mare plodded out of sight along the track and round the corner, and I began to think we had lost him for good. But after a quarter of an hour I heard a horse cantering towards me, and suddenly Bill reined up in front of me, wide awake but sorely puzzled. He had expected to see the tail of the column, rather than its head. Presumably the mare had become uneasy at getting so far ahead, and had herself turned back to see if the column were following. Bill had then woken up, and seeing no column concluded that he had dropped behind, put spurs to the beast and—met us head on. He was a perplexed man indeed.

The railway bridge was satisfactorily crossed and destroyed, and we drew near our objective. Every one was weary, and Sam Cooke resolved to dump packs in a safe bivouac under guard, and do the last twenty miles light, coming back for our kit after we had completed the "demolition" of the railway station. Rid of our packs, we seemed to march on air, and we reached the assembly area on time. Here the three columns of the group split; I was directed along the west side of the railway, parallel to it but a mile off, until I had the station abeam; then I was to swing into it, arriving at the signal box and station-master's office at eleven p.m. precisely. Other columns were to burst in from the south at the same time.

We had apparently slipped through the outer defences, and the only opposition we met was one sentry in a sentry-box, five hundred yards from the station. I suspect he belonged to some irregular auxiliaries, and had only the vaguest idea of the difference between an exercise and the real thing. Ba Than reported his presence, and I stalked him with a torch and my revolver. He failed to hear my approach, standing as he was in his box; and the first thing he knew was when I shone my torch through the window in the side wall. He immediately turned his head, and my left hand stole round the corner and caught him by the throat.

He fell to the ground pleading for mercy, and I had to

soothe him and give him a cigarette—most irregular—to show him I meant no harm. On we ran to the railway station, and, ignoring some desultory firing, claimed the day.

I rapidly made my dispositions for a counter-attack, lined up some thirty prisoners in two ranks on one side of the platform, and with rare perspicacity sited my headquarters in the refreshment room. I then ate three tins of sausages, cold, and a plate of tongue, in quick succession, and took over the Mohammedan tearoom as a sort of NAAFI for the troops. Fortified, I went out on to the platform to see how my sappers were getting on with preparing the signal-box for demolition, and to make sure that my defences were in order.

The most senior general in the neighbourhood came up.

"If you're Fergusson, I don't much care for your dispositions, what I can see of them. I don't mind telling you that you are pretty likely to be counter-attacked."

"I honestly think we're ready for it, sir," I said, and explained my fire plan. It was a little difficult to talk to him, because appalling bangs were going on all over the place, as my sappers let off crackers to demonstrate their doings. A train was in the station, and such passengers as were not hiding under the seats were enjoying the show. Some of my Burma riflemen, with a Bren-gun, were sitting on the roof of a carriage.

"I wouldn't be too sanguine if I were you," he said; but at that moment the attack came in. These troops were the rawest recruits from a local depot, and about all they had so far learned was how to fall in; so that when they saw my prisoners standing in two ranks on the platform, they thought their place must be beside them. With a smartness which did full credit to their drill instructors, they doubled to take their place on the end of the ranks; and then, seeing that the prisoners had their arms grounded beside them, they also complied, and stood at ease.

That was the end of the counter-attack, and of the battle. The demolitions were still continuing, but the general said, "I think we've had enough noise to-night." The words were hardly out of his mouth when the devil of a bang came from the signal-box.

This had the desired effect; the Cease Fire was blown, and we were reprieved from the withdrawal on to our packs twenty miles away. Instead we marched a mile to a camp which had been prepared for us, exhausted but happy; and our packs were collected for us by lorry the following day.

There followed a fortnight of feverish preparation by day and mild celebration by night. How long we were to stay in Jhansi nobody quite knew, but we expected to entrain for Assam the second or third week of the month. The next three weeks were far more leisured than the five days at Saugor; and though there was much work to be done on final equipment, we had a fair amount of spare time. There was, however, a certain amount of reorganisation to be done. The last exercise, though more gruelling *qua* marching than anything we afterwards had to do in the field, had disclosed a number of men (and I fear some officers) who were not up to scratch. The deficiency in British other ranks was serious; and after much discussion it was decided that, rather than get in new blood at the last moment, it would be better to break up one column, and distribute the manpower round the others. Until the decision was made as to which column should cease to exist, we all went about with gloomy faces. The lot fell upon Gim Anderson. We were particularly sorry for him, for he was one of the best of the column commanders; but there were other considerations to be taken into account.

We were short of officers, too. There was a hitch about Duncan's posting, and I had had to sack my sapper officer. George Borrow had already gone to Group Headquarters as Intelligence Officer,* but John Kerr, who on the exercise had proved himself one of my best officers, in spite of his minority views on welfare and unarmed combat, had taken over his platoon. David Whitehead, a small and spectacled sapper from Yorkshire, had come as technical sapper officer; he had had much excitement already this war, having done something mysterious in Holland, and Commando raids on Lofoten and Spitzbergen. Other newcomers who

* Note A: Lieut. G. H. Borrow.

joined me now were Jim Harman, who had been in Mike Calvert's Jungle Warfare school in Maymyo, and had come out through China; Willy Williamson, ex-regular N.C.O. of the King's, who went as longstop to Tommy Roberts' support platoon; and Gerry Roberts, ex-transport corporal in the Welsh Guards, and since then a professional footballer. He was officially a first reinforcement, but I attached him to Bill, as assistant A.T.O. Finally there appeared one Tommy Blow, a tall and powerful builder from Hertfordshire, who was in the Indian Army, and had not the slightest idea what he was coming to, but was delighted when he knew what it was.

Bill Aird, my doctor, at last came to rest in No. 5 Column at this time, having wandered from column to column during previous months. Until now, we had only had three doctors for the whole brigade, who were not allotted to specific columns; but Bill and I had long plotted that when the time came he should join me. He belonged to Glasgow and had a great sense of humour; the men were very fond of him, he and I had much in common, and altogether it was a most successful partnership.

Christmas was upon us, and a large and beautiful English church was two hundred yards from our lines, and numerous Welshmen in our ranks. With Sam Cooke's permission, I set to work to train a choir to practise Christmas hymns. The local padre and his wife were charming folk, who were delighted at the suggestion; and she played the organ for us on the two evenings when we were able to practise. Bill Smyly, Jacksie Pickering, St. George De la Rue and Pearce, a new officer in 8 Column, helped; but the loveliest voice belonged to a little Welsh miner in my own column, one Williams, who proved to be the owner of a tenor voice such as you hear three or four times in a long life. As often happens, the singing went better at the practices than at the service; but all the same the singing on Christmas morning was something to remember. I never heard "Hark! the Herald . . ." better sung; and Williams's voice, in the most beautiful tenor part in the hymn-book, I can remember now.

The difficulties over Duncan's posting were such that I had to go to Delhi, with the Brigadier's permission, to sort them out. He had already joined me, on Boxing Day; but was officially on a month's leave after his course. At Delhi I managed to get it fixed, though not without dust and heat. I went and had a good guffaw at the Joint Planners, still sweating away in that imitation cathedral at plans for the year 1950 or thereabouts; I enticed some of them out to luncheon, and they blinked in the open air like pit ponies. They were really envious, and so were all of the prisoners pent who knew what was in the wind.

I was back in Jhansi in time to celebrate Hogmanay Night, 1942-1943, with my column and with selected people from other columns. Sam Cooke was there, by virtue of being my group commander; Lieut.-Colonel Alexander, who commanded the Gurkha Group, was there, by virtue of being a Scotsman; L. G. Wheeler was there, by virtue of being one of the nicest men I had ever met, and one of the most amusing; George Dunlop in the Royal Scots, who commanded No. 1 Column, Peter Buchanan, Gim Anderson and a few more Scotsmen from outside Five Column; and Jacksie Pickering and David Hastings, by virtue of being born gate-crashers. I had promised Athole brose for all (Scotch whisky by virtue of the Black Market, at 45 rupees, or £3, the bottle); money seemed no object in view of what lay ahead. In their eagerness they all arrived early, and when a large jug of white stuff was put upon the table, I presumed it was the Athole brose, which Peter Dorans and I had been making and sampling earlier in the evening. We had been a bit short of cream for it; so I passed it round with a warning that although it might look innocuous it was pretty strong. Every one poured it out, waiting for the others to fill their glasses, and then reverently sipped it. . . . It was pure milk, which Peter had brought in for our post-prandial coffee.

The brose was forthcoming in due course, and we had a hilarious evening. In the Commando Serjeants' Mess, they were busy shaving off the moustaches of all officers who came their way. I gave them a wide berth.

The Brigadier had gone off to Imphal, and there was still no likelihood of the train being before the 11th or 12th. It seemed to me the column was getting soft in Jhansi, so I resolved to do a short march, half holiday, half training, for four days. We marched to the banks of the Betwa River, in Orchha State, and put our mules across the one place we could find where the banks were fairly clear of rocks: for most of them, this was the first time over.

We bivouacked on the far side, in a glade that might have been the Forest of Arden in *As You Like It*. Cheetal and sambhir, as friendly as the fawn in *Alice in Wonderland*, abounded, and nosed their way into our very camp. Next morning we had a leisurely start, and marched along the river until again we found a place which, being on pleasure bent, we decided was meet for another pause. We let the men enjoy aquatics in the two-man rubber boats which were part of our equipment; for the more they got used to handling them the better. John Fraser wanted to march some of his men home for some reason, and I gave him permission to do so. He began with one of his spectacular crossings of the river, with half the men in the column taking the time. His satisfaction at knocking two minutes off his previous record was tempered by the discovery, having just got his platoon fully dressed on the far bank, that he was on an island, and that all was to do again.

Duncan and I swam lazily across to the other bank, climbed out and picked our way delicately in our bare feet to the summit of the island to see what we could see. We found a number of haycocks—good, sweet, juicy hay, the very thing for the animals. We each picked one up, and, ignoring the deep scratches they inflicted, clasped them to our bosoms and staggered with them down the hill to the bank. There we hailed Bill Aird and Corporal Dale, who were rowing about in one of the rubber boats, to bring it across to act as hay-barge. The two haycocks filled it completely, and Bill and Dale swam behind it, pushing it before them across the lazy current, while Duncan and I clambered up the hill again for more. This time we came face to face with a couple of

Indians, who were considerably taken aback to encounter, in the middle of a respectable native state, two stark naked *sahibs* stealing hay. Duncan had some Urdu and murmured something at them, with the result that in a minute they were carrying the hay down to the bank and themselves loading it into the boat. When we reckoned we had enough, we swam back to our clothes and fished out of our pockets the very reasonable sum the men had asked of us, sending it across with Dale in the boat; and the two men disappeared satisfied. The real owners of the hay arrived to demand money with menaces an hour later.

I had planned to spend the night near the great Castle of Orcha, of which we could see the huge towers stretching high above the trees, even from where we were: and I sent on an advance party to choose a site. We arrived ourselves just before dark, in time to see a rabbit-hunt by the "Burrifs," as the Burma riflemen were familiarly called. They pursued it on foot, forecasting its twists and turns with astonishing accuracy, until at last it was exhausted and easily killed for the pot. Next day we returned to Jhansi.

It was astonishing how handy the men were in the jungle after these few short months. They had quite happily sloughed comforts which they had thought indispensable, and made themselves self-sufficient. As in the old song, they were "contented wi' little and canty wi' mair." A year before these men had been in England, stationed on the coast of Essex, and thinking themselves ill-used if they were two miles from a pub; now, although they enjoyed the cinema and the canteen as much as the next man, they were completely at home in jungle. By far the great majority of them were townsmen, from Liverpool, Manchester and Birmingham; and it is a fact that, in jungle warfare, the countryman has no advantage over the townsman after the first week of training.

It may be of interest also to know that the average age of these men was little under thirty; it had been higher until a draft arrived, just before I took over, which included younger men. They were a very good lot, though they had some habits which might have driven me to drink: I could not cure them of being litter-louts, nor could I make them properly silent; they would try honestly enough, and then forget. These things they learned in due course; and indeed they come more easily once across the Chindwin.

And to some extent the jungle had got under my skin also. I had enjoyed my trip to Delhi, and the two days of good meals, and sheets, and a bed; but I enjoyed the march round Orchha even more. It is the only time since I began playing in jungle that I have been able to say, "This looks a nice place: let's halt here a day." And the men had enjoyed it too; for when we got back to Jhansi, in time to write final letters and make our last preparations for the move to the forward area, one heard the men chattering excitedly to friends in other columns about how much they had enjoyed themselves. It had stopped us from becoming muscle-bound, and was a healthier way of spending four days than in a dull cantonment.

Orchha was jungle as it should be. It is a game sanctuary, and it was a sanctuary for men also. To me jungle has become a place of stealth, a place in which to wage war, a place which affords cover to approach your enemy, and for him to stalk you. In Orchha the river bustled over its boulders through free country, and in the great woods on either hand no shot could ring out to slay man nor beast; at night the stars were tranquil, and privy to no conspiracy against you. We often thought of Orchha afterwards.

For this was our last period of peace, and we knew it, although we knew little else of what was in store for us. The foresight of the Brigadier had been astonishing in every respect; the weapons and organisation of the columns proved exactly right, and exactly what was wanted for the campaign. We all knew the next few months would be desperately hard, and I always felt that the odds I had given Duncan on coming back—even money—was a fair bet;* but the actual nature of the fighting, and the hardships, nobody could picture except the officers of the Burma Rifles. Our

* The odds in No. 5 Column proved to be 3 to 1 against.

ignorance worried them at times, and I think they were a bit gloomy: they had every right to be, for they knew our job, and we did not.

The men were not much worried. Their faith in Wingate was implicit. My serjeant-major, Cairns, from Stranraer, used to get quite lyrical whenever he spoke of him; and the men were much the same. They certainly knew it was not going to be a cake-walk, but their only distress was the knowledge that they could not write home.

The officers also were happy enough. Duncan and I knew what we were letting ourselves in for when we joined; Denny had answered an advertisement for a "special mission," and was sick as mud when he found it meant walking; none of the others were volunteers except Jim Harman and David Whitehead: it had just come their way, and they looked on it as an unexpected reprieve from sitting in Secunderabad.

I gave the officers a talk the afternoon before we entrained. The thing that worried us all most was having to leave behind the wounded; but it was quite obvious that there was nothing else to be done for them; and that to linger with them meant risking the success of the show. All had been taught the rudiments of first aid, for what such rudiments are worth; all had been issued with morphia, and told how to administer it, according to need, and including a lethal dose. For the badly wounded, it might be possible to leave them in friendly villages, and every officer had copies of a letter in Burmese to be left with the villagers to whom they were confided. Having been taught at home all about the evacuation of wounded, it must have seemed hard that in the very first campaign on which they were engaged evacuation was impossible. Except for John, Duncan and Denny, none had been on service before.

But there was no doubt about their spirit. All were in fine fettle, full of confidence and well. I was conscious that I myself was fitter than I had been since the day when the great doors of the Grand Entrance closed behind me and I passed out of Sandhurst. Within us all, officers and men, were faith and fire alike.

A few days later, after a hard forenoon's work, we shut the truck door on the last mule, and waved good-bye to Alec and Bill Smyly, who were travelling on the mule train. That night, soon after midnight, our own engine whistled and our own train started. In the words of a current popular song, we were off to see the Wizard.

CHAPTER FOUR

FROM JHANSI TO CHINDWIN:

12th January—15th February

> "Ah, we were dauntless in those days, the moon on our bucklers,
>   Naught was amiss with the world then, we under enchantments—
> Better a day at the trout in the burn, or the moorcock in Appin,
>   Than years of this trade as a soldier!"
>   NEIL MUNRO—*Duror of Appin*.

NONE OF US could tell you much about the famous Manipur Road, for we marched up it at night. By day the long motor convoys went grinding up and down it, and we had to leave it free; but it was too dangerous for night driving, and then it became our property. The stages varied in length from seven to eighteen miles. We would start the march at dusk, have one halt of an hour sometime during the night, when we would brew up tea; and at three or four in the morning we would find our guides, sent on ahead by lorry to take over the staging camp. On the lorries would travel one extra blanket for each man; for the nights were bitterly cold, and the heights anything up to 5500 feet. Meeting our guides, we would sleepily draw our blankets, roll up in them and fall asleep; and not till nine or ten in the morning would we wake up to see whither our night's march had brought us.

Sometimes the view which thus burst on us was enough to take one's breath away. Huge mountains rose across the valley, and mists curling up from far below betrayed the line of the streams. Sometimes one would be minded of the West Highlands, set up on thrice the scale. Sometimes Duncan would exclaim, "Just like Gippsland!" wherever that may be. On occasions we were disappointed, as when we found ourselves gazing into the side of a hill two hundred yards away, or when the whole landscape was blotted out in swirling, stinging, blinding rain.

50

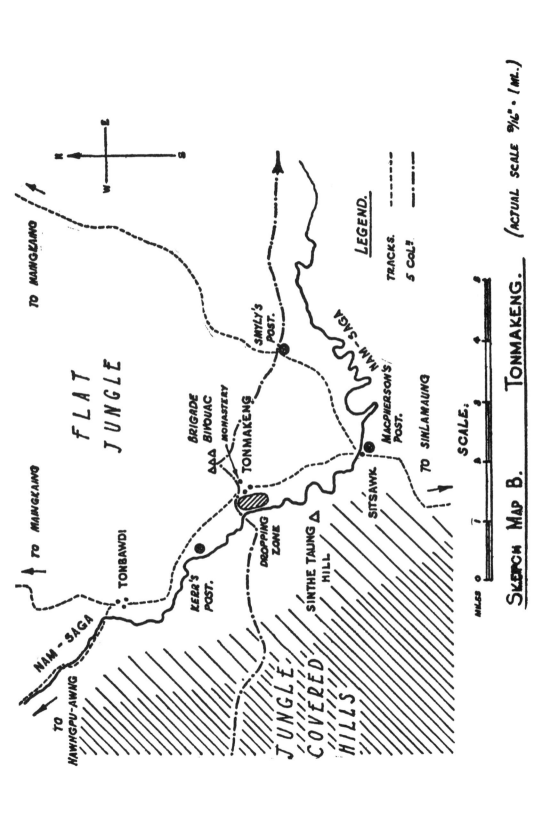

SKETCH MAP B. TONMAKENG.

(ACTUAL SCALE 9/16" = 1 ML.)

LEGEND.

TRACKS. ....

5 COLs. .—..—..—

SCALE.

MILES 0   1   2   3   4

FLAT JUNGLE

TO NANGZANG

TO MAINGKANG

TONBAWDI

KERR'S POST.

NAM-SAGA

TO HAWNGPU-AWNG

JUNGLE COVERED HILLS

SINTHE TAUNG HILL

DROPPING ZONE

BRIGADE BIVOUAC

MONASTERY

TONMAKENG

SMYLY'S POST.

MACPHERSON'S POST.

SITSAWK

TO SINLAMAUNG

NAM-SAGA

Once, at Kohima, I was roused from my beauty sleep by an orderly who said I was "wanted." I pulled on my trousers, and went down the hill with a poorish grace, to find General Sir Alan Hartley, the Deputy Commander-in-Chief, and General Mallaby, the Director of Military Operations—two of the only people in the world to see whom I would willingly be thus roused. I assured them that, whenever I found myself saying "This is damned uncomfortable, would I rather be in Delhi?" the answer was still, "Not on your life!" At Kohima also I got a message from the station staff officer to say that he would like to entertain to supper up to four officers, Scotsmen preferred. John, Duncan and I went down, and had a most amusing evening with an elderly tea-planter from Assam, thrust back into uniform for the war. He was a native of Bute, and we swapped West Highland stories until it was time for us to go back to the column and renew the march.

Often it rained, and the staging camps were under water, and the air dismally dank and cold. Marching on the hard road was sore on the feet; and it was a great relief when Brookes, my bugler, sounded his blast to signify that the moment had come for the fifteen minutes halt that I had every hour. We had collected at Jhansi a young Indian armourer called Abdul Khaliq, a handsome, cheerful but helpless youth who was dubbed Abdul the Armourer, Abdul the Bulbul (Tommy Roberts), or Abdul the Damned (Duncan) as the fancy of the moment suggested. Abdul was one big grin, and he spoke no English; but the men with whom he marched, not far behind me, taught him to call out, whenever they were feeling tired, "Blow the bugle, Mr. Brookes!" a refrain which Duncan and I incorporated into some frivolous verse.

One of the bullock-drivers was Akerman, a little Welshman with whom I often passed the time of day. He used to stump along with an old pipe stuck in his mouth; in accordance with the custom of my own regiment, I always allowed pipes on the line of march. Once I asked him how he was getting along with his bullock. He replied, in his singsong Welsh voice: "Sir, I am so bewildered, I do not know which is the bullock, myself or the bullock!"

Those nights of marching seemed interminable. They were tolerable only because we were able to march in threes instead of the single file, or "Column Snake", which was our normal tactical formation (the only one possible in jungle or on jungle tracks); and because we were able to sing. Up at the head of the column marched Duncan and I and John Fraser; behind us came Cairns, the ideal serjeant-major, in temperament as much as efficiency, of all time; Peter Dorans; Serjeant Rothwell, the animal transport serjeant; L./Cpl. Lee the clerk; Horton the cipher operator, known throughout the column as Jimmy 'Orton; Foster and White, the two signallers; Serjeant Skillander, Irish ex-jockey and spare serjeant in column headquarters; and Brookes the bugler himself. They were a witty and cheerful lot, and John, Duncan and I were often in fits of laughter at what we overheard from just behind us.

Rothwell led all the singing; his two favourites, sung every night, and often two or three times a night, were "I've got Sixpence, Jolly, jolly, Sixpence," and "When Johnny comes Marching Home Again." Peter and Cairns would exchange long reminiscences about the Rhins of Galloway, whence both came. Peter had been my servant almost continuously since 1931, and is something of a legend in my regiment; Cairns, a Territorial in the K.O.S.B., used to drive and work the threshing machine, which travelled the Rhins from Corsewall to the Mull; he knew many farms and farming folk whom I had known in my youth, and had a story for each. Jimmy 'Orton had a quick wit; and I remember him saying one night, "This column's marchin' so perishin' fast the Major 'as to give ' 'Alt!' three 'undred yards before w'ere 'e wants us to stop."

At the long halt of an hour, Peter used to produce tea, whatever the weather and however wet or scarce the fuel. I used to snatch a half-hour's sleep. At the short halts, Duncan and I would either study the stars with the help of a torch and a book I had, called *The Yachtsman's Week-end Book*; or would learn a few phrases of

Burmese from John. Best of all, though, I recollect lying flat
on our backs in the muddy road, and making out the different
constellations which we had learned on previous nights. Then
Brookes would blow the warning signal, and we would haul our
packs on to our shoulders, and go on with the second half of the
march.

Frequently we came to places where the engineers were at
work on bridges, or clearing landslides, or hollowing away more
of the overhanging cliffs. Their great arc-lights lit up the dripping sides of the hill, while the bull-dozers and angle-dozers
jerked screaming to and fro, shoving slithering tons of earth over
the edge and down the hillside. Like ours, their work began when
the traffic ceased.

At last, the summit far behind us, we came out, one cool clear
morning, on to the Imphal plain. We had marched 120 miles in
nine nights, and attracted little attention. (Indeed, the security
was so surprisingly successful that even when we came out few
people round Imphal knew we had gone in, and some of the
junior staff officers at the headquarters there knew nothing of us
at all.) Behind us, the mountains over which we had come were
hidden in cloud; before us the plain was in sunlight. We turned
off the road a mile or two, and were told to pitch camp, since we
would be there for an indefinite time.

The rain, however, was security-minded, and before the afternoon was far advanced it flung its cloak about us again. Six or
seven months ago, the men would have been helpless; but now
before evening every man was housed in a hut made of grass and
bamboo, and roofed with banana leaves. The downpour that first
evening was very heavy, and George Bromhead, the brigade major,
came out from Imphal, where the Brigadier had set up a temporary
headquarters, to find out if we wanted to move in there; but we
spurned the offer; and indeed, when he saw our neat village,
sprung up in two or three hours, he felt himself that the offer was
superfluous.

Here we stayed for twelve days, and, thanks to the kindness of
General Scoones, we lived like fighting-cocks, in spite of the many

anxieties about supplies which the unprecedented rain had thrust upon him, owing to landslides on the road. Rum was issued every evening; and though we were usually wet and cold, we were always cheerful. I held various tactical or other exercises, and marched both mules and men a short way every day, to keep feet and backs in good condition; at night we could have held sing-songs or other entertainments, but the rain always intensified.

Every other day, parties of officers went into Imphal to study the maps, air photographs, intelligence summaries and other things which brigade headquarters had gathered there in an improvised operations room. The Brigadier used to hold "map exercises," using an enormous one-inch map which covered the whole floor; all officers had to remove their boots, and crawl over it in their stocking soles. There the campaign was finally planned, and there he confided to me for the first time that my job would be the destruction of the Bonchaung gorge, and a bridge in its neighbourhood.

Still everybody was cheerful and full of optimism, not to say ribaldry. One day, lying on the chimney-piece of the Ops Room, we found a Wild West novel, in which occurred the remarkable phrase: "Howdy, buckaroos! Which way're ye ridin'?" This passed into our vocabulary, and was used chiefly for mocking John Fraser, who, for the first time in his life, was trying to master the way of a man with a horse, aided by his Karen groom Nelson, who had never before seen one.

John's daily hack was a sporting event. He had little say in where his horse would take him; and when it was fresh it used to go all over the shop, so that the countryside seemed full of horses. Somebody chose to assume that he and his horse were a complete cavalry regiment, and the term "Fraser's Horse" was taken as referring to this imaginary unit, rather than to the single intractable animal. John would arrive, his horse passaging quaintly, to be greeted with a chorus of "Howdy, buckaroo!" which drove him to fury.

Nelson took to it like a duck, and, being a conscientious man, quickly became an excellent groom. He even learned to ride, entirely through his sense of balance; and when one day we held a gymkhana he was second in the grooms' race. The officers' race was a proper shambles, since few of us knew how to ride, and hours of misery in the riding-school at Sandhurst had not helped me much. Bill Smyly was a born horseman, and Duncan, with his Australian background, pretty fair; Alec and John Kerr rode in the same manner as Crawshay Bailey played football—with determination. I regret that the officers' prize of twenty-five rupees was won by a guest-artist, Peter Buchanan; but I don't think he has been paid yet. I fell off.

There were still no signs of a move, and the delay was becoming vexatious to people who, like us, were all keyed up. One day I was told in confidence that General Wavell was coming. I do not know if Wingate guessed—I certainly did not—that he was coming to cancel the offensive to which our operations were to be complementary. For various reasons which could not be surmounted, it was not possible to stage the hoped-for advance; and it was suggested that to send us in unsupported would only be to throw us away, and could do no possible good.

This was calamitous. True, our whole object was to precede and aid in an offensive; that was the purpose of our existence. But Wingate had still to prove his case to the world: not only his belief that we could help an offensive, but the very methods and manner in which he proposed to fight. India and the world were full of sceptics, whom his brusque manner and intolerance of argument had done less than nothing to convert, and much to alienate. Offensive or no offensive, for him it was now or never; and there was the further point, that he had brought his brigade to the boil, and by no stretch of the imagination could it be kept simmering until next cold weather. I know that doubt has been cast on his wisdom in pressing to be allowed to carry on independently, and even—an intolerable impertinence, it has always seemed to me—in the wisdom of the commander-in-chief in allowing him to do so. I can only say that every column commander was in agreement; so would have been every officer had they been consulted; and not one of us, even in the light of after-events, has ever regretted the decision.

So it was on. General Wavell inspected and addressed every column, and it was one of the proudest days in my life when he inspected mine. For the past seven years I had been almost continuously under his command, and had spent five periods, varying from two years to one month, on his staff; and now for the first time I was showing him troops which I had trained, on the eve of the battle. They looked splendid. Every man was paraded with his pack on his back, and all his worldly goods for as far ahead as the imagination could penetrate. I introduced him to all my officers and many of the men, and he had a word for each. He had a word, too, for Peter, standing in his place in the ranks.

"Hallo, Dorans, what are you doing here?"

"Just the same as usual, sir: followin' the major!"

I think it was the 12th of February when at last we set off from the camp, and celebrated the end of our rest with a twenty-two mile march which fairly knocked the nonsense out of us. It was a blazing day, and the tar macadam of the road made our boots twice as big and thrice as heavy as Nature (if her responsibilities include boots) intended them to be. The next day was almost as long and just as bad, and when we arrived at Palel even Duncan was whacked, the first and only time I had ever seen him so. Perhaps the unpleasantness of the marching will be appreciated still more vividly when I say that John Fraser voluntarily rode Fraser's Horse for two stages. The road between Imphal and Palel was over the easy country of the Imphal plain, and therefore a two-way road; so that as far as Palel we were able to march by day at the same time as convoys were using it. At Palel each column spent twenty-four hours resting from the long stages before it, and then resumed the march by night up the winding road to the Saddle; so that at Palel, when we arrived in the evening, we met Scotty's column just moving out. John had friends from Burma there, so we turned all social and went out to dinner.

Another day or two brought us to a height from which we could see across the Kabaw Valley, and discern hills far away across the Chindwin.

" There's Japs in them thar hills!" said Cairns, and we looked at them respectfully.

At Lokchau, where the bridge had been repaired, there was in those days a divisional headquarters; and there I had my last meal off a tablecloth, with Jack Dalrymple, the G.S.O.I., with whom I had been an instructor at Sandhurst before the war. At Tamu I found the Seaforth Highlanders and had luncheon with them, together with some good nostalgic conversation about the Northern Meeting and kindred subjects. Greatest joy of all, I found among them a lad from my home, newly commissioned; and with him I talked of the Auchengairn Drive, and the pheasants that come high over the last of the Five Glens from behind the Heather-House, and the duck that come down to the mouth of the Toddy Burn when the lochs in the hills are frozen. After that, I went back to my column with a renewed idea of what I was going to war for.

And now for some strategy. Wingate had decided that he could not hope to conceal for a long time, if at all, the fact that he was crossing the Chindwin; the best he could do, he thought, was to conceal the whereabouts and strength of the real crossing, by providing a feint one elsewhere. He had therefore ordered Lieut.-Colonel Alexander, with Nos. 1 and 2 Columns of the Gurkha Group, to cross the Chindwin at Auktaung, while he himself with the main body crossed at Tonhe. He provided a feint even for the feint, by sending Major John Jeffries with a small party still farther south, to make inquiries as to Jap dispositions in that area, and to order rice and other supplies to be held in readiness for the advance of a large force. Jeffries was attired for this purpose as a brigadier, and took to himself the pomp and pomposity befitting that exalted rank.

These parties, therefore, continued on south from Tamu, moving without undue secrecy, while the main body avoided Tamu altogether and sneaked off across country by night, on

to the main track running north from Tamu up the Kabaw
Valley. Once again we marched by night and lay hidden by day.
L. G. Wheeler and his headquarters, which numbered three British
officers and about a hundred mixed Karens, Kachins and Chins,
crossed the Chindwin at Tonhe about the time that my column
left the Tamu area, to arrange for our first supply drop a few
miles beyond. He crossed without incident, and found that such
few Japanese as were in the neighbourhood had reacted according
to plan, and sped off southwards to investigate the rumours
coming from Auktaung.

Two nights' marching from the Tamu area brought us to
Thanan, the last point to which lorries could be got. I arrived
there to find Sam Cooke with his group headquarters, and Ken
Gilkes with No. 7 Column, already there, waiting to start over
the hill to the River on the night of the 14th February. I was the
tail column of the whole brigade; the Brigadier had already
gone on.

At four o'clock that afternoon, I assembled the whole column
round a tree, whose roots provided a small elevation on which
I could stand, and read out to them the Brigadier's Order of the
Day. They were stirring and noble words, and although the last
paragraph has often since been quoted, I feel that it can bear
repeating; for it did gather up the sentiments of most of us, and
I can imagine no more fitting committal to a great enterprise
than these words:

"Finally, knowing the vanity of man's effort and the confusion
of his purpose, let us pray that God may accept our services and
direct our endeavours, so that when we shall have done all, we
may see the fruit of our labours and be satisfied."

Just before dark, we said good-bye to those who were not
coming with us, and set off on the last stage to the Chindwin. In
our packs we had five days' rations, of biscuits, raisins, dates and
cheese, tea, sugar and milk. A few men carried a last luxury, in
the shape of a tin of bully or half a loaf of bread; for we were not

to see these again, and consequently they had taken on a new value. So laden, and with one blanket a man carried on mules, we turned up the steep footpath that led over the last hill to the River.

Before darkness fell, we bumped the tail of the next column ahead. Word came back to us that the track was appalling, and that the loads of all the mules were slipping. I went forward, and found that it was true. Every fifty yards was an unloaded mule, with its load on the track, and men resaddling it. Now this is shame and disgrace, for ninety-nine times out of a hundred a slipping load means one that has been badly or carelessly put on, or a saddle-girth that has not been tightened after the mule has "blown." I am proud to boast that during that appalling pull uphill only four loads in the whole of No. 5 Column had to be adjusted.

But it was in truth a bad track. The gradients were steep, but that was not all; for the recent rains had loosened much earth, and the track was apt to give way and slither down the hillside. Rex Walker in 7 Column lost his pony in this way, and before venturing past the spot I had more of the inner edge cut down with pick and shovel to widen the track. It was three or four in the morning when, after a really nightmare march, we bivouacked two miles over the crest at the only waterpoint which existed before the Chindwin—two columns and group headquarters all in serried ranks, and with a good chance of a mule swishing your face with his tail as you tried to sleep.

Next morning, the 15th, at about eight o'clock, Sam Cooke, Ken Gilkes and I set off with our horses ahead of the columns. The track was not fit for riding, but we thought it might be later on. After a couple of miles, we saw a clearing on the right hand side, and leaving our chargers with the grooms, we climbed twenty yards or so to see if there was a view.

There was. Below us the Chindwin stretched away north and south, separated from us by about five miles of jungle-covered hill, sloping gently down to the River. Due east, the way we were facing, the jungle stretched as far as the eye could see, unbroken, featureless, flat and dense; only on the horizon did it climb into low, ragged hills. Eighty miles to the north-east rose the volcano-like shape of the Taungthonlon, the mighty hill which dominates all the country round, and on whose summit dwells the *nat* or demon of the hill, to whom all the Shan-Kadus pay homage. On our left, and immediately to our north, rose other and higher hills, the continuation of that on which we stood: these were the mountains behind Homalin. Only at two places was the jungle interrupted: immediately opposite where we stood, where a village was discernible on the far bank of the River: and about eight miles north of us where a green smudge running away from the River, its light emerald contrasting softly with the savage green of the jungle, showed the valley in which lay Myene. There, even now, L. G. Wheeler's advance party was waiting to collect the first supply drop that night.

Ken Gilkes was the only one of us who had his glasses with him, and we looked through them in turn, realising that, far though we had already come, the real adventure was only just beginning. The Narain Nullah and the Betwa River belonged to another world. Far away, only to be seen through the glasses, was a range of pale grey mountains, it seemed a lifetime away; and we knew that our objectives lay beyond that and beyond that again. It made me tired to look at it.

We pushed on down the track, passing on the way a Jemadar and six men, of an Indian regiment, who started to their feet when they saw us appear, and hastily put on their equipment again, like schoolboys surprised when they should have been working. A little beyond them we checked at a fork, where one track went left and the other right. As we stood, the Indian patrol came up and turned off left; but by then we had seen the footprints, half obliterated with rain, going off to the right, and followed them instead. Another mile, and we met a sentry on the track who told us that brigade headquarters was just off to the right; and we turned in thither.

Squadron-Leader Longmore, the senior R.A.F. officer, met us and took us along to Wingate. As we went, he told us that the

SEE MAP ON PAGE 39

crossing was going very badly; there had been no interruption, but it had taken a long time to get a power-rope across, the stream was wide, the current swift, and the mules were jibbing badly. Wingate confirmed this, and said that, although things were now going better, we were badly behind schedule; 3, 4 and 8 columns, and brigade, were all on each other's heels down at the bottom of the hill. It was a poor lookout for me, as tail column; and I asked if I could try my luck at a village marked on the map some three miles farther upstream called Hwematte, which looked as if it was on the track where I had just seen the Indian patrol go down. If the hold-up at Tonhe was as bad as it sounded, I would have plenty of time to fail at Hwematte if it were no good, and still come down to Tonhe afterwards, to resume my place at the end of the queue. He agreed, ordering me to march independently to Myene if I got across all right; and I turned back along the track, resolving to take the whole column down to Hwematte on spec.

The column was just reaching the fork when I got there; and I led them off down the northern track, leaving a bamboo sign for late comers, reading " Gilkes right, Fergusson left." The track had obviously never before been used by animals, and there was a good deal of clearing to be done and detours to be cut; so I put Duncan in charge, and pushed on with John Fraser (whom I had appointed second-in-command and heir to myself), a section of his Burrifs, and Peter Dorans. We passed a number of skulls and skeletons, and realised that some of the luckless refugees of 1942 must have tried to escape this way.

About an hour before dark, we crossed a small stream which led into a paddyfield. At the far end of it we could see the dark trunks of tall trees, and there seemed to be a space between them and the end of the field, which might be the River. We quickened our pace to see—and it was.

We had come out at Hwematte, as we had hoped. The village consisted of about eight houses, all derelict and deserted, standing parallel to the river at the top of the bank. Under one of them the Indian patrol, which proved to consist of Assamese, was cooking, for a thin column of blue smoke was rising placidly into the damp, still air. I looked up and down the River. The banks were high, the River about four hundred yards wide where I stood, but a good deal wider both above and below. It reminded me of the Thames at Cliveden. Looking north, it ran straight for a good three miles; southward was a bend, but not sharp enough to blot out the view, perhaps three miles away, of boats crossing and re-crossing—presumably the main body of the brigade. As I looked, I saw coming lazily downstream towards us, less than four hundred yards away, a native boat, with three of a crew. We needed badly all the boats we could get; all we carried was four two-man rubber boats, and two round R.A.F. pattern dinghies; so I told John Fraser to get hold of it somehow, and got everybody under cover.

Jameson, one of John's Naiks (Corporals), skipped into a place of hiding near the water's edge, from which he could hail the boat, and everybody else threw themselves on the ground. The Assam patrol, seeing the excitement, got into a fire position, Bren-gun and all.

"Don't shoot, don't shoot!" cried John urgently in Urdu. I never saw such a look of disappointment as came over their faces.

The boat came abeam. One man was steering with an oar, and the other two drowsing. Jameson hailed them softly, and they looked up. He motioned them to the shore, and they came, lazily but without suspicion. As a piece of piracy, it was an anti-climax.

I slithered down the steep bank with John to listen to him questioning them; they were the first Burmans I had ever seen apart from those in the brigade, and were of a different race— Shans. They were fishermen, they said, going down to Thaungdut to sell their fish. No, they did not know of any Japs nearer than Homalin, but many British had crossed the River two days ago (Wheeler). Yes, certainly we could hire their boat. Would we like to buy their fish?

I willingly agreed to buy them, in order to acquire the right to fling them into the River, for they stank to high heaven; but the Burrifs' hands were already in their pockets, and the whole cargo bought up in no time—not to dump, but to eat. This problem disposed of, and nobody else being in sight, I looked at my surroundings with more attention, and tried to see it as a crossing-place. The near bank was all right; there was a little track down which mules could be got, and a good beach, and a patch of deep water near the edge into which the mules could be shoved (for they like a gradual immersion no more than I do). But the far side was tricky: although there was a beach, it looked muddy, and was backed by steep banks. I resolved to go across and have a look.

With Jameson, who spoke English, I stepped into the boat and had myself paddled over. Engrossed as I was, I found time for satisfaction that I was the first in my column to set foot on the far bank. I found it less muddy than I had feared, but the steep banks presented a problem. I found a dry *chaung* (stream)* running back into the bank for a couple of hundred yards. It seemed to me that its banks looked less formidable than those of the main stream, and that with a little pick and shovel work it would be possible to get the mules up all right. I cast up and down the Chindwin shore for a little way, but I found nothing so promising.

I got back into the boat again, and was paddled across to Hwematte beach. As I reached the top of the bank, and was accepting a cup of tea from Pa Haw, I saw the head of the column emerge on to the paddy, Duncan leading. It was now just on seven o' clock. I gave orders for covering parties to be put out, and for a meal to be cooked and eaten; and said that the process of crossing the "Jordan" should begin at 9.30 p.m. Everybody was to rest till then. I myself carried out a hasty reconnaissance, made up my mind on certain points, and then lay down to snatch an hour's sleep.

* I hate the habit in travel-books (particularly those dealing with countries I do not know) of putting in native words with an English word in brackets after it. But I feel that where the native word is so common that it is adopted by the British soldier, the practice is legitimate. I hope the reader will agree.

CHAPTER FIVE

FROM CHINDWIN TO ZIBYUTAUNGDAN

15th February—28th February

"But Charon, the last gillie,
    Answer makes none:
Slow through the dark valley
The dark waters run."

JOHN MOORE.

AT NINE-THIRTY we roused to work. The moon was up, and the waters of the River and the dark woods beyond were most beautifully dappled. David Whitehead was already busy with his river-crossing equipment—1½-inch manila rope (alleged), his blocks, his snatch-blocks, and his rubber boats. He had selected the tree on which he wanted to make fast the hither end of the power rope, and his sappers were all ready for a hard night's work. I allotted jobs to various platoons, and gave out my orders for the crossing (including a *sotto voce* one to Peter to keep me well supplied with tea at intervals throughout the night). I ordered the houses to be stripped to make rafts, since the matchboarding which comprised the walls looked as if they would make admirable decking. Then we started to get the power-rope over.

The Chindwin was a good deal wider than anything we had previously tackled, and though we had had stronger currents to deal with, the combination of current and width proved formidable. The intention was to tow a light line over in one of the small rubber boats, made fast to the heavy line; and once the light line was across, to tow the heavy line over by hauling on the light. But the heavy rope kept being caught by the stream and whisked off to leeward, and the light line parted every time. After strenuous efforts, we got the heavy line over, the far end coming ashore a long way down stream; and then we could not eliminate the sag. At last it became apparent that we had fouled the bottom. That began a weary cycle of twitching it, diving for it, dredging for it, and then starting again. Thompson, Berger, Serjeant Pester of the sappers, I and anybody else who at all fancied himself at swimming, were at it all night long. We had put a small party across to the other side in rubber boats and the fish-boat, together with a signal lamp and operators; and lamps winked furiously at each other across the water. All night long pairs of people hauled themselves out along the rope in a rubber boat to the place where the obstruction seemed to be; and then, while one hung on to the rope, the other dived or hauled himself down it to the river-bottom, struggled to cast it off as long as his breath held, and then shot to the surface with lungs bursting, to take over the job of holding the rope while the other had a shot at it. Sometimes one would triumphantly cast it off and rise from the waters squeezing out a cheer with one's last breath, only to find that it was still foul a few yards farther on. I remember pulling back to the shore hand over hand with Berger after half an hour's effort, with barely enough breath left to pull, and the boat full of water.

Meanwhile the fish-boat which held about six men with their packs, had been patiently ferrying Tommy Roberts's support platoon over to the far side, since I had detailed them for the first elements of the bridgehead. At 4.30 in the morning, the moon had sunk so low that we could hardly see at all; and so I despondently called a halt until 6.30, when it should be light enough to start again. Bitterly cold in spite of my latest cup of tea, I rolled up in a blanket and was asleep in a second.

But with dawn our luck changed. Bill Aird and Lance-Corporal Thompson went out in a rubber dinghy, Thompson went down the rope and cast it off a snag, and, lo and behold! the rope was running free right across to the other side. Half an hour's hauling with men and mules, and it was as taut as could reasonably be hoped for. From then right through the day the fish-boat and the rubber dinghies went to and fro across the River, carrying loads and towing mules, while the raft, completed, with decking laid

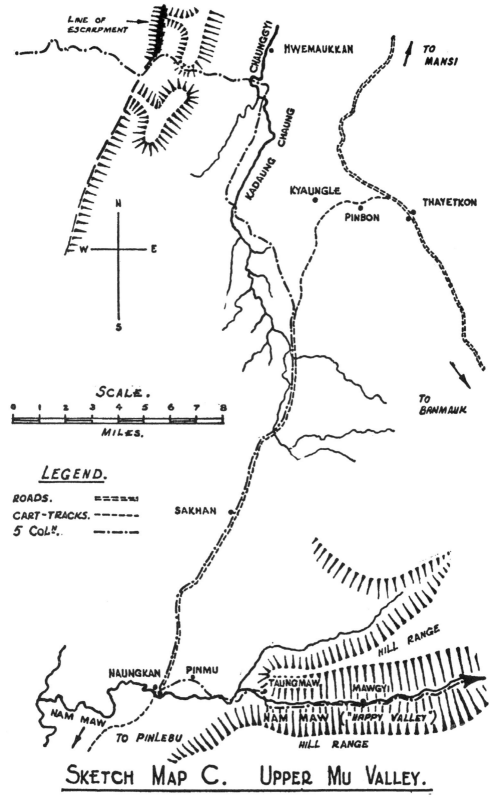

LINE OF ESCARPMENT

CHAUNGGYI

HWEMAUKKAN

TO MANSI

KADAUNG CHAUNG

KYAUNGLE

PINBON

THAYETKON

N
W — E
S

TO BANMAUK

SCALE.
0 1 2 3 4 5 6 7 8
MILES.

LEGEND.
ROADS. ════════
CART-TRACKS. --------
5 COLⁿ. ─ · ─ · ─

SAKHAN

HILL RANGE

NAUNGKAN   PINMU

TAUNGMAW

MAWGYI

NAM MAW

NAM MAW "HAPPY VALLEY"

TO PINLEBU

HILL RANGE

SKETCH MAP C. UPPER MU VALLEY.

(ACTUAL SCALE 4 MLS TO 1 INCH.)

on two of the rubber boats, was hauled on the power rope. A second was established farther upstream without difficulty; this was used for the outward journey, and the other for the homeward. In addition to the raft, the R.A.F. dinghies (which could take fourteen men and their packs, provided some of the men hung on to the side and let themselves be towed), were also using the power ropes. Mules which were reluctant to swim—there were not many—were lashed on to the raft; most were towed behind one or other of the queer assortment of vessels; some few swam willingly and free. Judy, the column dog, trained in message carrying, took a great interest in the whole performance. She would travel on the raft or boat, and, whenever she saw a mule trying to turn back to the shore or seize control, she would leap into the water and swim beside his head to turn it in the right direction. She certainly did her share of the work.

When night fell, the crossing was almost finished. I had intended to move away as soon as it should be, for although we had seen nobody, it seemed incredible that news of our antics should not have reached the Japs. Instead of the whispers of the previous evening, there was now a lot of noise going on. But our southern flank was covered by the crossing of the main body, while any threat from the north was more likely to go for Colonel Wheeler's party at Myene than for us; and Subedar Ba Than had taken patrols well out to the eastward and heard of no Japs anywhere. So, as we were all dog-tired, I decreed that we should stay where we were for a bit of sleep and move off at five in the morning.

The decision to stay was all right; it was the decision to move at five which was foolish. The moon had set, and dawn was not till six-thirty or later; and after struggling for a few hundred yards in the blackness of the night, I was compelled to give the order to go to sleep again. Even the Burrifs, who had reconnoitred the route the previous evening, could hardly find it in the inky darkness.

As soon as we could, we saddled up again and moved off, reaching the group of houses at the mouth of the Myene valley an hour or two later. We noticed a couple of boats hidden under the houses as we passed. The people seemed friendly, and told us of all the British troops up the valley. It began to rain, and a cold, chilling rain at that. Ba Than and a small party had gone on ahead to meet Colonel Wheeler's force, which had with it my colour-serjeant and a small administrative party. They had left with Wheeler from Imphal, in order to watch our interests at the supply dropping.

Myene proved to be a small village in two halves, lying in its own paddy, which was pretty well under water with the recent rains. I met Ba Than, who said that the supply drop had been successful, and that the villagers had co-operated in bringing in outlying parachutes. (Ba Than had a *flair* for becoming rapidly acquainted with gossip.) He led us to a bivouac which he had selected, among dripping trees but with good water, and not too far from the area where the food had been dropped.

Scotty's column had arrived just before me, coming by a different route. Mike Calvert (3 Column) had got in the night before, just after 4 Column. He was now busy picking up his supplies ready for a move. Wheeler had left a couple of days before for a place called Tonmakeng, some forty miles to the eastward, which Wingate had told him to make for; since from there we knew of a forest track, whose existence was supposed to be unknown to the Japs, but which led right through their forward positions to the Mu Valley beyond. This Wingate hoped to use, reaching the area by forced marches while the Japs were still worrying about the Auktaung feint.

An hour after me, the leading elements of brigade head-quarters arrived, led by Wingate himself. We had an informal conference, at which I was ordered to hand over my inglorious place as tail column and move off first thing in the morning, just ahead of brigade headquarters; Scotty would come next, and Sam Cooke and Ken Gilkes, who were still engaged in crossing at Tonhe, would bring up the rear. The expedition was taking on some of the characteristics of a bumping race.

That evening, Lieut. Toye, of the Burma Rifles, rode in from

Tonamakeng with the news that Wheeler had arrived there all right. He had information about enemy dispositions which was of the greatest value. Toye's ride, in which he was accompanied by a single orderly, was something of a feat. He had only just joined the Burma Rifles, and knew nothing of the language; so a ride of forty miles through hostile country was for him no mean undertaking.

The rain stopped in the evening, and I put on my spare shirt and trousers which were comparatively dry. I went down to brigade headquarters to get Spurlock, the signal officer, to come and look at one of my sets which was giving trouble. I saw him part of the way home, and then in the dark got lost in the paddy-fields. I picked my way delicately over some boggy ground, and at last saw ahead of me, shining in the moonlight, what I took to be the track. I jumped down off the paddy-bund along which I was walking, on to the track, thanking my stars that I had found it. I hadn't. Some of those streams that run across paddy-fields are quite remarkably deep.

The column filled up with rations to six days' worth, before moving off. In all respects except one, it had been a successful drop. The one failure had been in the matter of mail. The air-craft scheduled to drop it had had a rough ride and arrived in the area in a thunderstorm. Anxious to get back over the hills as soon as possible, the pilot had thought he recognised the sandbank in the Chindwin, which was the clue to the dropping area, and had let go the mail. Only a few seconds later he realised his mistake, and discovered his correct position. He had dropped the mail near an enemy post in the neighbourhood of Thaungdut.

As soon as this was known, Scotty was ordered to send off a fighting patrol to retrieve it, and to catch up the brigade at Tonmakeng. It was not so much that we were keen on recovering private mail, but that its capture by the enemy would immediately divulge our whole order of battle. My personal fear was lest the Brigadier should order no further mail to be dropped; and the thought haunted me for several days to come.

Wanting to see the Brigadier, I left next morning half an hour before the column; and at brigade headquarters I found Gim Anderson, who told me he had been attached there. He did not think he was going to enjoy it one bit; he had no definite job, and was merely extra cipher officer and bottle-washer.

He told me a conversation between him and the Brigadier which had happened in the middle of the night. It went something like this:

WINGATE: Major Anderson, why is that mule braying?
ANDERSON: I'm afraid I don't know, sir.
WINGATE: Well, go and find out.

Gim went over to the mule lines, but by that time the mule had stopped braying. For one wild moment he thought of asking all the mules which of them had been braying, and why; then he returned, without an answer, wondering what he would say to the Brigadier. But he had gone back to sleep.

I offered Gim my sympathies, and just then Wingate roared "Major Anderson!" "Sir!" cried poor Gim, once a column commander, and bustled off at the double.

We marched that day through flat teak forest, at that time of year very pleasant marching, with great shady leaves to keep off the sun. Later, when the leaves are down, from the middle of March onwards, to march in teak is a purgatory of dust and thirsty heat, for streams are few and far between. But that day we found some water about noon and made the most of it. During the noon halt, I got my first definite news about the enemy. It came over the wireless, but was later amplified by a mounted officer, who cantered up the track from brigade headquarters behind me.

Mike Calvert, nearly a day's march ahead, had heard of a Jap patrol of two hundred in a village called Metkalet. The route the brigade was to follow ran through Tonzi, a village with a gold-mine on the Nam Karun;* Metkalet stood on the same *chaung*

---

* *Nam* is the Shan word for a stream, whereas *chaung* is Burmese. In Chingpaw the Kachin language it is *hka*: all very confusing.

some five miles farther south. Calvert had characteristically asked permission to give chase; I could if I liked. Of course I liked! Besides the chance of complete surprise, we had all of us realised that the one thing needful to complete our training was a successful early brush. Our easy crossing of the Chindwin and lack of interruption until now was having a bad effect on the men; they were becoming too easy-going and incautious. I looked at the map: there were no distressing contours between us and Metkalet, and the fact that there were no tracks did not worry me unduly, since cross-country through teak is easy meat. There appeared to be no obstacles whatever.

I chose off the map a point of departure about a mile ahead, where the track we were on turned a few degrees farther north. I did not know where Mike had left it, but I fancied about five or six miles farther on. I hastily told the officers what was in the wind, and gave them a chance to pass it on to the men. Metkalet as the crow flies (or as we used to say, as the snake crawls) was about ten miles, and I hoped to reach it early next morning. I reckoned Mike would have about the same distance to do as I.

We duly left the track, and after about three miles of marching met a patrol of Mike's. They were out from the bivouac where he had left his rear elements, and from which he had taken his battle group in search of the enemy. They were not confident about the best way back to their rear bivouac, or I should have liked to accompany them to learn Mike's plans, concerning which they were vague; so after travelling in company with them for a bit I pushed on. Unfortunately this was one of the few occasions when our maps let us down badly; for instead of the free run through teak which they promised us, we came suddenly to a long narrow marsh of oozy black mud, covered with surface water and fringed with tall dry reeds. We followed it for a good mile in an endeavour to find a way round it, but it seemed not only to be endless, but to be heading us back on our tracks.

I have met these marshes since, and learned to dread them. They seem to be forever coming to an end, but always one finds a little arm sticking out which you have to go round, and then another, and another, till you fancy yourself on an island, and wonder how the devil you got there.

At last it became obvious that there was nothing for it but to build a causeway. This we did by felling small trees and spreading them crosswise (that is, parallel to the banks), and filling up the holes with small branches, brushwood and rushes. They shiver ominously as you cross, the mules do not like them one bit, and they take a good half hour to make. Once over, we felt as though reprieved—until after going three hundred yards we came across just such another. Again we could find no way round. In the next twenty-four hours we built fourteen such causeways, and broke our hearts. Let the Japs in Metkalet do as they please: all we wanted was to get out of this nightmare swamp. While we floundered in it we got a signal from brigade: "Suspect you are on wildgoose chase stop on to Tonmakeng." Had I been brought up on any fare other than G. A. Henty, I should have burst into a fit of uncontrolled weeping. I could only pray in my jealous fashion that Mike was in the same fix.

The following afternoon at four o'clock, covered with mud and in vile tempers, we burst out of low scrub jungle into a clump of high trees, and gazed moodily across some paddy and the Nam Karun, at the village of Metkalet on the other side. Suddenly one of the Burrifs came running back, and chattered in Burmese to John Fraser, who listened intently and then, followed by myself, aflame with curiosity, went forward fifty yards to see what it was all about. Everywhere in the clump of trees there were ashes and mountainous elephant droppings. The ashes were still warm.

The Japs—fifty of them rather than two hundred, with four elephants—had pushed off to the south in a hurry four hours before. Whether they had news of our advent it was impossible to say; the villagers had not. We stirred up the Jap ashes and made tea off them, watered the mules, had a quick wash, and carried on through the village. With Pam as interpreter, I had a talk with the headman, who was leaning on his gate. He seemed friendly enough, and I gave him a silver rupee, which made him almost dribble with ecstasy: he had nearly forgotten they existed.

Two miles beyond, at the top of a long pull, I bivouacked for the night, which passed without event—just as well, since one of the sentries fell asleep at his post. Here I set you a problem: how do you punish a man for an offence like that, in circumstances like these? Shooting, thank goodness, is no longer the recognised punishment; to hold a field general court martial and give him penal servitude hardly helps towards making him a useful soldier during the next few months; detention, loss of pay, stoppage of leave, confinement to—column?—none of these seem applicable. To deprive him of some of his already meagre rations lessens his usefulness as a soldier, for in all conscience they were meagre enough already. Yet you cannot let him get away with it lightly: he had all our lives in his hands, and put them in pawn. I pose the problem; I do not provide the answer. I only want it appreciated that Long Range Penetration has some problems peculiarly its own.

The next few days were without incident, except that we met Gillow, a young officer who had joined Scotty's column at Jhansi, more or less wringing his hands. Scotty had somewhere picked up four elephants shortly before crossing the Chindwin, complete with *oozys*. Exclaiming at his good fortune, he had piled all his men's blankets on them, and given them Gillow and a section of infantry as escort, to move in rear of the column. The previous evening Gillow had become benighted before catching up the column, and, not certain that he was on the right track, bedded down where he was, to wish for the day. The day came, but the *oozys* went: they had got off their mark in the night, leaving their elephants. Although Gillow addressed them in every language of which he was a master; although he said "Gee-up," "*Chelo*," "*Iggiri*," and "Come hup"; although he pushed them and prodded them and held hay in front of them, and stuck them with bayonets, those elephants were just not moving, and he had had to abandon both them and their loads. I was a bit sorry for Gillow.

Of the last few days before we got into Tonmakeng I have little recollection. All the columns had got on to the same track, and were treading on each other's toes. We had reached the bumpy ragged hills we had seen from beyond the Chindwin, and the teak had given place to bamboo. I found that one column had forbidden talking, and was making all men converse in whispers. I was shocked to find this, for I am convinced it is bad psychology, and leads to undue nervousness. Talking in a low voice is another thing altogether, and can easily be acquired with training; but whispering is hard on the voice as well as the nerves, and leads moreover to misunderstandings. It is a bad rule, and this column, I know, did away with it after a bit.

Tonmakeng stands on one of the most important north and south tracks in the district, and is an attractive village, fairly large by local standards. It lies on the Nam Saga, and is the most upstream of a series of villages whose paddy areas are almost continuous. Above Tonmakeng, the *chaung* runs through jungle, and the flat lands on either side are crowded out by hills. The track by which we had come was poor and precipitous, not easy to follow. The last hill, the Sinthe Taung or Dead Elephant Hill, dominates the village. To the north, low rolling hills spread away to the Uyu River, a considerable stream that has its source up in the north near the Hukawng Valley.

At Tonmakeng we met Wheeler's party, which was camped on the Nam Saga about a mile from the village. He and Peter Buchanan were both in good form. A patrol had been sent to Sinlamaung, twenty miles south-east along the track and had found it held: one Burrif had a bullet in his leg to show for it, our first casualty. We were in need of more food, and the country ahead was thought to be unsuitable for supply dropping; so the Brigadier had decided to have a mammoth supply drop at Tonmakeng for his whole force—brigade headquarters and the five columns with it. The few aircraft available for supplying the expedition would need three whole days to complete the drop. Rather than waste these three days, he would leave two columns to run the drop, and send three to beat up Sinlamaung, where the garrison was believed to be three hundred strong.

Orders for this operation were given at a conference on the

SEE MAP ON PAGE 51

bank of the *chaung* on the 23rd of February. Sam Cooke was to command the expeditionary force, which would be made up of 3 Column (Mike), 7 Column (Ken) and 8 Column (Scotty). 4 Column was to be the first to ration up, and push out along the so-called "Secret Track"; I was to have the not very honourable task of running the supply drop. Until they were ready to move, 4 Column's support platoon and various other platoons were to come under me to help me in the defence of the area, for which I was made responsible. The more unwieldy parts of the expeditionary columns were to be left in a safe bivouac, which I was to select and protect. Brigade headquarters was going off for a little peace and quiet by itself in the jungle.

I found a secluded place for the bivouac, and a use for the telephone, which everybody had mocked me for bringing. I had a permanent defence centre on the dropping ground (the big paddy near the village); and I put Tommy Roberts in charge. John Kerr I sent off with his platoon about a mile away to stop the track down the valley, and gave him Judy, the message-carrying dog, and one of the two men between whom she ran. Bill Smyly, who was always pestering me for more militant employment than A.T.O., I sent off with ten of his Gurkhas as a stop on another track; Macpherson of the Burma Rifles with his platoon of Chins was already blocking the only other approach I knew of.

The march to Sinlamaung and the supply drop both began next morning. Hopes were high of doing some good at Sinlamaung; Alex's group down south had already drawn blood without loss to themselves, and we were hoping to do better. The fighting patrol sent to recover our mail had returned empty handed, and their report left little room for doubt that the Japs had got it.* This meant that they knew our order of battle, and could probably have a fair guess at our strength: which was to be regretted, but, since there was nothing to be done about it, not to be unduly mourned.

The supply dropping was excellent. Everything fell on good ground, and I distributed it all round the columns as it came, the

* Note B: The Loss of the Mail.

representatives of those columns on their way to Sinlamaung collecting it on their behalf. I was anxious that if the Japs should interrupt the performance before the curtain, the rations available should nevertheless be evenly distributed. Denny Sharp, who was running the technical side of the drop, gossiped most of the day with Tommy Roberts, whose half-section he had become, and took photographs of the scene.

The Sinlamaung expedition was abortive, in that the Japs got wind of it and skedaddled before the village was reached. They hurtled eastwards, spreading alarmist tales and causing much marching and counter-marching; so some benefit accrued. The columns, thwarted of their prey, solaced themselves by destroying a large rice dump and other stores, and burning down some new and half-finished hutments which were apparently intended for monsoon quarters. They returned on the 26th tired, but not ill-pleased with themselves.

Meanwhile, we had had our own minor excitements. A patrol had come into Tonbawdi, the next village downstream from Tonmakeng, from the south-west. It must have crossed our recent track; but it continued on its way north without showing any interest in us. I made inquiries in Tonbawdi, and found that it had had no interpreter with it, so presumably it had come through villages teeming with gossip about us which it had failed to overhear. As a patrol, it sounded rather inefficient.

Another patrol had passed through Macpherson's post, but instead of coming towards Tonmakeng had kept on up the track towards Bill Smyly's. I sent him a warning, to keep a sharp look-out, but it never showed up there. There was no other known track up which it could have turned; and our complete loss of contact rather worried me. Mac was positive the Japs had not seen his men (with whom incidentally he was furious for not having opened up: he had been snatching a sleep at the time), and Bill had had his finger on the trigger for twenty-four hours. Long afterwards, we heard that they had tumbled to our presence in Tonmakeng, and were so frightened that they hid starving in the jungle until sometime after we had moved on.

By the time the Sinlamaung columns had got back, the supply drop was over and everything issued. The Brigadier held a conference in the monastery* and gave out his orders for the next stage. 4 Column was to thrust on and make good the "Secret Track" to the edge of the Zibyutaungdan escarpment, twenty miles to the east; they were to start at once, and be followed by Scotty, brigade and Wheeler the same afternoon. I was to leave at three next morning, when there would be a moon; Sam Cooke and Ken Gilkes later next day. Mike Calvert wanted to travel by a route he had heard of on the way to Sinlamaung, which ran through a village called Namza: permission was granted to him. The object was to reach the Mu Valley without going through any of the known defiles, which might easily be blocked; therefore, with the exception of Mike we were going to march in line ahead along a single track off which one could not deploy. It was a complete gamble—a gamble on the Japs not knowing that the track existed.

Next morning at three a.m., with packs once more heavy from the supply drop, we left our bivouac; and as soon as we came into the dry *chaung* bed along which we had to travel to reach our starting point on the "Secret Track," I became aware of another column moving parallel with us. This was Mike, who had chosen the same hour to start as I had been given the previous day. Never at my most equable at that hour of the morning, I sent him an extremely rude message by the mouth of Taffy Griffith, his Burrif officer, whom I happened to meet.

"My compliments to Major Calvert," I said, "and ask him another time to be so good as to adhere to the timings laid down by brigade, so as to avoid inconvenience to those who take the trouble to do so."

This sentence seemed to me magnificent for the next half-hour. After that I woke up, and then I felt rather a fool.

I don't know how it is, but as soon as I get a pack on my back I begin to develop a grievance. Woe betide anybody who talks to

---

* The *hpongyi-kyaung* in a Burmese village combines the functions of monastery and school.

me as I march along, especially anybody who tries to be funny; I remember that very morning snubbing poor Pam Heald for some perfectly innocent and probably quite funny remark. I don't say I always have a grievance; sometimes I walk along with beautiful castles in the air: wonderful reviews for a book; a speech by the Lord Provost of Edinburgh, as he presents me with the freedom of the city; arriving home on repatriation; choosing a Lucullan meal at the Berkeley; walking round at Lord's; making my speech from the balcony of the county buildings in Ayr, on being declared elected Member for South Ayrshire by a record majority. But far more often I am hugging a grievance; inditing a crushing letter to *The Times*; winning an insubordinate correspondence with the Army Council; flooring an unpleasant general with some such remark as Midshipman Easy's—"discipline is a matter between officer and officer, but manners is a matter between gentleman and gentleman." On all these occasions I win hands down. If there is any grievance at the back of my mind, the weight of my pack (which is after all close on half my own) is sure to bring it out; and I stalk along, bent double, nursing my wrath to keep it warm. This goes on until I halt, when my pack comes off my back, the restriction on my blood-vessels is eased, and the milk of human kindness courses through me to such effect that I would offer the Devil himself a cup of tea.

John Fraser tells me—I have forgotten the incident, but I have no difficulty in believing it—that once as we walked along I said to him:

"Where are you?"

He knew at once what I meant, and answered:

"In the Cally Hotel in Edinburgh—I am just trying to make up my mind if I know that girl on the sofa over there. Where are you?"

"In Prunier's. My brother's late for luncheon."

Another freakish trick of my mind when I march is its method of assessing distances. It insists on comparing them with distances known to me at home in Scotland. Sixty miles becomes "as far as from home to Glasgow," eight miles "from home to Cassillis station"; two and a half, "from home to Dailly." Thus, an hour's stage, our normal march between rests, corresponds almost exactly with the Sunday walk to church. When twenty minutes are gone, I think of myself as having reached the Old Toll, while half an hour marks the top of Bellman's Brae. I have never induced any one else to admit to this curious mental process.

Mouthing poetry is my great standby on these occasions. Psalms and paraphrases come in handy, and so do the long wedges of Shakespeare taught me at my private school by one Mr. Money. The day we left Tonmakeng, however, I could not get into my stride; for we had done only four miles, picking up Bill Smyly *en route*, when we ran into Macpherson and the tail of the Burma Rifle headquarters. For the rest of the day we kept bumping each other, and whenever I cursed them they answered that they were bumping brigade in front of them, that brigade in their turn were bumping 8 Column, and that 8 Column could not get on because of 4 Column. Several times I halted for half an hour or an hour, and moved on again for fear of being bumped by Sam Cooke; but always, and however long I halted for, half an hour's march would bring me up against Macpherson again. The reason was, of course, that 4 Column were doing all the pioneering, clearing fallen logs, reconnoitring odd tracks that went off at a tangent to make certain that we followed the correct one, and so on. To be the first of an impatient line of columns is a rotten job.

At intervals I met a Burrif messenger coming back from John Fraser, whom I had sent on ahead with 4 Column to look after my interests in the matter of bivouacs, and to keep me informed; water shortage was the burden of his reports. Although the best and most consistent going is nearly always to be found on watersheds, water is always a difficulty, since one of the inscrutable ways of Nature is never to have water flowing along watersheds: usually a stiff downhill scramble, beyond the powers of a mule, is necessary to reach it. That night, however, we bivouacked just above the Nam Kadin, and found ample water for all columns.

Next morning, 8 Column dropped back two places, so that the

order of march was now 4, Brigade, Burrif H.Q., 5, 8, Sam Cooke's
2 Group, 7. It was unpleasant marching, since three out of the
first five miles were along the Nam Kadin, splashing through the
water, and thence up a long feeder of the same stream, much
obstructed with bamboo. We had a bad climb out of it, too, with
mules and mule-loads giving a heap of trouble. But it was a
short day: no later than three o'clock I found the Burrifs halting
for the night, and received orders to pass through them and
bivouac anywhere I liked ahead of brigade.

John Fraser was waiting for me, with a good bivouac area
already laid out. 4 Column, he said, had reached the escarpment,
and were trying to find a way down it. Before nightfall a message
came back to say that they had succeeded, and were busy improv-
ing it with picks and shovels. Wingate sent for me, and told me
that next morning I was to shove on ahead, down the escarpment,
and leave the brigade. I was to move independently with all
speed for the Bonchaung, pull down the gorge on to the line,
and do any other damage in the neighbourhood that I could.
Then I was to cross the Irrawaddy and move down towards
Mogok, where it was his general intention to concentrate the
brigade.

Mike was being given similar orders by wireless, except that
his objective was the railway at a point farther south. 4 Column
was to attack the Japanese garrison known to be at Pinbon, to
facilitate the rapid move southward down the Pinlebu road of
brigade headquarters, 2 Group and 7 and 8 Columns. There was
no news whatever of Alex's group, and had been none for several
days: this was a little worrying, but as yet there was no cause
for alarm. Wingate finished by saying that he would almost
certainly catch me up next morning for a final word.

It was my practice, in case anything untoward should happen
to me, to pass on all orders to John and Duncan as soon as I
received them, even the most confidential information which was
not for the ears of others. I did the same thing that night before
going to bed; but I also told all the officers the rough outline
of the plan in so far as it affected us, and was necessary for them

to know. According to John, who had already been forward to it, we were only half a mile from the escarpment, and the track to and along it was easily negotiable by moonlight; so anxious to get ahead of the bumping and boring contest, and quit of it for good, I gave orders for a start at 4.30, pulled my Balaclava over my ears, lay down, and I rather suspect went to sleep in the middle of a sentence. . . .

CHAPTER SIX

FROM ZIBYUTAUNGDAN TO BONCHAUNG

1st March—5th March

"The red-coats march at the skreek o' day,
  An' we maun lie on the brae the night;
Then here's to them safely on their way,
  Speed to the mirk brings the mornin's fight."

CHARLES MURRAY—*Hamewith.*

THE MORNING of the 1st March dawned as we moved northward along the edge of the escarpment, seeking the track down it which 4 Column had reported. On our right hand lay a deep valley, out of which clouds of mist were already rising like fluffy cream. What appeared to be a single valley was in reality the headwaters of two: the Chaunggyi or Great Stream, which went off northward for a few miles, and then, turning abruptly west, broke through the Zibyutaungdan in a deep gorge; and the Mu Valley proper, of which the waters drain away to the southward past Pinlebu. The watershed between these two streams (which, though small, draw their tributaries from over a wide area) is so low and ill-defined that it is hard to trace it even on a map; and from our viewpoint on the edge of the escarpment the whole depression appeared as one broad valley.

Across it, bold and impressive, rose the high hills of the Mangin Range, running up to the 3700 feet of the Kalat Taung exactly opposite. Beyond those hills was the Meza Valley, and beyond that the railway and the important communications centre of Indaw. One more range of the same calibre, the Gangaw, was still to cross before the Irrawaddy.

The Mu Valley, separated as it is from the railway by a range of hills with few passes, was the ideal line on which to place outposts for the protection of the railway. It possessed a good road, motorable in dry weather even before the Japs came, running

83

SEE MAP ON PAGE 67

from Pinlebu in the south to Mansi in the north, not far from where the Chaunggyi carves its way through the escarpment to find the Uyu. There were reputed to be garrisons at Pinlebu and Mansi, and also at Pinbon and Thayetkon, to cover the one motorable road leading through the hills to the railway at Indaw. This road ran through two moderate gorges, one on either side of the town of Banmauk, and from the map it looked an ideal target for harassing operations. At the twentieth milestone, in particular, the map seemed to hint broadly at an ambush; for here the road was cut out of the side of the hill, and a stream in a deep bed ran close below it. So tempting was it, that while we were at Imphal I sought out a similar place and practised it with my column, in the hope that an opportunity might offer during the campaign. It did not; and M.S. 20 remained inviolate for that year.*

4 Column was therefore required to attack Pinbon for two reasons: first, to make the enemy cover up Banmauk: secondly, to give the other columns a free run down the Pinlebu road. The object of these other columns was to make the enemy apprehensive for Pinlebu, while Mike and I slipped over the hills to cut the railway.

We descended into the Valley at a brisk speed. We knew that, thanks to Wingate's bold march along the "Secret Track," we had dodged whatever force the Japanese had put out to block the only routes over the escarpment known to them; and it behoved us to move quickly before they could adjust themselves to a new threat. I confess that I thought, as we twisted and turned and slid down the steep track which 4 Column had made, that the period of our uninterrupted march must now, after a fortnight, have come to an end; and my ears were ready for the outbreak of firing which would signal that 4 Column had already bumped trouble. But none came.

The word passed quickly up the column from behind, "Brigadier, Brigadier"; and Wingate, mounted on a pony, arrived as he had promised. He was annoyed with 4 Column for

* Note C: Milestone 20, Road Banmauk—Indaw.

some sin of omission and was not in the best of tempers. He gave me final orders, and marched with me for twenty minutes while somebody led his pony. I was not precisely sure of my position, and he showed it me on a one-inch map which he carried (the rest of us worked off half-inches). At the bottom of the escarpment, where the ground became suddenly flat and the going easier, he wished me good luck, bade me hurry and went on down the track after 4 Column, while I struck off across country.

It was blissful to breathe, for the first time since Orchha, the pure air which surrounds the commander of an independent column. The continued jostling with other columns, and, to be frank, the constant liability to thunderous reproaches from a great leader with unattainable standards, were preying on my mind, and I was happy to get away. But it proved less easy than I had thought. The going turned bad, and we found ourselves being forced down a spur running due east instead of south-east; as so often happens, the jungle was thin on the top of the ridge, but impossibly thick in the *chaungs*. Soon we stumbled on a broad and beautiful stream, beside which was a group of roughly built huts. Ba Than went to question the inhabitants, who proved to be the first of many colonies which we afterwards found—colonies established in the jungle to get away from Jap repression and requisitioning. They confirmed that the stream was the Chaunggyi, and said that there were Japs in Hwemaukkan and other villages near by.

Later in the day we met "Fish" Herring of the Burma Rifles, with his platoon of Kachins. Originally attached to 7 Column as its Burrif platoon, they had been sent by the Brigadier on a special mission, and were henceforward independent until a rendezvous which they were to keep at the beginning of April far away beyond the Irrawaddy, right down towards the Burma Road. "Fish" had left the main body of the brigade after I had; and he told me that George Bromhead had just been sent to take over the command of 4 Column, and that Gim Anderson had been appointed brigade major in his room.

I was delighted for Gim, but a little sorry for George's promotion; because to take over a totally strange column, and a

Gurkha one at that, on the very eve of a battle, was a bit of a tall order. I wished "Fish" the best of luck, and went on my way.

The "colonists" had so little contact with the outside world that they had not been able to tell me precisely which villages held Japs and which were free of them. As the going on top of the ridges was almost as quick as the road would be, I decided to stick to them, and selected from the map a line of ridges running almost parallel to the road but gradually converging. By nightfall I had reached a point on the Kadaung Chaung, where it was evident that timber-felling was in progress during the day; tree-stumps were still damp with sap, and fires were smouldering. I found a bivouac in the standing trees beyond, and was settling down for the night, when Peter Buchanan, with a small patrol of Burrifs, stumbled on me. He was laughing at an adventure which had just befallen him.

Wingate had suddenly said, "Go and do propaganda in some of these villages, and join us farther down the road." So Peter had obediently walked into a small village, and begun a speech to the inhabitants in his best Burmese, which was rudely interrupted by a volley of rifle fire. Apparently this was one of the villages which was held. So Peter closed down his meeting, and was now looking for the Brigadier to warn him that the district seemed unsuitable for electioneering. As I was over a mile from this inhospitable village, I reckoned I was all right for the night where I was. Anyway, thank goodness, I was clear of the brigade.

Alas for my hopes; for hardly had I said good-night to Peter, when Sam Cooke and Ken Gilkes arrived with their respective armies. I told them of Peter's adventure, and they went on to bivouac somewhere beyond me. I gave orders for a move at first light, and went to sleep again.

After a short march next morning I came to a motorable road running east and west across my line of march. This was shown on the map as a track, and had obviously been recently improved to motorable standard. There were recent footprints of rubber shoes with Jap treads going west. I dropped a platoon under Philippe Stibbé to block the track in either direction while we crossed; for a column takes ten minutes to pass a point, and is a thousand yards long. I had not gone five hundred yards when a message came up from the rear to say that a party of coolies had walked into our block carrying kit for the Japanese patrol whose footprints we had seen, and which the coolies said was ten minutes ahead of them. We pinched some documents which came to light in a rapid search, and pushed on, leaving the rest of the baggage intact, and bribing the coolies not to say they had seen us.

Going got slower and slower, as the jungle grew thicker. Our ridge was petering out as it got nearer to the Pinlebu road, and I was afraid we should be losing our lead on the brigade. At that moment came again the ominous whisper up the column, "Brigadier, Brigadier!" and dash my wig if he had not caught me up again. Very forcibly he told me that I was going far too slowly, and would lose all that he had gained for me. Instead of two or three men in front to cut the way, he showed me how to use a whole platoon, a lesson which I have never forgotten. The leading two or three men cut a path just wide enough for themselves, and the remainder coming along behind each do a little more, until at last you have the path five foot wide, which you need if your mule-loads are to come through without damage.

We were now a bare quarter-mile from the main road, and the Brigadier allowed me, rather grudgingly, to have a short halt for a rest and a cup of tea before reaching it. While the tea was brewing, we heard two loud explosions about a mile to the north-east; I thought I had heard one half an hour before, but the noise of marching through the jungle had made me a little uncertain. We hurried up, and soon burst through on to the main road, while the Brigadier waited for his headquarters to come up: they were following on the track which we had cut.

Once on the road, I resolved to move at speed, to make quite sure that we got clear of the brigade this time. The sensation of walking along a main and motorable road, for the first time since the Kabaw Valley, was a strange one. Men with anti-vehicle grenades led the column and brought up the rear; for the possibility of meeting truckloads of infantry, or even armoured cars, was by no means remote. Bill Edge, I remember, was walking beside me; and the column was closed up into threes instead of its usual "snake." It was a pretty road, with a brown surface, and tall trees on either hand; it rather resembled a national park I once saw in the redwood district of California; it inevitably reminded Duncan of Gippsland. It was a solemn thought to think that the road ran ahead of us straight into Pinlebu, with nothing on it between us and the enemy.

The thought was not only solemn: it was quite erroneous. We had marched a bare mile, with fingers practically on the trigger, when dash me again if we did not run into Sam Cooke, Ken Gilkes and Scotty. The idle devils had marched boldly down the road, blowing up the timber bridges, while I had been struggling virtuously through jungle. I felt it was only a matter of minutes before the Brigadier said that, as I did not seem to want to be an independent column, I needn't be, and Scotty could go off instead.

The Brigadier arrived at that moment on his pony, and ordered us all to push on. I was to lead; I was not to halt until after dark, and then only for four hours; thereafter not again until I had reached the point on the main road where he had told me to turn off to the eastward: if he saw me again he would be very cross. So I pushed off quickly in case he should change his mind, and marched as if the Devil himself were after me.

About four in the afternoon, it came on to rain in torrents, and we were soaked to the skin in thirty seconds. Even on the road it was heavy going, and the mules slithered and slipped in all directions. I halted soon after dark near a village called Sakhan where a small track went off to the east and west; the rain had eased a little, and we were able to cook. At eleven p.m. I pushed on again; the moon should have been up, but it was still heavily overcast, and marching was thoroughly unpleasant. I took a nasty fall into a ditch and twisted my kneecap so badly that it bothered me the rest of the campaign; Willy Williamson did the same thing, and had to ride a charger for some days. It was about four in the morning when we turned off the main road at last, and up the valley of the Nam Maw. We looked in vain for a suitable bivouac; the whole area seemed to be paddy. At last, an hour after daylight, we found a small wood perched on a hill; tactically and in every other way it was thoroughly unsound; but the main body would soon be marching between the point where we had turned off the road and the garrison of Pinlebu, and we had done thirty-two miles since the bivouac where Peter Buchanan had met us. I decided to take a chance, and ordered Reveille for noon. So ended about the nastiest march of my life.

This was the third of March, and my rations were due to last only till the following evening. I could have another drop if necessary, but to do so would mean delay, and would lessen my chances of reaching the railway without interception. If I could possibly buy enough foodstuffs locally to do away with the need for a supply drop, all the better. I was at the mouth of a long valley with many villages and large paddy-fields, and with any luck I should get as much as I could carry. Three miles away was Taungmaw, the largest village of the lot: and I set out for it after a meal, at half-past one in the afternoon. All of us were stiff from the long march of the previous day, and our frequent wettings; and we moved like a squad of wooden soldiers.

At Taungmaw we heard that twelve hundred Japs had marched down the road towards Pinlebu during the night; but we realised that the "Japs" were brigade headquarters and the two remaining British columns. At last we were free of them. Taungmaw was able and willing to supply us with rice: they had never seen either Japs or British before, and I doubt if they knew which we were. At the entrance to the village was a police post *cum* air-raid shelter, with a notice outside it in Burmese saying that it was for the use of Jap soldiers: the headman said that all villages had been ordered to build one. We spent three-quarters of an hour there while they brought us rice for ourselves and unhusked paddy for the mules; we took (and paid for in silver rupees) as much as they were willing to give us, promising ourselves more from the villages farther up the valley.

The map showed us the main track following the *chaung*; but the headman said it was very bad for mules, and advised us to

retrace our steps for a couple of miles and go round a more
northerly route. Pressed, he said that the track we were on would
be just passable; and so, always reluctant to go back, I said we
would go on. I foolishly failed to ask for a guide, and we had
only done three-quarters of a mile when the track, which had
been getting steadily worse, plunged across the *chaung* on a series
of stepping stones, consisting of large, round, slippery boulders.
Much search failed to find an alternative route suitable for mules;
and I made a decision which deserved retribution: to stay where
we were for the night, while a reconnaissance party went back to
the village to find the correct route for the morning.

I could hardly have done a more stupid thing. Had we been
followed up, as we might well have been, we were caught in a
deep glen from which the only way out was the way in. I was
bitterly ashamed of myself; and when morning came without
our having been disturbed, as I deserved to be, I swore a solemn
oath that never again would I chance my arm in that fashion.

The headman reported that the way we had tried to go was
passable for men on foot, so I sent Duncan and Jemadar Aung Pe,
with a party of about ten British and Burrifs mixed, straight on
up the *chaung*. With the column I retraced my steps till just short
of the village, and followed the guide over the shoulder of the
hill, above the glen, and round. We caught up with Duncan later
in the morning; he had all our rice and paddy ready, and we
stored it in our packs and feedbags with the minimum loss of
time. We put in a good march that day. It was a beautiful,
peaceful valley, with trim villages and well-kept paddy and
banana trees; the hand of war had not touched it, and the hills
above it shielded it completely from the outside world. We
dubbed it "Happy Valley," a name which, though obvious enough,
caught the fancy of Wingate; and all Old Boys of the expedition
talk and think of it as "Happy Valley" to this day.

The Mankat Pass, at the head of Happy Valley, was such an
obvious route into the Taung Chaung valley, which lay beyond
it and offered access to the railway, that one hardly dared to hope
that it would not be held. When at last we reached the top, and

found it empty and innocent, the relief was greater than I can describe. It was a perfect spot and beautiful beyond words. Behind us lay the contented villages of Happy Valley, with the turbulence of the Pinlebu road far off, and the hills beyond. On either hand, the thinly clad, broad back of the Mangin Range climbed again towards the sky, after stooping to afford the Pass. Ahead lay the wide flat basin of the Taung Chaung, where the jungle was often interrupted by stretches of paddy. Beyond it, some fifteen miles, were the low tumbled hills through which ran the railway. Six miles to our left, but hidden by the broad shoulder of a hill which intervened, was Banmauk, with its reputedly formidable garrison.

If I seem too fond of describing views, it is because in jungle country views are hard to come by, and every one is precious. Submerged in jungle for days at a time, to reach the top of a range of hills and to see the view is as precious as the sight of the sea to the engineer of a fishing boat; who once in an hour thrusts his head through the hatch, looks around him, and gulps a few lungfuls of salt sea air. Whenever possible on such an occasion, I used to halt the column in the most advantageous place, where the most people could see; to give a chance to all officers to identify landmarks on their maps, and point them out to their men. In days of long and weary marching, the more the men can be told, the better; they always took a great interest. At every midday halt, Duncan would pin a marked map to a tree, showing our position, our route, and our distance from the last bivouac; and, whenever there was no reason to be too fussy about security, the positions of other columns so far as we knew them. The day's news, as heard on the wireless, would also be posted. Around this information board, there was always a small crowd.

It was in the Happy Valley that we had our first casualty. A man was found to be missing at the evening bivouac; an idle section commander had failed to check his section, and nobody could remember having seen him since half-way through the morning. It is my belief that he fell asleep at a halt; every one was very tired, and it might easily have happened. We hoped he might catch us up, but he never did, and nothing has been heard of him since.

A couple of miles below the Pass, the track forked by a small stream. On a tree was a note, in Burmese, pinned to the bark with a shaving of bamboo. John looked at it, and found it was merely a note from a traveller to someone he was expecting to follow him; so we carefully put it back. We had not gone half a mile, when a message came up from the rear asking us to halt; and a panting soldier, pop-eyed with excitement, came rushing up from the tail with the note in his hand, saying, "I found this pinned to a tree, sir!" We could not be bothered to go and put it back; and I have often been haunted by the thought of the upset we must have caused in that unknown traveller's arrangements.

We did twenty-two miles that day, and eighteen the next. A friendly priest told John that the only Japanese post near the Bonchaung was one of about twenty men at Nankan, the next railway station south from that of Bonchaung itself. There was another post at the railway station at Meza, but he did not know its strength. The Japs had built a motor road from Nankan through Tatlwin up to Indaw, using conscripted native labour; they occasionally sent patrols along it as well as along the railway. Otherwise, the valley of the Taung Chaung saw little of the Jap. In the evening we passed through Tatlwin and marched three miles southward along that same road, bivouacking for the night 5th-6th March, a little way off it to the east.

We were now only three miles from Bonchaung station. In the eighteen days we had been across the Chindwin, we had not seen a Japanese. For two days we had been out of touch with brigade, but had to-day received a short message to say that 4 Column's ciphers were compromised; and this sounded gloomy, for compromised ciphers usually mean that a disaster has happened. Otherwise the outlook was bright. We lay beside the fire, Duncan and I, and discussed the incredible good fortune that had brought us so far. If only it held for to-morrow, we did not care what else might happen. Duncan thanked his stars for the lucky chance of the *maidan* at Saugor, and quoted "And gentlemen in

England now abed shall think themselves accursed they were not here." I thought of the big operations room in Delhi, and wondered how far behind us was the chinagraph smudge, recording our march on the huge map.

I had already made my plan, and given out my orders. To blow the bridge and gorge by daylight would be far quicker and better than to do it by night; and although never until to-day had it occurred to me that a daylight operation would be possible, the unexpected scarcity of Japs in the area put a new complexion on it. Our successful extrication from the area, and crossing of the Irrawaddy without interception, were going to be much harder propositions than the actual blowing of the bridge and gorge. I had thought this out long before; and it seemed to me that as all our moves so far had been hole and corner, the enemy would expect us to be even more stealthy when withdrawing. Even though in all probability he was not expecting us to cross the Irrawaddy, but to withdraw to India, he would quickly become aware of his mistake; and, with the new network of motor-roads which he had been building everywhere, it would not take him long to switch his troops from one area to another as information about our movements reached him.

Therefore, instead of trying to slink across the Irrawaddy with our pitiful collection of rubber boats—an operation which would probably take several nights—I resolved to make for some town where boats were likely to be plentiful, and to try to cross in one bold stroke. My choice fell on Tigyaing, which lay to the south-east, and which was boldly marked on the map as a steamer-station. It was some twenty miles from Katha and still farther from Wuntho, the two garrisons most likely to come out and hunt us. Wuntho was in any case more likely to be taking an interest in whatever was happening at Pinlebu. Tigyaing be it: and I ordered John Fraser to make his way to that neighbourhood, and report by wireless on its possibilities. This was the night of the 5th March; I aimed to cross at Tigyaing about the 9th.

Jim Harman, with Serjeant Pester and half the Commando Platoon, was to blow the gorge. With him I sent Philippe Stibbé and his platoon as escort. The Jap post at Nankan ought to have its head kept down, and for that task I selected Tommy Roberts. He was to take with him the mortar half of his support platoon, without their mortars (I thought I might need the Vickers M.G.s at Bonchaung), John Kerr complete with platoon, and Pam Heald with a detachment of Burrifs, the others going with John Fraser. Tommy and Jim were to go as far as Kyaik-in village together; it was only a mile south of my bivouac, along the motor-road. Thence Tommy's party would carry on the six miles to Nankan, while Jim's struck off across country to the gorge. I would follow with the main body into Kyaik-in, moving about an hour later, and turn east along a small track shown on the map as running direct to Bonchaung station, a distance of about three miles. There, Alec Macdonald would go on ahead with the mules and all the unwanted items, to make a safe bivouac three or four miles beyond the railway. Duncan and I, the machine-guns, the half-platoon of Commandos under David Whitehead who were to do the actual job, and the remaining infantry platoon would remain at Bonchaung station until the bridge was blown. The bridge we knew to be a three-span steel girder affair at the southern end of the station.

David Whitehead wanted two or three hours before moving off to get his various toys in order, so I decided to push off John Fraser at first light; Tommy's and Jim's parties about eleven, and myself with the main body at noon. The rendezvous for everybody was to be a small stream in the Kunbaung valley, about twenty-five miles away, up till noon on the 8th of March; I had also a rendezvous with John Fraser nearer Tigyaing for that same evening. Finally, I decided that as Tommy Roberts was running the greatest risk of casualties, he should take with him Bill Aird, the doctor; and Bill Edge, now Cipher Officer, elected to go with him for fun.

CHAPTER SEVEN

BONCHAUNG

6th March

"Now, God be thanked who has matched us with His hour."
                                    RUPERT BROOKE: *1914*.

ON THE MORNING of the 6th of March, everybody got off to time;
but before I had marched four hundred yards along the road,
Fitzpatrick, Tommy Roberts's groom, came up at a gallop,
somewhat flustered. He had been up and down the road for
fifteen minutes, unable to spot the point in the jungle where our
bivouac had been. (I never bivouacked within five hundred yards
of a track). Tommy was engaged in Kyaik-in village with some
Japanese; he had sent Jim Harman back and round to go straight
for the gorge, and was fighting it out himself. I asked Fitzpatrick
(in civil life a buttons in a Liverpool hotel) for details, but all he
knew was that there was a lot of shooting going on, and a lot of
bangs, and Tommy had sent him back to warn me.

I hastily decided to send the main body straight off across
country to Bonchaung. I sent the remaining rifle platoon, now
commanded by Gerry Roberts, down the motor-road to the village
as fast as it could go, to back up Tommy, while I gave Alec and
Duncan their orders. When I had finished, I took Peter Dorans,
and followed Gerry. As I drew near the village, I could hear light
machine-guns in action, and the occasional burst of a grenade.
The jungle was continuous on the right of the road, but there was
a small strip of disused paddy, with some scrubby bushes, on the
left; and by the time I arrived (for it took a minute or two to
give out the orders to the main body) Gerry's leading Bren section
was already in position, and had fired on a small party of Japs.
Obsessed with the importance of avoiding a fight with our own
troops, I begged him to be careful, and to work gradually along

95

SEE MAP ON PAGE 97

the track. I saw two men of the original party in the bushes on the right, one of whom was Bill Edge's servant, who had been with Tommy: he told me that Bill Edge had been hit, had gone off with Bill Aird to get his wound dressed, and told him to stay by his pack.

By this time all was quiet, except for one light machine-gun firing at us from the south-eastern end of the paddy; but its fire soon ceased, and somebody found the gunner dead by his gun half an hour later. I pushed gingerly forward with a section, and found a fork in the road; one branch, which seemed to be the main road, ran over the hill, and the other went into the village. In the point of the wood at the fork, I saw Private Fairhurst, who called to me that John Kerr was there, wounded.

I crossed the road, noticing as I did so two dead Japs, and found John with a painful wound in the calf of the leg, right in the muscle. Beside him were half a dozen Japanese dead and two or three other British dead or wounded: among them was poor Lancaster, the boy who had been one of my swimming instructors, unconscious and almost out. I offered John some morphia, but he refused it until he had told me his story, in case his brain got muddled—very typical of his devotion to duty. They had walked head-on into a lorry-load of Japs standing in the village: he thought they had just climbed into it after cross-examining the villagers. They had killed several of them at once, but the driver had driven off immediately, with at least two bodies in the back, to the south. They thought they had killed everybody, for the loss of two killed and Bill Edge and one or two others wounded; and Tommy Roberts had gone on. John was waiting only to collect his platoon, when suddenly a new light machine-gun had opened up, and hit him and several more.

While he was telling me this, there was a sudden report just beside my ear, and I spun round to find Peter Dorans with a smoking rifle, and one of the two "dead" Japs in the road writhing. He had suddenly flung himself up on his elbow and pointed his rifle at me. Peter shot him again and finally dispatched him.

What to do with the wounded? The problem we had all so

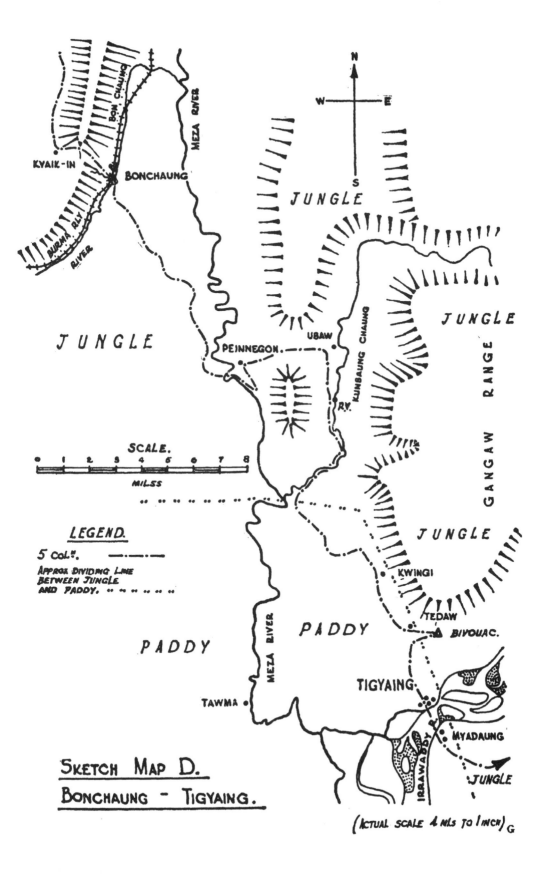

long dreaded had at last arisen. There were five of them unfit to move, and by bad luck they included not only John but his platoon serjeant and two of his section commanders: they had all been together at the fatal moment. The truck had got away, and there was no knowing when the Japs would come back on us. We hoisted three of them on to mules, and bore them down to the village a hundred yards away; and there we left them with their packs, and earthen jugs of water, in the shade under one of the houses. One of them said, "Thank God, no more walking for a bit"; one, Corporal Dale, said, "See and make a good job of that bridge;" and John Kerr said, "Don't you worry about us, sir, we'll be all right." The other two were too sick to move, and we had to be content with telling John Kerr where we had left them.

Sixteen dead Japanese were counted in and around the village. It was thought that the one who got away in the lorry was the only survivor. One Gurkha Naik, by name Jhuriman Rai—one of six whom I had sent with Tommy as a change from muleteering— killed no less than five of them, three with his rifle and two with his *kukri*. Five bullet-holes were found in his clothing and equipment afterwards.

With Gerry Roberts's platoon, and with the much saddened platoon of John Kerr, I sought the track to Bonchaung, but could find no trace of it. To the south we heard various explosions; we knew it could not be Jim Harman already, and rightly guessed it was Mike Calvert celebrating his thirtieth birthday on the railway. I became more and more anxious to hurry to Bonchaung, and so I told Gerry to come on with men and animals as fast as he could, while I pushed on ahead with Peter Dorans. We got there just after five o'clock, to find everybody in position. David Whitehead, Corporal Pike, and various other sappers were sitting on the bridge with their legs swinging, working away like civvies.

I found Duncan, who told me that Jim Harman had had a bad time in the jungle, and had turned up at Bonchaung half an hour before, having got hopelessly bushed: he had now set off down the railway line towards the gorge. David hoped to have the bridge ready for blowing at half-past eight or nine; he had already laid a "hasty" demolition, which we could blow if interrupted. Until he was ready there was nothing whatever to be done, bar have a cup of tea. I had several.

Duncan had everybody ready to move at nine, mules loaded and all. David gave us five minutes' warning, and told us that the big bang would be preceded by a little bang. The little bang duly went off, and there was a short delay; then . . .

The flash illumined the whole hillside. It showed the men standing tense and waiting, the muleteers with a good grip of their mules; and the brown of the path and the green of the trees preternaturally vivid. Then came the bang. The mules plunged and kicked, the hills for miles around rolled the noise of it about their hollows and flung it to their neighbours. Mike Calvert and John Fraser heard it away in their distant bivouacs; and all of us hoped that John Kerr and his little group of abandoned men, whose sacrifice had helped to make it possible, heard it also, and knew that we had accomplished that which we had come so far to do.

Four miles farther on we met Alec's guides; and just as we were going into bivouac we heard another great explosion, and knew that Jim Harman had blown the gorge.

CHAPTER EIGHT

BONCHAUNG TO IRRAWADDY

7th March—10th March

"Stone upon stone he laid them down
Until the boat would hold no more;
The freeboard now was scarce an inch:
He stripped his clothes and pushed from shore."
ROBERT BRIDGES—*Screaming Tarn.*

WE AWOKE with a sense of exhilarated guilt. What was it we had done the night before? Ah, yes: blown the Bonchaung. Perhaps we had better be moving.

As we marched, I was worried about Tommy Roberts: although John Kerr had said he had pushed on, it seemed odd that he had not heard the subsequent shooting and come back. The more I brooded over it, the more likely it seemed to me that he might have got into trouble, perhaps with reinforcements summoned by the solitary Jap who had got away in the lorry. Without John Kerr's platoon, his force amounted only to about thirty men, half of them Burrifs, and at least two wounded. We could only hope he would turn up at the rendezvous.

I halted at twelve to get on the wireless. John was getting along towards Tigyaing: he reported no signs of Japs and prospects good. Then brigade came up on the air, and I passed them an exuberant message, "Bonchaung bridge blown good and proper 21.00 hours stop explosion heard from direction gorge 24.00 hours." David had indeed done a good job on the bridge: of three spans, he had blown one clean off its piers, on to the dry stream sixty feet below; and another longer one, of 100 feet, he had dislodged so that one end rested in the *chaung* bottom, while, thanks to a skilful twisting charge, he had warped it like a corkscrew. A good portion of the piers themselves had also been blown away.

About noon we reached the Meza River at a village called Peinnegon, where there was a ford four feet deep. There was also a timber-raft, which we used for ferrying such delicate loads as the wireless sets and the column commander; while the rest of the column, turned fastidious in the absence of Japs, removed their trousers before wading. Aung Pe, the Jemadar, whom we had with us, reported smallpox in the village, so we went through rather hastily, and turned southward along the east bank of the river. In less than a mile we had come to a complete halt; the jungle was exceedingly thick, and all of us tired: we had marched 113 miles in seven days, and had a considerable emotional strain as well: while our loads weighed on an average 60 lbs. The country seemed Japless, and if attacked we could always get out by one of several timber-hauling tracks which ran back in the general direction from which we had come. So that evening we halted at four o'clock, and were all asleep before dark.

The rendezvous closed at twelve noon the following day; and, as I was in some doubt as to whether I could get the animals there by then, I sent Duncan, Aung Pe and a few men over the hill across country, while I went back with the column to Peinnegon to follow the track. Twelve noon, when we were due on the air to brigade, caught us a mile short of the rendezvous, but I was particularly anxious to establish contact; so I halted for the midday meal and wireless period, knowing that Duncan was on the rendezvous to intercept other arrivals. We told brigade where we were, and received a high priority message in return which read as follows:

"Owing no news received from No. 1 Group for ten days crossing of Irrawaddy possibly hazardous stop no news Four Column stop leave it your own discretion whether you continue movement or make safe bivouac in Gangaw Hills to harass reconstruction railway."

This message was distinctly unsettling. With 4 Column apparently gone,* and a good deal of doubt about Alex's party

* Note D: No. 4 Column.

in the south, it meant that the only columns still definitely in the hunt were my own, Mike's and the two with Wingate. However, he was leaving it to me, and it was a problem which needed a little thought. I wirelessed back, in clear, an interim answer:

"Grateful your confidence stop let you have answer five o'clock to-night."

I closed down my wireless, and marched on thinking. John had reported the Tigyaing prospects favourable. The Japs were almost certainly expecting us to break back towards India, and making their dispositions accordingly. For the brigade to concentrate in one area now would greatly ease the enemy's task of dealing with us. All these points were in favour of crossing the Irrawaddy as originally planned. On the other hand, the crossing was itself a tricky operation, and the longer it took the trickier. My column was still scattered, and I was not sure that every one would find the rendezvous punctually. Once the other side of the Irrawaddy, how precisely did one eventually get back? It was quite a pretty subject for an appreciation of the situation, such as one was taught at Sandhurst. However, I still had four hours in which to make up my mind.

We duly found Duncan at the rendezvous: he had been there since ten o'clock, but there was no sign of anybody else. I promptly fell prey to the worst fears. It was now three and they should have been there by twelve, both Tommy's and Jim's parties. I caught John Fraser on the air, having luckily arranged a time to do so, and told him that I was all alone at the rendezvous, but would wait an extra twenty-four hours there. He reported that he had had spies in Tigyaing, who reported it entirely free of Japs, and full of boats. He was distressed to hear that we must put the programme back a day; but he was obviously confident, and this made up my mind as to the answer I must send to Wingate. At that moment also, Tommy Roberts came marching briskly in, though minus nine men. They had got separated from him during the scrap, and he hoped they were with John Kerr, with whom he had also lost touch.

I broke to him the news about John Kerr, and he was terribly distressed, reproaching himself for having gone off in such a hurry, and full of remorse. I had the greatest difficulty in persuading him that he was not to blame, and that John Kerr himself had been perfectly happy about it. The missing men were all from his mortar team, and included both serjeants.* Finding himself so short of troops, he had not gone on to Nankan, but had got badly bushed on his way to the rendezvous. Pam Heald had lost one of his Burrifs, but was otherwise complete, and Bill Edge was in good form under the care of Bill Aird, though he had been hit below the shoulder-blade.

I sent an answer to Wingate saying that the auspices for the crossing were so good that I proposed to try it, and then to march for the Shweli bridge on the road running from the main Burma Road up to Bhamo. If this could be destroyed, and as a suspension bridge its destruction would not be a difficult job, then the isolation of Myitkyina would be complete, now that the railway had also been cut. I reckoned I could get there by about the 20th, or the middle of the next moon period, when bombers could be used in support. To this signal I never got any answer, and there is some doubt as to whether the Brigadier ever saw it.

I slept that night in a fever of worry about Jim Harman. I had already sent a signal warning brigade that I hoped to be able to receive a supply drop on the 12th at a village called Pegon, about twenty miles the other side of the Irrawaddy; choosing it on account of its remote location, at the head of a valley among a horse-shoe of hills. The food problem was rather acute, for it was now ten days since we started on our last five days' supply, and we were all heartily sick of the rice bought in the Happy Valley. A mule which had been shot in the action at Kyaik-in showed no signs of recovering, so we killed and ate it. This was only the 8th, and we had four days more to go before the supply drop. We should be able to get food in Tigyaing, but our wireless batteries were running low, and we had no more petrol left with which to run our charging engine.

* Note E: Missing men of Captain Roberts's Party.

The ration at the best of times was not too good: it was too meagre, at any rate, to try and make one day's last a day and a half without loss of stamina. The dieticians were horrified at our using it at all, since it was originally designed for parachutists to live on for a maximum period of five days. It consisted of twelve Shakapura biscuits, 2 oz. of cheese, some nuts and raisins, some dates, twenty cigarettes, tea, sugar and milk. In addition, there was supposed to be chocolate; but two packets out of three had acid drops instead. Such was one's frame of mind that when one got acid drops instead of chocolate one wanted to burst into tears; and such is my luck, I only got chocolate twice. I should add that there was also that extremely important item, a packet of salt. One day's rations weighed exactly two pounds.

Next morning, John popped up on the wireless at noon, just as I was preparing to move, and said that Jim Harman's party had joined him late last night. Relieved but fuming, I marched off towards Tigyaing.

It was a nervous march, since it all ran across open paddy. The Kunbaung Chaung ran into the Meza Valley four miles south of the bivouac, and one could be seen for three miles in any direction. Our marching raised a cloud of dust, and we seemed to be covering the ground very slowly. A prominent white pagoda on a hill just south of us never seemed to get any nearer. I felt as if I were sailing a boat with the tide against me. About five in the afternoon, we saw a native coming towards us on a bicycle. He hopped off it as he got near us, and to our surprise we recognised Robert, one of our own Karens, in plain clothes. He led us, bicycling slowly like a schoolboy, to a spot where we met John; who told us that he had shifted his bivouac because he did not like the look of the headman in the nearby village. These suspicions were confirmed when later in the evening one of the Burrifs intercepted a runner from him, who was carrying a written message to the Japs in Katha, telling them that we were in the neighbourhood. I am bound to say that this was the only occasion throughout the whole campaign when we definitely knew that we were denounced to the Japs.

Jim Harman had reached the rendezvous about ten o'clock on the previous day, and for some reason had been worried to find nobody there. He knew of my next rendezvous with John, and had hurried on to find it. He must have missed Duncan by only a few minutes.

However, here we were, united again, with only those few men of Tommy's unaccounted for. I was not unduly worried about them, since they had level-headed N.C.O.s with them; but their loss was a great nuisance, since it meant abolishing one mortar-team, leaving only one which we could work.

We went to bed that night fairly certain that our hiding-place was unknown; but we were rudely disillusioned next morning when a party of Indians walked in on us bearing presents of eggs, milk, bananas and other delights. They were rather pathetic, poor fellows: the Indian in Burma is the community creditor, and there was now nobody to protect them from the unpopularity inevitable to the creditor. The local police chief had befriended them so far as he could, but had been unable entirely to prevent their being plundered; while the Jap, of course, had systematically mulcted them as being the richest portion of the community, and best able to contribute to his support.

Duncan mistrusted their appearance, murmuring, "*Timeo Danaos et dona ferentes*": but I could see nothing sinister in the elderly, grey-bearded Sikh and rather tremulous Punjabi Mussulmen who comprised the delegation. I told them in no way to commit themselves to helping us, since we were only birds of passage and the hour of their deliverance was not yet at hand. They were bitterly disappointed. The best we could do for them was to take their names, and notify their kinsfolk in Lahore that we had seen them alive and well; but unfortunately these were lost with the rest of our documents later.

Since the coast seemed clear, I considered that the sooner we whisked ourselves over the Irrawaddy the better. I sent off John Fraser with his complete platoon, Jim and the Commando platoon, Philippe Stibbé and his platoon, to take over the boats and make a cordon round the entrances to the town; I would follow with the main body in about an hour. The die was cast, the crossing was on; but it felt distinctly precarious.

John was gone less than fifteen minutes when an aircraft came up from the south and circled between the bivouac and the town. It hovered over Tigyaing itself for some minutes, not aimlessly but purposefully; and then flew off in the direction whence it had come. I had arranged with John that as soon as he was in possession of the town he should open up on his wireless; and when he did the first question I asked him concerned the aeroplane. He answered that it had dropped leaflets demanding our surrender. It struck me at once that the Japs would hardly go to all that bother had they been confident that they could intercept us: however, it confirmed that they knew our whereabouts, and once more it behoved us to get moving. John said that all was quiet; but that fifty to five hundred Japs were reported at Tawma, eight miles south-west across the marshes. There was nothing to be done about that. The mules were ready loaded, and we stepped off at something like light infantry pace.

Now again we had the sensation first experienced on the Pinlebu road: instead of hole and corner creeping, we were marching boldly in the open. There was something exhilarating about thus throwing off all pretence, and showing ourselves men: morally it felt far healthier than the continual hiding, which one never felt to be really effective anyhow. For the better impressing of the inhabitants, we marched in threes, and when we reached the post which Philippe had left at the police station, the first building of consequence in the town, I made the men march at the slope, swing their arms, throw out their chests, and look like soldiers—despite beards and buttonlessness. So we marched through the town. At first the inhabitants kept mostly to their houses, but those few who did not and watched us nervously were soon reassured by our broad grins, and the cheery greetings of the men; and by the time we halted, in the main street, the children first, and then men and women in their hundreds, poured out of their houses; the shutters came down off the shops, and the town of Tigyaing took on a festive air.

We had noticed, as we marched out of our bivouac, a series of smoke fires, south and west; up the Meza and Kunbaung valleys, and away down river. Columns of smoke rose high in the air, and flattened out into clouds. There must have been five or six of them. John asked me if I had noticed them, and I admitted it.

"I don't like it," he said. "I saw fires like those just before the Sittang Bridge battle, and again several times during the withdrawal. We thought they were signal fires, lit by fifth columnists whenever they had seen troops, so that the Japs knew that in the middle of the circle of the fires there were British troops."

This produced a nasty feeling in the pit of my tummy; but that was not going to help us cross the Irrawaddy, and the important thing was that the troops should not know what the smoke-columns betokened; unfortunately the Burrifs had seen them before and knew them for what they were, so that it got out to the men in no time. Meanwhile John showed me some of the pamphlets which the aircraft had dropped. They were printed in English, Urdu and Burmese, and read something as follows:

"To the Pitiable Anglo-Indian Soldiery.

"Your forces have been utterly destroyed in the battle of the 3rd March, and not a man has been able to recross the Chindwin. The powerful Imperial Army of Nippon is all around you, and you cannot possibly escape. Do not again trust your brutal and selfish British officers, who will leave you to starve in the jungles as they did last year. Come to the nearest Nippon soldiers with this leaflet in your hand, and we will treat you well."

There was also another pamphlet in Burmese, addressed to the native population, saying that we were stragglers, and were to be apprehended and taken to Shwebo.

I gathered round me such troops as were handy, and read them the proclamation in full view of the inhabitants. I thought it would do them good to see how the troops took it and I was not disappointed. As to the other pamphlet, I asked every one in the crowd who spoke English if they thought we looked like stragglers, and they all laughed.

Meanwhile, Jim Harman's platoon was already across, and John said the boats were ready for the next lot. I told Tommy Roberts to reconnoitre various hills that lay in the middle of the town, as sites for his machine-guns and his remaining mortar; and then, with John, I moved down the street to the waterfront. There for the first time I saw the Irrawaddy River. My first reaction was to thank my stars I had come to a ferry-town; for getting across without the help of proper boats was obviously out of the question. It was fully a mile wide; although much of the space was filled up with sandbanks, the actual channel was not less than half a mile.

On the main sandbank, opposite where the principal street of the town debouched on to the waterfront, there were a couple of huts, by which lay half a dozen boats. Others were at that moment being brought round from the main bank of the river just above the town, where they had been moored. John had enlisted something like twenty boats of various sizes to come and help, and they were all congregating. We were to splash across the shallows that intervened between the waterfront and the main sandbank, over the sandbank to the huts, and embark there. I detailed two platoons to be the next to go, and walked back into the town to see my dispositions.

Tommy Roberts had sited his machine-guns where they commanded the whole stretch of paddy to the south and south-west. Their field of view was at least three miles, over completely open country, to the very edge of the marshes which lay between us and Tawma; and back also the way we had come. There was nothing to fear from there. On the north side of the town, the jungle-covered hills—the last of the Gangaw Range—subsided into the plain at the very outskirts of the town itself; there we had to take a chance. I stood on Tommy's hill, and admired the scene. Immediately to the north was the main street down which we had marched, and two streets beyond that was a long ridge, running at right angles to the river, crowned with a tall pagoda, the biggest I have seen. It was a blue, sunny day, and the pinnacles of the pagoda, gold-tipped, sparkled and shone. A long covered way led from the pagoda to the monastery, incongruously reminding me of the covered way from Turnberry Station, at home in Ayrshire, to the Turnberry Hotel; but instead of being painted with the familiar red of the L.M.S., it too was ornamented with gold pinnacles, and flashed merrily in the sun.

To the north, the broad river disappeared behind a projection of the hill: beyond it were the flat forested lands running up to the Shweli River. Immediately opposite was the village of Myadaung, with a big warehouse and a monastery as its principal features. Beyond it, blue in the distance, were the hills around Pegon, where we hoped to have our supply drop in a few days' time. South, the river ran entirely through flat country, paddy-lands and marshes on this side, jungle on that: somewhere, if one could only see it, about ten miles away was the mouth of the Meza: and somewhere, doubtless, marching towards us, the Japs of Tawma. Bidding Tommy keep his eyes skinned, and taking an orderly from him who could summon him when the time came, I went down again into the town.

The first person I met was Bill Aird, sitting on his pack eating a banana, among the other officers and men of Rear Column Headquarters.

"Could I go and have a look at this Irrawaddy, sir?" he asked. "It would be a pity if we didn't get across, and I couldn't even say I'd seen it, after coming all this way!"

I said he could.

Next I met Cairns.

"There's a very nice Burmese gentleman here, sir, who'd like fine to speak to ye. He speaks good English. Will ye see him?"

I said I would.

Next I met one of my platoon commanders.

"Would you be rather worried if the Japs came down this bank from the north?"

I said I should. But what did he propose I should do about it? I returned to the waterfront, passing the time of day with various

English-speaking shopkeepers as I went. They had been doing a roaring trade, and were so surprised at being paid for their cheroots, nuts and so forth—and overpaid at that—that they were beaming all over their faces. I talked also to a quite beautiful and very *soignée* girl, a Burmese from Rangoon, who had been in the telephone exchange there: she wore European clothes, and spoke excellent English. She was sitting at an upstairs window.

"It is wonderful to see you all," she said, in a voice which was only slightly singsong; "and so many! But you haven't come to stay?"

I said I was afraid not: we had come to do mischief to the Japs, and to see how the people of Burma were faring under Japanese rule. We could not stay this time, but the day would come when we should be back for good. Poor girl! She was near tears, and gazed wistfully at the troops as they cheerfully went buying in the shops. She said she would pray for us, and I bade her cheer up. I met a man also, an ex-post office employee, who shook hands with me, and called out, "God save the King! Long live the King!" I felt near tears myself, at all this loyalty still flowering under the yellow blight.

Pam Heald stood at the end of the main street on the water-front, looking like a harvest festival, or Ceres, the goddess of plenty. (I hope that's right.) He had been entrusted with the buying up of foodstuffs to see us through until we got our supply drop. Among other things he had amassed 137 eggs, rather less than one per two men; potatoes, rice, vegetables in great quantities; cheroots; fruit of all kinds. He had also indulged in one or two private purchases, out of (so he assured me) his own pocket: Scott's Porage Oats, Polson's Butter, and some tinned oysters, for which he had paid fabulous prices. They were the last in Tigyaing, and I should think the last in Upper Burma. He had also bought a lot of sugar. He had always a prodigious appetite, and at intervals a man from a nearby restaurant was bringing him plates of pork and potatoes. Duncan and John afterwards confessed to having had some too, but they never gave me any.

The flow of men and animals was being maintained at an even

rate across the sands to the embarkation point. I was naturally loth to expose the whole column there at once, and Duncan was responsible for seeing that they came forward as boats were available. From the top of Tommy's hill, I had seen a steamer apparently moored on the opposite bank, about a mile downstream half concealed by a little point; and I decided to send Gerry Roberts's platoon, which was in process of crossing, to destroy it. When they reached it, they found it had been destroyed long since.

I took my leave of Tigyaing, and, with Peter, splashed in my turn across the warm shallows and arrived at the huts. The crossing was going smoothly and quickly; the mules were behaving well, and the native boatmen working hard. The afternoon was wearing on, but it looked as if we would be over complete before dark. Peter discovered that one of the huts was an eating house, and he brought me a plate of a quite excellent dish: melon and marrow fried in batter. I have often meant to try it since. There was a signal lamp on the far bank, through which we talked when we had occasion; and Alec Macdonald was in charge there.

Three-quarters of an hour before dark, I sent for Tommy to withdraw from his eminence, and come down to the beach. One platoon only, Philippe Stibbé's, still remained in position, and I brought it in to hold a smaller and more compact perimeter on the waterfront. Tommy's people were just in process of crossing, when there was a sudden chill in the atmosphere. The crowd on the waterfront melted away, and the boatmen, instead of bringing their boats back to the landing place by the huts, disappeared far away down river. This could only mean one thing: Japs!

The word had come so suddenly that we had only one boat under our hand at the moment of the defection. Luckily one of John's Karens on the far side of the river tumbled to what was happening, and with great presence of mind he leapt on to a boat which was just shoving off, and forced the crew to bring it to the proper place by covering the helmsman with his rifle. John Fraser argued with the crew of the boat with us, but had to pull a gun on them also before they would resume work. He extracted from them that two hundred Japs were marching up the Tigyaing bank from the south.

The situation was suddenly serious: only two boats, luckily fairly large ones, and about sixty men and ten animals still to get across. Some Karens found another boat, deserted, and took one load over; while the crews of the other two boats were urged to greater efforts by a judicious brandishing of firearms. I got Philippe out of the town, and put two Bren guns in position on the sandbank in the gathering dusk. (Never was I so glad before of the speed with which the tropical night falls.) The boats seemed to take an age in their crossing and turn round.

Two mules and their loads, and Fraser's Horse, still remained to go. Suddenly to the south we heard the sound of an aircraft's engines. I bellowed to every one to stand stock still. It came over so low that Fraser's Horse took fright and galloped off into the dusk towards the town. It seemed incredible that the aircraft should not see us, but it showed no sign of having done so, and went on northward up the river. Nelson the Karen groom ran off to see if he could find the horse. He had been gone half a minute when the shooting began.

It came from the main bank of the river just south of the town, and I think the first shots were directed into the town itself, for we could hear nothing over us. There were machine-guns, and I think a mortar; but even an hour later, when we discussed it, we could not agree if we had heard a mortar or not. There was so much to think about. We had nothing to fire at, and we just kept still. Nelson came doubling back again, but had seen nothing. All we could do was to wait for the boats; and we thought we could just get everybody into one trip.

It was now almost wholly dark. The shooting had stopped and we did not know if we were being stalked or not. It seemed probable that by now the Japs realised that we were no longer in the town, and had been told where we were crossing.

Out of the blackness came the creaking of a boat. We filled it with the remaining Bren gunners, with Cairns, Peter Dorans, and a few more odd men. As they were getting in, the other boat came creaking and whispering over the water, and grounded softly. The rest of us got in—Duncan, John, two or three Karens, including Po Po Tou the colour-serjeant. Nelson and I and one of the native boatmen shoved off. The shooting began again from the direction of the town, this time aiming generally at the river, but nowhere very near us. Cairns called out to us from somewhere out on the river, "Are ye all right, sir?" and we shouted back, "Yes."

The boat, laden to the gunwales, was almost fast on the sand, and we had a job getting it off. By the time she was afloat, I was over waist-deep, and wearing my pack, the weight of which was enormously enhanced by all the good things Peter had been putting in it during the afternoon. When at last I tried to heave myself aboard, I found I could not; I got my elbows on to the little poop, and that was all I could do. With a great effort, Po Po Tou and Nelson, now safely on board, got me by the seat of my trousers and the underside of my pack, and heaved. The boat rolled perilously, shipping water over either gunwale, but I was safely aboard.

A matting canopy spread over the boat except at the extremities, where a small poop and forecastle allowed the crew to stand and work their poles and paddles. I found myself kneeling on the poop with my head under the canopy, trembling all over with a mixture of cold and fright. Whenever I tried to change my position to something more tolerable—even to sit—the boat rolled horribly and everybody cursed me in a hoarse stage whisper, in English, Burmese and Karenni. It was not that so much as the influx of water at each attempt that made me desist. It was thus, to the accompaniment of shots, with my head under the canopy, and my behind hideously exposed; with the boatmen heaving away at their paddles, the water chuckling under the boat and swirling among the floorboards—that, shivering with cold and fear, the solemn thought came to me that has been my proudest boast ever since: I am the first British officer ever to have crossed the Irrawaddy on all fours.

We lost contact with Cairns's boat. On the far beach, we

handed a handsome sum in silver rupees to the boatmen, and it was no more than justice that those who had run away got nothing for their afternoon's work. For a short time we could find no trace of anybody. Some of us cast downstream and some up: for the current was strong, and in the darkness it was impossible to know where we had landed. The upstream search party was successful: we found not only Cairns's party but also Tommy Roberts, who had come to look for us. Alec had gone on an hour before to find a safe bivouac, and Tommy was now the senior officer on this side. Hearing the shooting he had not been certain whether to expect us or Japanese to cross next; and to him as to us the turn round of the boats had seemed unendurably long.

Tommy, bless his heart, had every one ready to move; and in ten minutes we were marching through the village and along the track which Alec had taken. We marched for an hour, and then a dark figure rose out of the bushes by a paddy-field. It was Tommy Blow and his runner, who had come back to meet us. He too had heard the bursts of shooting, and then a long silence of over an hour; and he had not greatly enjoyed the thoughts which occupied his mind while he waited. Another half-hour of marching in the inky blackness brought us to Alec's bivouac; and it was not long before we were bedded, after the most exciting day of my young life.

CHAPTER NINE

FROM IRRAWADDY TO NAM PAN

11th March—23rd March

"A pilgrim in a land unknown,
A thirsty land whose streams are dry."
JAMES MONTGOMERY.

To HANG ABOUT in the neighbourhood of the Irrawaddy was obviously unhealthy; to march away from it as fast as we could almost equally foolish; for the enemy would expect us to do so, and, crediting us with so many miles a day, would have a fair idea where to seek us. I resolved, therefore, to have a rest for a day or two; finding a safe area in which to lie up. The first day after the crossing, we put another two or three miles between us and Myadaung; the jungle was thick and going difficult; and after marching and hacking our way for an hour or two, we subsided and went to sleep. We made an effort to get on to brigade, but got no answer.

In Tigyaing, John had heard that other troops had crossed two or three days previously some twenty miles south, at a place called Tagaung. We guessed—rightly as it turned out, though I cannot remember on what we based our conjecture—that this was Alex, from whom nothing had been heard of for so long. We did not know in which direction he would go, but fancied that he had also been ordered to the area of Mogok.

The far side of the Irrawaddy seemed a positive paradise of peace and safety; we should never have believed that in a few short weeks it would seem to us a prison. True, the Shweli River bent round in such a way as to form something very like an island: had we realised how long we were to linger in that area, we should have been reminded of the island on to which John Fraser had crossed, during those peaceful days in Orchha. But at the moment, all seemed to be splendid; and our only worry was that we could not get our indent for air supplies through to brigade. Having lost a day on the far side of the Irrawaddy, we could no longer hope to reach Pegon by the 12th without bursting ourselves; I planned therefore to have the supply drop one day later.

On the eleventh, I began moving seriously on Pegon, but the jungle was very thick—about the thickest we had seen up till then. On the twelfth, we got into a dry *chaung* with occasional pools called the Myauk (or Monkey) Chaung, which seemed to head in the direction we wanted. There was only one road to Pegon from the north-west, and I thought it best avoided: I had therefore resolved to descend on the village by way of the mountains which hedged it around.

Half-way up the Myauk Chaung, it being noon, I decided to call up brigade on my fast dwindling wireless: we had tried to get petrol in Tigyaing without success, and we had not been able to run our charging engine for several days. I reported our location; and as I did so I heard aircraft a little to the south of us. The location message was queried, and we repeated it. The answer came in clear :

"Well done stop did you get anything to-day stop if not you must wait until 14th."

It dawned on us that the aircraft we had heard had been the supply drop at Pegon for which we had put in a provisional indent for the twelfth, never dreaming that they would honour it without confirmation. They had; and I was torn between annoyance at their being so premature, and gratitude that, not having recent news from us, they had sent over the drop on spec.

By now we had long since settled down into our daily routine, and the time wasted at halts, or at getting into or out of bivouac, was negligible. I used to try and make bivouac just before dark. If we were marching on a track, Duncan or I might ride on five minutes ahead to choose a site; but more often we just halted

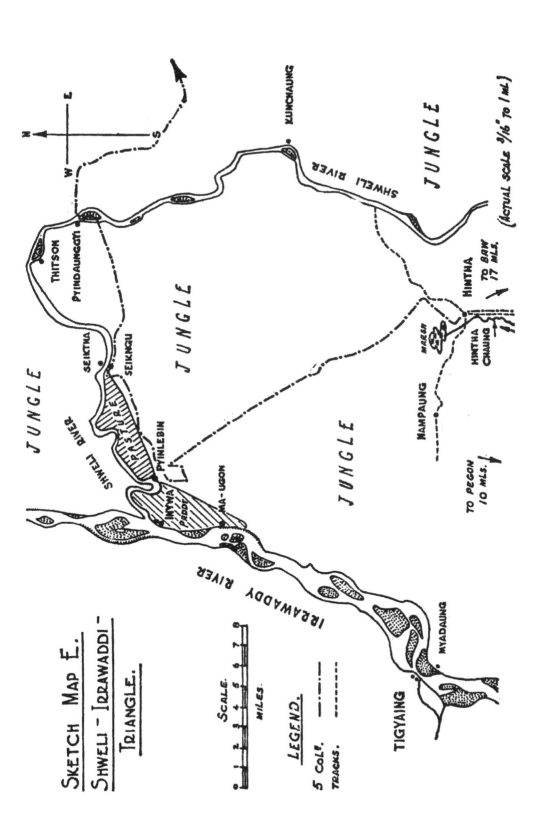

Sketch Map E.
Shweli - Irrawaddi -
Triangle.

SCALE.
0 1 2 3 4 5 6 7 8
MILES.

LEGEND.
5 COL^S. ————
TRACKS. -----

(ACTUAL SCALE 3/16" TO 1 ML.)

JUNGLE

JUNGLE

JUNGLE

JUNGLE

SHWELI RIVER

SHWELI RIVER

IRRAWADDY RIVER

KUNCHAUNG

THITSON
PYINDAUNGGYI

SEIKTHA
SEIKNGU

PYINLEBIN
INYWA
PADDY
MA-UGON
PASTURE

TIGYAING

MYADAUNG

MARSH

NAMPAUNG

HINTHA
HINTHA
CHAUNG

TO BAW
17 MLS.

TO PEGON
10 MLS.

N
W   E
S

where we were. Always, however, we left the track, whether an existing one, or one that we were making ourselves as we marched; and moved off it in small parties for six hundred yards, so that any patrol which might be following up could not see where we had gone. Then either Duncan or I would turn and face the column as it came, pointing out to each group as it arrived where it was to settle for the night. The duty of finding sentries went by roster to each platoon, so that men could count on having at least two nights out of three in bed without interruption. The only orders to be given out were, first, what was to be our rendezvous should we be surprised and scattered; and secondly, at what time I intended to move off. There was no Reveille, but each platoon would be roused by the sentries in time to move at the hour named. Woe betide them if they were late.

In the morning, we moved at or before first light, and marched two stages before halting for tea. Each stage of one hour was followed by fifteen minutes' halt. At the tea halt, mules would be unloaded, and tea brewed; two biscuits would be eaten (when we had them). A whistle would blow ten minutes before we were due to move, when mules would be loaded again and packs put on: a warning whistle blew at one minute, and then another to signify "March." We would cover another two or three stages before noon, when we would invariably halt for three hours.

This noon halt was the pleasantest period of the day. Too hot for marching, it was the ideal time for internal economy. Bill Aird would hold his sick parade, and the platoon commanders would inspect their men's rifles, feet, and so on. Signals would get brigade on the air, and the cipher people work away at their mysterious craft. Duncan would shove a marked map on to a convenient tree, where the men could study the "day's run," as if they were aboard a luxury liner. And we would eat. At three we would carry on until the time came to enter bivouac. Everything was done on the whistle, and one or two licensed people half-way down the line had the responsibility of passing on, with their own whistles, what they heard from the front. Routine, thoroughly well known, means a happy column; and from a good routine they get the maximum rest.

I had a standing order that all fires would be out one hour after we reached bivouac; and we used to get in not less than eight hours' sleep a night, more often nine.

We slept the night of the twelfth near the head of the Myauk Chaung, and next day climbed laboriously out of it. The thirteenth looked like being a short day; we had less than four miles to cover to Pegon, and I promised every one an easy afternoon, making and mending and washing. I spent the rest of the day wishing I hadn't; for the mountains down into the horseshoe valley were so precipitous that we could not get the mules down; and by four in the afternoon I was no nearer than I had been in the morning. Ba Than and Aung Pe led numerous reconnaissances to find whether it was possible for mules to get through, but came back each time with the lugubrious message: "Mules can't go." The roots of the trouble were the steep descents into *chaungs*, where the rocky sides grew so close together that mules and mule loads could not squeeze between them; or deep bottoms where men could go if they got wet to the breast, but where mules could not get a footing.

At last, on Duncan's advice I led the column along the watershed to the point where the track from Myadaung led over the hill, and sent on Denny Sharp, Philippe Stibbé and Philippe's platoon, with two or three Burrifs as interpreters by the rough route I have described. The column slept the night on the Irrawaddy side of the watershed, Duncan having discovered the track just before dusk; and at dawn I rode on over the track on my pony while the column followed. The aircraft were expected at 10 a.m. and I arrived there at 9, to find everything under control, with Denny's signal fires already built, and Philippe's platoon enjoying a belated breakfast. They had had a devilish walk, and had made it an hour after dawn, having had a sleep *en route*.

The aircraft arrived before the column, and they were good to see. It was fifteen days since we had last seen them dropping at Tonmakeng, and a good deal had happened since then. Down floated the parachutes, beautifully and symmetrically in the middle of the paddy, while the Hodges and Gileses of Pegon goggled at them. Out of that drop we got five days' rations and the petrol, as well as much mail, newspapers and Penguin books. The only things missing were the boots and clothing for which we had indented, and of which we were in dire need. Doubtless, we thought, these would arrive later.

That afternoon we spent reading and re-reading our precious mail; graduating thereafter to the newspapers, and thence to the local papers. I have remarked during this war what an enormous proportion, fully 90 per cent, of the newspapers received from home by the troops are local papers. Personally, I get more pleasure out of a local paper of a district I have never known than out of a so-called "National" newspaper two or three months old: the local ones are ageless. In them I can read every paragraph, from the "Very Pretty Weddings" to the "5s. for No Tail-Light," from the "Children's Column" to "Retiral of Station Master." I read with delight the *Galloway Gazettes* produced by Serjeant-major Cairns, and discussed with him and Peter the blackface prices of every sheep-farm in Galloway; and having disposed of them, I read Alec Macdonald's *Bootle Times*. Alec was Scots-bred and Bootle-raised, but, like so many of his kind, indignantly denied any affinity with England: so that Duncan and I used to taunt him with verses of a poem to which we were for ever adding:

> "How the pipes will skirl and tootle
> When Macdonald comes to Bootle,
> When he dons a tartan plaid instead of a jersey;
> They will drink hot toddy daily
> And will hold a special ceilidh
> When Alec's boat is signalled in the Mersey."

Teasing Alec was like pulling the ears of a spaniel: he used to pretend to get furious, but cheerfulness kept breaking through. The argument usually ended in a rough and tumble, in which

Alec was in the awkward position of having to disdain, for reasons of pride, offers of help by the English, and having at the same time to submit to severe pummellings by the Scots.

Knowing we were well ahead of brigade, and believing that only Alex was ahead of us, I had little sense of urgency, and was quite resigned to waiting for the clothing to come (as I expected) in a subsequent drop. We had hoped to have leisure to wash clothes and bodies, but unfortunately Pegon had no stream, only a well; and it was now that lice began to put in an appearance. New clothes would have made all the difference, but when we asked if a further drop were coming, we were told that more aircraft could not be spared: they would try and drop us clothing next time. This was a disappointment, but there was nothing for it.

I observed next morning also as a holiday, and spent a portion of it myself having my hair cut and my beard trimmed by Corporal Litherland, an ex-barber; I told him to take as his model the sailor on a Player's Cigarette packet, and the effect was much admired by my sycophantic colleagues. I have often been asked why we grew beards, instead of shaving in accordance with army custom. The answer is threefold. First, even the small saving of weight represented by not carrying shaving kit was precious. Secondly, a beard makes better camouflage for the face than all the fancy screens in the world, apart from being permanent. Thirdly and most important, the beard is a very real defence against mosquitoes, ticks and similar abominations. Provided it is properly looked after, hair on your face is no more unhygienic than hair on your head; and if you want to take the line that beards and discipline are incompatible, I would refer you to the Senior Service. Some people, it is true, feel more respectable clean-shaven; although in our style of living, for lack of time to shave, the "clean-shaven" usually had one day's stubble which I find more untidy and more unpleasant than the whole-hearted beard. Wingate himself was a strong apostle of the beard: indeed, in his own case, he looked genuinely apostolic. At one time he ordered people not to shave; but I induced him to relax this ruling, partly out of sympathy for those whose beards were loath to grow.

At 2.30 I called in the various outposts, and at 3 p.m. we set off in a south-easterly direction, intending to clear the horseshoe by the easiest route, before turning south for Mogok. Just as I was preparing to leave, John told me that he had heard from a villager that a party of Burman troops, with two British officers, had spent the last two nights in the forest rest house at Yingwin, the village about five miles away, but had left that morning. John and I racked our brains to think who this could be, and finally came to the conclusion that it must be "Fish" Herring and that the second British officer must be local exaggeration. Anyway, we had no time to investigate.*

At four o'clock in the afternoon, we were just crossing some paddy when a Jap aircraft came over us at about a thousand feet. It was a chance we had taken fifty times without being seen, but this time we were caught well and truly in the open. The aircraft circled us twice; one could imagine the little, malevolent yellow face of the pilot, staring down through his goggles and counting us as he banked; and then it flew off southward, while Denny Sharp growled, "If I'd been him, and that had been a Hurricane, and he'd been down here. . . ."

This encounter was the very worst of luck, for up till then the Japs must have lost track of us completely ever since we crossed the Irrawaddy. The people of Pegon were simple folk, who did not even know there was a war on, and who were not likely to have sent runners with information of our presence; and except for them we had not seen a soul since our crossing. Luckily at the moment we were spotted we were heading east, whereas our true direction was south: I derived such comfort as I could from that, but it was none the less annoying.

The country to the south of us was shown on the map as completely without villages; and although a good number of *chaungs* were marked John warned me that they would probably be dry: otherwise there would almost certainly have been villages

* See Note F.

beside them. He was quite right; the next few days of marching
were desperately thirsty, and only the strictest water discipline
got us through them. The soil was red laterite, and the jungle
low dry teak; the only life that flourished there was red ants,
with the most vicious sting imaginable. They would stand on
their heads and burrow into you as if with a pneumatic drill.
If you were unlucky enough to brush a tree with your sleeve,
you would spend the next fifteen minutes in a torture compared
with which the martyrdom of Saint Sebastian was a holiday
with pay.

We found some waterholes at noon on the 16th: they were
stinking but acceptable. That night we found two moderately
good holes, one for mules and one for men; but we drank both
dry, although enough water had seeped into them again by morning to fill our waterbottles.

The morning of the seventeenth was again a fearful march,
with a blazing sun and no shade. At a halt, Denny Sharp pinched
the slender tree I had in mind for my own shade: I remember
and am still ashamed of the way in which I told him to go and
find another. At noon we found no waterholes, but halted at a
dry river-bed where at some of the corners the sand looked mildly
sticky. We fell to digging: I have never seen Jim Harman display
so much animation. At two feet it was moist, and at four feet
we stopped to let the water seep in. Two of the six holes were
productive; and after waiting patiently, and trying to sleep to
take our minds off our thirst, we managed to get half a bucket
for each mule, and a drink and a full waterbottle for each man.

It was no pleasanter that afternoon, without any protection
from the sun whatsoever; and the *chaung* on which we had set
our heart for the night's bivouac proved bone dry. The Burrifs,
whose unerring noses for water had led us to the previous places,
were baffled this time, and assured us that they could neither see
nor smell anywhere worth digging. We had to pin our hopes
on the Nam Pan, a stream marked in encouragingly large letters
on the map about three miles' march farther on.

Incidentally, the navigation of this part of the trip had been exceedingly difficult. Normally, I compare navigation in jungle to navigation in a small boat on compass and leadline. You cannot usually see anything on which to take a bearing, and you have to steer by dead reckoning, checking only on the contours and *chaungs* which you cross, corresponding to the deposit that comes up on the arming of your lead. To Duncan is due the credit of these two or three days. Our last point of departure had been a ridge a little to the east of the village where we had been spotted by the enemy aircraft, on the afternoon of the fifteenth; on the morning of the eighteenth, we halted within what subsequently proved to be half a mile of Duncan's estimated position. This was after having crossed a multiplicity of *chaungs*, but no hills or possible contour lines. Duncan without doubt was the best jungle navigator I have known, except General Wingate himself, who was uncanny. I have known even him to be lost; but Duncan never. It does not normally matter in jungle whether or not you are sure of your exact position, provided you know that sooner or later you will come to something you can recognise; but on this particular occasion the line of the Nam Mit, a prominent river, was one which the enemy was likely to watch, and it was important not to come out in a village. The Nam Pan, a few miles short of it, was big enough to be almost certainly recognisable, and we were pretty sure of picking up our exact position on it, by the direction in which it ran, before blundering on to the Nam Mit itself.

Our hopes of water in the Nam Pan were justified, and we had a cup of tea before moving on. Two miles beyond the Nam Mit was a main road which we believed to be motorable, leading to two others which we knew to be so. Out from our wilderness we were coming into an area of good communications, where it behoved us to watch our step. We were entirely without information about this district; it was too far into Burma for our Intelligence in India to have knowledge of, and the desolation through which we had just come, being uninhabited, acted as an insulator and prevented any gossip about the Mogok area reaching the neighbourhood of Tigyaing. I had therefore resolved to spend a day on or near the Nam Mit, while John Fraser's Burrifs sent out small parties in twos and threes, wearing plain clothes, to pick up the talk of the neighbourhood. I was pretty sure that, with the knowledge that we had crossed the Irrawaddy, and with the easy movement which the motor-roads afforded, the enemy would certainly have brought troops up to the area from his reserves near Mandalay and Shwebo.

About half a mile from where we expected to stumble on the Nam Mit, we stumbled instead on sixteen wild elephants. Elephants are the only creatures in the Burma jungles to be treated with real respect. They take offence much too readily, and prosecute trespassers with the full rigour of the jungle law. I was relieved, therefore, when these sixteen decided to admit the existence of a right of way, and shambled off grumbling to the westward. They had been drinking at some pools which, though muddy, were good enough for the mules, who are normally fastidious about what they drink; and so, putting aside some pools for the mules and some for the men, I resolved to make my bivouac here.

After a short rest and a cup of tea, John dispatched three patrols of Burrifs in plain clothes to different villages, one immediately south of us, one west and one east. I sent out a reconnaissance party to find the river, which returned in twenty minutes with a glowing account of a flowing stream some two feet deep and twenty yards wide. By now almost every one was lousy, and felt, as an Italian prisoner of war once said to me, that a *bagnio* was *indispensablo*. I allowed two platoons to go bathing at a time, exhorting everybody to take the greatest care not to make a track between the river and the bivouac. For if patrols are seeking you in a waterless country, it is by the water that they will look; and a suspicious track leading down to it will be the sign that you are there.

Up came brigade on the wireless, with the astonishing and quite unexpected news that they had crossed the Irrawaddy with 7 and 8 Columns. The message said that I was to go for the Gokteik Viaduct under the orders of Mike Calvert, who was appointed local Lieut.-Colonel; No. 1 Group was to march on Mogok, under the orders of Lieut. Colonel Alexander, if still with them, and under the orders of Mike, if he were not; No. 1 Group to confirm whether Alex was or was not with them.

This was a complete surprise, although I knew that Mike had always wanted to blow the Gokteik: he had prepared it for demolition in 1942, and had sat on it for ten days awaiting the order to blow. Whosoever orders he was under knew their Mike; for they had expressly forbidden him to blow it without word from them. This never came, and Gokteik, Demolition of, was written on Mike's heart. I looked at the map, and looked away again hastily: the mountains between us and our goal were stinkers, nothing less; and we only had one blanket between every two men. I asked for a supply drop on the twentieth, which would mean one day without rations; but I could see no suitable place near at hand, and instinct told me the area was Jappy.

With my mind full of the Gokteik, I went off to have a wash, and found Bill Smyly also bathward-bound. The Nam Mit was indeed a stream of pure delight, and the ablutions of Bill and myself took a full half-hour. Then I went back to see if there was any answer to my request for a supply drop, but brigade had gone off the air.

Next day, just before noon, the two scouts whom John Fraser had sent into Myitson (a village four miles east of us, where the Nam Mit joins the Shweli), returned in great excitement, saying that there were seven hundred Japs in Myitson, and that they were being reinforced by troops coming up from Mong Mit in lorries. We encoded a message, and had it all ready to send when brigade came up on the air at noon. They were keen to pass us a message, but we thrust this news across in their teeth first; and were rewarded two hours later by the father and mother of an air-raid on Myitson. The message they passed us in return was a change of orders: Mike's and Alex's tasks remained as given, but I was to remain in my present area, and cover the advance of brigade and its two satellite columns to the same neighbourhood. The message added that I could be given no supply drop until the twenty-third. This was the nineteenth and officially our last day in rations, though I had warned the men to keep something in hand as in any case I was not expecting a drop till the twentieth.

I wirelessed back :

"O.K.; but see Psalm 22 verse 17." ("I may tell all my bones: they look and stare upon me.")

The answer came back directing me to the reference of "It is expedient that one should die for the people." I was not amused.

But the supply problem was now serious. Not only could I get no drop: I could not forage; for if the Japs had patrols in the neighbourhood, I could not enter villages without its becoming known, and attracting further attention to the very area which brigade should reach in three or four days. I gave an order to tighten belts.

Bill Aird and John Fraser now both came to me with long faces. They had been putting their heads together, and decided that it was their duty to tell me their opinion of the state of the troops. In Bill's professional opinion, they were, physically speaking, only sixty per cent effective. The long marching on short commons had, in his opinion, so undermined them that they must have at least a fortnight's rest on decent rations before another effort was asked of them.

This communication came as a complete shock to me. The very fact of being the commander lends a certain exhilaration to one's acts, and helps one to ignore physical decline. I knew we were all hungry and losing weight, but I confess I had not thought of it in quite such a gloomy light as this. Further, Wingate had led us to expect that we would very probably be staying in for the monsoon. I had always been against this, because I believed it impossible to preserve health throughout such a prolonged effort. Bill now said that with reduced resistance, to stay in for the monsoon was, from the medical point of view, out of the question. I could hardly dispatch this on the wireless, but I hoped to see the Brigadier in a few days, and to have a chance of discussing it then.

Meanwhile, entirely by chance, we had intercepted No. 1 Group's wireless on the air. Lance-Corporal Foster, the signaller, said they sounded very close, and we began talking to them in clear. They had heard the bombing of Myitson, so we knew they must be near us, but we could not say in clear where either of us were, and we had no common cipher. It did not in any case greatly matter; but it gave us a nice friendly feeling to know that we were not entirely alone.

I went down to the river again to have another wash, and was shocked to discover that, despite my warnings, a definite track had been made by people going down. To my mind a move was now imperative, although I liked this particular bivouac, and had been intending to stay there until brigade caught us up. The only thing against moving was that one of John's patrols was still out, and would not know where we had gone if we shifted from our present location. I told John to leave a standing patrol to watch for their return, and moved off at three in the afternoon to a stream about a mile farther west, the Bawbe Chaung. This was a partly dry stream in which a few pools remained, and though less pleasant was much safer than the old location.

That night a runner came in from John's standing patrol to say that an hour after we had left our bivouac, taking great pains to leave no trail, a Jap patrol of fifty strong had come up from the Nam Mit along the track made by the water parties. They moved very cautiously in three sections, working parallel to each other. They spent nearly an hour trying to decide which way we had moved out of the bivouac, and at the end of that time returned whence they had come. Ten minutes later, the standing patrol who had watched the whole performance heard two grenades go off; and shortly afterwards they were joined by two of their number who had been to a village to see if they could get any news of the missing patrol. These two had met the Japs on their way back, had dodged into the jungle, chucked a couple of grenades into them as they passed, and lit out for bush. They were thoroughly pleased with themselves. They had, however,

1. Major-General Orde C. Wingate, who founded and led the Chindit Long Range Penetration Groups, boarding a Dakota. On his right is Brigadier Michael Calvert.

2. Men of No.5 Column in a bamboo jungle clearing brew up during a midday halt.

3. No.5 Column troops light camp fires among teak trees during a midday halt.

4. Wounded and weary, two platoon commanders: Lieutenants Jim Harman and Bill Edge.

5. No. 5 Column commander Major Bernard Fergusson.

brought no news of the missing patrol; so John arranged to send out another a little farther afield.

I spent next day and night still on the Bawbe Chaung—the only occasion during the whole campaign, except for Tonmakeng, where I spent two consecutive nights in one bivouac. During this period of enforced idleness, we amused ourselves in various different ways. I wrote a short story, which alas! never got back to India; I look on it much as a fisherman looks on the fish that got away. You wouldn't believe how good it was. Bill Edge and Philippe Stibbé held a literary competition on the lines of those in the *New Statesman*: the following prize-winning entry, which is good jungle as well as good jingle, came from Bill:

"If elephant droppings are brown and hard
Your plans for a bivouac will be marred;
But if elephant droppings are soft and moist,
Then you'll find water to quench your t'oist."

On that day, the twentieth, I had further orders from brigade about my supply drop; it was to be no farther south than the Nam Pan. This meant retracing my steps, but there was no help for it. I decided next day to send Denny with one platoon to the area on the Nam Pan which I had chosen, and to lay a false trail myself to the north-west. Again John had to wait for his patrol, and we arranged that he should join us later.

Next day's was a dull, hot march, with no water until we reached the Nam Pan late in the evening, some eight miles above the point where I proposed to have the supply drop. We marched there dispersed in platoons, so as to make the task of anybody following up more difficult. Next day at noon John joined us; having regretfully given up all hope of recovering his patrol. Further inquiries in a village had established that the Japs had seized two Karens in plain clothes, and it seemed certain that these must be Havildar Tun So Ne and his companion. Gossip said that one of them had escaped, but had he done so he would presumably have come back. We were all very sad, because Tun So Ne was one of the best and most popular of all the Karens in the column.

We marched downstream parallel to the *chaung*, but we were having unaccountable trouble with the mules; three had to be left and their loads abandoned. Bill dropped behind with them, and when he caught me up, he confided in me his almost certain fears that it was anthrax. We had with us an Indian veterinary havildar who had no doubt about it. I have always supposed that they must have picked it up at the elephant wallow. It was a sore blow, and they went on dying at the rate of two or three a day for the next three days, when the epidemic stopped as suddenly as it had begun.

What with this delay and the bad going, we did not reach the rendezvous until after dark; and then the guides whom Denny had left for us on the *chaung* lost themselves. At last we found Denny, who told me the welcome news that he had run into No. 1 Group in bivouac on the other side of the *chaung*. They were proposing to leave at six in the morning. He said that they were horrified to hear we were having a supply drop there, since they had been chased by Japs and had only that afternoon managed to shake them off. They had had a supply drop four or five miles farther downstream the night before. I was very tired and had had nothing to eat all day, and I proposed waiting to see them till next morning; but Duncan, a very strict adjutant if ever there was one, refused to hear of this, and shamed me into going by threatening to go himself if I wouldn't. That put the lid on it, and grumbling I walked over, telling Peter to keep the fire going, so that I should know where I was when I came back.

In No. 1 Group's bivouac, all the officers were asleep, but I found George Dunlop, the column commander of No. 1 Column, and had no qualms about waking him up. I yarned with him for half an hour, and arranged to come back at first light to see Alex, who was asleep. Back in my own bivouac I was just settling down when the mules started plunging about. I leapt up and ran towards them, in time to see a low dark shape run away into the night. I fancy it was a panther. None of the mules was attacked, though one was particularly nervous. I made the line piquet build up a decent fire, and went back to bed. This was the only occasion during the whole expedition when we ever looked like having trouble with wild animals; and I never saw a snake the whole time.

At a quarter to six, I was over with No. 1 Group talking to the colonel, and watching the mules being loaded. I saw also Vivian Wetherall, a young officer who spoke Gurkhali as well as he spoke English, and who had an extraordinary ascendancy over the Gurkhas; Bill Edmunds, an R.A.F. officer from New Guinea, a magnificent fighting man with a family feud against the Japs which he was burning to avenge; St. George De la Rue, whose brother had been at school with me, and whom I had first met celebrating with the Gurkhas just after I joined the brigade; and Chet Khin, better known as "Chicken," a young Karen subaltern, whose smile was never known to fail, and who was one of the best reconnaissance officers in the brigade.

They told me briefly their story. Emmett's column had been caught in ambush, and except for a few scattered men who had joined Group Headquarters they knew nothing of what had happened subsequently.* Group and No. 1 Column had duly blown up the railway where they hit it, and crossed the Irrawaddy at Tagaung two days before my own crossing. They had had one supply drop on a sandbank in the middle of the Irrawaddy, when they saw some Dakotas passing over them: they had made the appropriate signal and got a drop they had not indented for. And their last drop had been the biggest of all time: they had had rum, and fish, and bread, and bully. . . . Seeing me drooling at the mouth, Bill pressed on me half a loaf of beautiful, fresh white bread, only three days old.

"Don't be afraid to take it," he said. "We've got so much I had bread-and-butter pudding last night!"

They had had trouble with their wireless, and until recently

* Note F: No. 2 Column.

had been out of touch with brigade for over ten days. It was now working all right, and they were getting good communication.

They warned me about the Japs who had been on their tails yesterday morning; they thought they had thrown them off all right, but advised me not to linger too long after my supply drop. I told them all I knew of local gossip, as gleaned by John's patrols, and then I watched them move off, cheerful and with six days' rations.*

* Note G: No. 1 Group.

CHAPTER TEN

FROM NAM PAN TO HEHTIN

23rd March—26th March

> "The Englishman's kyte is a great tribulation,
> He must hae kitchens, and puddins, and wine;
> A pokefu' o' meal frae the Lothians for Donald,
> A faggot o' wood, and a well, and he'll dine.
> Gie us the meal and we'll soon find the collops,
> But if they're no in it, ye'll no hear us squeal;
> Our fathers before us were dour folk to meddle
> Wi' naething but bannocks o' barley meal."
>
> NEIL MUNRO—*Bannocks o' Barley.*

THE AREA we had chosen for the supply drop was far from perfect, but it was by no means bad. It consisted of a stretch of five hundred yards of straight *chaung*: entirely sand save for one small pool which was our water supply. Two aircraft arrived at 11 a.m., and dropped three days' worth of food, boots, shirts, socks and trousers. They also dropped what was supposed to be a bag of bullion; but in actual fact what arrived was, first, a shower of silver rupees, loose, very painful to those whom they struck on the head; and, second, a bag with the bottom missing, but with a note tied to it reading: "Enclosed please find Five Thousand Rupees." Pam Heald and a search party of Karens recovered about three thousand of them.

But three days' rations was not much good to us. I had asked for seven, and had already promised the men two days' food that day to make up for the involuntary fast which had already been forced on them. I quickly countermanded this permission, and wirelessed brigade, who were on the air, to know if more aircraft were coming. The reply came, "Presume drop completed stop previous orders cancelled stop march north to meet us rendezvous point on track one and a half miles west of Baw."

Three days rations only! There must be some mistake. I wired back in clear, for brigade were obviously in a hurry to get off the air:

"Incredible stop only three days rations received."

They replied:

"Never mind hurry north we will organise drop for you here."*

Just before the drop began, I had been joined by Major John Jeffries and his party, who had been with Colonel Alexander. They were the party entrusted with the original double bluff when No. 1 Group first crossed the Chindwin. Their task accomplished, they had rejoined the group; but hearing that I was expecting to meet brigade in the near future, Jeffries made up his mind to join me, and to report to the Brigadier for fresh orders. Put slightly on my toes by No. 1 Group's warnings about Japs, I asked him if he would very kindly look after a portion of the perimeter which I was laying out while the supply drop was in progress. This he most obligingly agreed to do. With him were two officers, Lieut. Vivian Earle and Lieut. Millar; they too had been helping me out.

Hoping against hope that I should soon hear the drone of another aircraft coming with the balance of my rations, I postponed the time of my start to five o'clock in the evening. John Jeffries decided to go by another route, and left at three, having learnt from me where my rendezvous with brigade was to be. No aircraft turned up, and, quite fairly thankful to get away from a place where so many people had prophesied the early arrival of the Japs, I moved off at the time arranged. When darkness fell, there was no moon; and I bivouacked for the night, resolving to carry on again about four in the morning.

I had no notion what lay behind the Brigadier's instructions to join him at Baw. Baw, on the map, was a village some five miles west of the Shweli, and some fifteen miles south-east of

*Note H: Supply Drop at Nam Pan.

Pegon; had I not turned south after the aircraft had seen me on the fourteenth but carried straight on, I should have reached Baw. Once again I was having to go through the distasteful process of retracing my steps, and this time it was through the barren water-less country which we had already traversed; but our line lay rather farther east than before, and our speed was quicker. There had been an element of urgency in the Brigadier's summons, and we put our best foot foremost.

At 8.45 a.m. we stopped for fifteen minutes' halt. We were on the edge of a plateau from which we had a good view to the north; and while we sat and smoked the cigarette which the halt just allowed time for, we heard mortar fire opening up. Duncan and I rushed forward to the edge of the plateau, and took a bearing on the sound: it was a little bit east of north, and just about where we made Baw to be. Something in a recent signal had led me to think that brigade was going to Baw without its usual escort of 7 and 8 Columns: I immediately leapt to the conclusion that brigade was in trouble, set up my wireless and asked how I could help. No reply, however, was forthcoming; and I told Duncan to prepare a light striking force to go ahead of the main body under my command, while the rest followed at mule pace to the agreed rendezvous. Then, while the sound of the mortars was at its noisiest, three Dakotas appeared from the direction of India and circled as if about to yield a supply drop, about eight miles away.

After circling for some little time, they began dropping; and it was during this drop that the well-known incident occurred of the two signallers joining the brigade by parachute. They arrived in the middle of the dropping area, to find a sharp action in progress and both sides beckoning them: they fortunately chose to run for the British, and reached them safely. Unfortun-ately, neither of the two eventually got out to India.

The drop was not concluded, the Japanese having succeeded in dominating the dropping zone. From our viewpoint we guessed that the full drop had not been made, for after a few dropping circuits the aircraft resumed their circling at a greater height, as

SEE MAP ON PAGE 117

if puzzled, and then went off homeward. I was reluctant to split my column into two parties, and so, although the light striking force still marched in a body, so that it could leave at a moment's notice, I took the whole column on together, towards the rendezvous west of Baw.

I had signalled my estimated time of arrival as half-past six in the evening, but it soon became apparent that I had been over-optimistic. The men were showing signs of physical weakness, and at five I gave them an hour's rest, while I myself prepared to push on with a small escort. I told John Fraser to take command of the main body, and gave as a rendezvous a confluence prominently marked on the map about two miles south of my rendezvous with brigade. Not knowing the outcome of the action at Baw, I did not wish to hazard the whole column on the track. I had to cater, also, for the possibility that brigade might have been scattered, having no column to defend it; and I had in mind, if this should prove to be the case, a crossing of the Shweli at a lonely spot some ten miles north-east of Baw. It was already apparent that we had lingered too long in the triangle formed by the Irrawaddy and the Shweli, and that we might have a difficult task in getting out of it. So I told John Fraser that if I did not meet him at the confluence by four in the morning, he was to move the column to a second rendezvous some ten miles north, which looked from the map to be a good assembly area for the crossing of the Shweli which I had in mind.

There were therefore three rendezvous current: the first, that with brigade, on the track one and a half miles west of Baw, where I was due at 6.30 p.m.; the second, that between me and the column, at the confluence, open up till 4 a.m. on the morning of the twenty-fifth; and the third, also with the column some ten miles farther north, open up to an unspecified time. I flattered myself that I had catered for all contingencies.

I took with me as escort Pam Heald, Aung Pe and a section of Karens. With a foolishness that I cannot explain, I left my pack to be carried on my charger, taking in my pocket only a packet of biscuits: I was counting on seeing the column again in a few hours. We were rather short of maps, and Duncan and I, being normally together, always shared one; and on this occasion I left our joint map with Duncan, trusting to Pam Heald's.

Pam and I, with our escort, walked hurriedly to the rendezvous, and found, just after dark, what we believed to be the very spot. The map showed the track as running about a hundred yards beyond a *chaung*; we found a *chaung* about where we expected it, and a track just beyond. Admittedly we did not reach it till about seven, but it was a blow when patrols for three-quarters of a mile up and down the track each way disclosed nothing. I left two men to watch, and settled Pam in a bivouac by the stream. At eight o'clock I determined to go and pick up the column at the confluence, and studied Pam's map intently so as to engrave on my mind all the features within a radius of several miles. I gave Pam orders similar to those which I had given John: to stay where he was until seven o'clock on the morning of the twenty-fifth; and if we had not joined him by then to march to the third rendezvous to await us there.

The walk to the confluence seemed simple enough. I had to march due south for a mile and a half, until I hit a broad and well-defined *chaung* and then turn along it to the east: half a mile should bring me to the spot. I borrowed as companion Jameson, the Naik who spoke English, and who had crossed the Chindwin with me five weeks before; and I took consummate care to march on an accurate compass bearing so that I could find Pam again if I wanted to.

I duly struck the big *chaung* and turned east to find the confluence. The *chaung* took me straight into a vast thicket of prickly bamboo, the biggest curse in Burma; whereof the leaves and stalks alike tear your clothes and flesh into ribbons. My going was very slow; and what was more disconcerting was that I could see no sign of a column having passed that way. I struggled on for a mile in the light of the rising moon, but failed to find anything remotely resembling a confluence.

With a sinking feeling I reckoned that I must be on the wrong *chaung*, so I turned back to the point where I had first struck it, and laid a new and equally careful course due south. I went on for two miles before I came to the watershed, and descended into the next valley; and I went down as far as the watercourse, though by this time certain that I was wrong. Back I came to the original *chaung*, convinced that it was the right one, and then along to the prickly bamboo thicket again, only twice as far this time, still without finding the confluence. Then I turned back once more, and went down the *chaung* in the other direction; still without result. I was that forlorn creature, a column commander who had lost his column.

I had been walking all the previous day, and all the night. I was desperately weary. It was now long after four o'clock; as that hour had drawn near, I had pictured the column waking up, loading up, Duncan and John conferring whether to wait another half-hour for me and deciding not to; and the column at last moving off. Well, there was nothing for it but to go back to Pam, collect him and his party, and push on to the third rendezvous to meet the column. And I had until seven o'clock to get there.

I went back to the original point on the *chaung* where I had first hit it, and whence I had taken my departure for each of my ineffective casts. I set off carefully due north, but soon became aware that this was very different country to what I had traversed last night. We were having to cut our way, whereas last night we had been able to walk free. Jameson was positive that we had mistaken the point of departure; and so certain was I that we were wrong, that I consented to go back to the *chaung* and try again. We did, and I let Jameson have his head; Karens are normally far better in jungle than I, and my first shot had obviously been wrong. But we fared no better, and I was convinced that Jameson's point of departure was not correct.

The moon was high, but all the shadows looked different to what they had looked last night; still I was convinced that my point of departure was right, whatever else was wrong. Soon the first light of dawn was beginning to appear, the weariest and most hopeless dawn that I can remember. I was quite certain that we should never find Pam by seven o'clock, and that I had lost both him and the column for good. I had no map, and only the haziest idea of how to find the third rendezvous; the only village in the neighbourhood was Baw, which I had reason to believe was held by the Japs; and we had no food. I reckoned we had walked twenty miles since last night at five o'clock; if I was tired, Jameson was whacked; and now he sat down and said he could go no farther. I gave him five minutes, and then hauled him to his feet, and we started off again, striving hard to keep on our northward bearing, but being deflected from it every few yards by impassable jungle. Jameson sat down twice: once ostensibly to draw my attention to a wholly uninteresting plant, and once from frank exhaustion. The second time I had to drag him up by the collar. At seven o'clock, the moment when Pam was due to move, I was near tears: the whole jungle was strange, and we were irrevocably lost. At that moment we stumbled on a mere, which seemed vaguely familiar; there were many of them about, but this looked liked one I had seen the previous evening. And then suddenly we heard the unmistakable sound of a column marching through teak undergrowth: we crouched on the ground and held our breath, and then Jameson cried out, "There is our adjutant! It is our column!" And out of a bush on the right, in the same second, popped the head of Pam.

It felt like a miracle, and I have never been more aware of God's mercy. Duncan, too, had spent most of the night looking for the confluence, and had twice searched the bamboo thicket, but his visits had not coincided with mine. Jameson and I were both done, and I had to order an hour's halt for our benefit; I was asleep the moment my head touched the ground.

When I was wakened, it was ten o'clock and I began to curse Duncan for having let me sleep in an extra hour; but he told me that while I had been asleep he had managed to catch brigade on the air, and get a new rendezvous out of them, on the Shaukpin Chaung, only six miles away. They were having a supply drop there at three in the afternoon, and would have some rations for us too.

We crossed the track, and in due course came to another *chaung* and another track, which probably accounted for my failure to find brigade last night. I found afterwards that George Astell of the Burma Rifles had been waiting for me most of the previous day and far into the night; and having come from Baw instead of out of featureless jungle, he was more likely to have struck the correct rendezvous than I. At three o'clock we were on the Shaukpin Chaung, and heard the aircraft circling and dropping within a mile of us; but although I sent out three officer patrols we did not find the spot until five in the evening. I always quote this as an instance of how hard it is to march on a sound in the jungle; a comforting thing to remember when one is playing hide-and-seek with Japanese.

It was Denny Sharp who finally found the dropping area. One day's rations only had been left for us, all that could be spared, in charge of David Rowland, an officer in 8 Column. He was very glad to see us, and we to see him, and to feel we were once again in touch with brigade and the other two British columns. He told us that they had moved two miles north-west to the Hehtin Chaung, and that they would be staying there for the next twenty-four hours; he was going to push on there straight away and get in to-night, but thought it would be all right for us to join in the morning. This I resolved to do, because we badly needed rest; and though it was disappointing only to get one day's rations when we had hoped for five or six, the rations included bully, which we had not seen for many weeks.

But the most momentous news which David produced was that the decision had been taken to return to India. This was wholly and absolutely unexpected. I quickly asked David if his men knew, and if so would he tell them not to say a word of it to mine; but it was too late, and the word had quickly spread around the column.

This was the most unfortunate thing which could have happened. As long as the men knew that they were staying in and carrying on with the campaign, they were perfectly all right; but so soon as the news got round that we were homeward bound, one's first reaction was to think: "Splendid! Now it would be too bad if I got pipped on the way home. I must start taking care of myself." And that is a disastrous frame of mind for soldiers whose whole safety depends on prompt, resolute and unhesitating action. I shall always wish that we had told them instead that we were going to another area to operate. It is not always easy, however, and even since then I have been obliged to make a similar disclosure to troops against my better judgment: on that occasion, however, it was to encourage weary men to produce a last physical effort before being withdrawn from a campaign.

Next morning at seven o'clock we walked in on the brigade bivouac on the Hehtin Chaung. From all sides came greetings and chaff. 7 and 8 Columns turned out in force, and Burrifs from Colonel Wheeler's party greeted our own Karens. All day long visitors came to see us, and Sam Cooke brought two bottles of Scotch whisky which Arthur Tuck, the King's quartermaster, knowing a reunion to be imminent, had dropped the day before. But I am anticipating: the whisky was not drunk till evening. We will forget it till then.

The column settled in, I went to pay my respects to Wingate. I found him naturally a bit depressed, but quite certain, as I was, that the decision to go back was a sound one. He had, in fact, been ordered back; but he was not the man to comply with such an order unless he himself was convinced of the necessity for doing so. He had been impressed with the fatigue of the troops (I did not have to labour the point about which I had been primed by Bill Aird, for he had seen the same physical decline in the two columns with him); he had gained for us invaluable experience; and he had demonstrated for all time that he could substantiate his claims about what could be done by a force of Long Range Penetration.

He was a little anxious about the recrossing of the Irrawaddy; I was in favour of remaining together as a brigade, and as such crossing the Shweli. Although it was obvious that the Japs were watching it, I reckoned that with the 1200 men of whom we disposed in the immediate neighbourhood, we would outnumber anything against us in any one area. But Wingate produced good reasons against this; and he had made up his mind that the best chance was to go straight back to Inywa, where he had crossed a few days before, and cross there again. It was unlikely that the Japs would expect us to move back on our own tracks so soon after the first crossing.

He had made up his mind also that we must harden our hearts and dump all mules and equipment, except for a few to carry the wireless and one or two other essentials; because otherwise the crossing would take too long, and the Japs in the area would be able to concentrate against us. He had information that the enemy had brought up large reserves, and that very soon the net round the Shweli and Irrawaddy Rivers would be impenetrable. He told me that he was having a conference of column commanders that afternoon at four, and bade me go and sleep till then. The columns would start moving out at one o'clock in the morning.

I tried to get some sleep, but there was a constant stream of visitors, and it was such fun to see them, that I did not grudge my loss of rest. There was Sam Cooke, with his whisky—but that comes later. There was David Hastings, the adjutant, and Jacksie Pickering, and Ken Gilkes and Scotty, and L. G. Wheeler and Peter Buchanan, all with stories to tell and to be capped. It was like a Bardic festival.

There was also one source of embarrassment. An officer whom I will call "Donnelly," had been sent before the supply drop at Baw to seal off part of the area from possible enemy interference. He had failed to reach his allotted position by nightfall, and had bivouacked short of it. When he moved on at dawn, he found the Japs already in the village between him and the supply dropping area. He was adjudged guilty of having failed to carry out his orders through negligence and summarily reduced to the ranks by the Brigadier. It was obviously impossible for him to stay in his own column, where he had been a captain; so he came to me as a private soldier.

I did not know him well, having come so recently to the brigade; but others, like Bill Edge and Tommy Roberts and Alec

Macdonald, had served in the same battalion with him for three years and knew him very well indeed. I talked to him for five minutes and to my relief found that he had taken this shattering blow most creditably, though he felt he had been hardly done by. I brought him into column headquarters, ostensibly as an intelligence private; and warned him that he was to be treated as a private soldier in every way.

I mention this incident for several reasons, but chiefly because it shows how one had, in the matter of discipline as in many other matters, to make decisions not normal in the army; and also because I want to pay tribute to "Donnelly," both for the fashion in which he took his degradation and for his extreme usefulness to me in the weeks that followed.

At the column commanders' conference that afternoon, the Brigadier repeated in the form of orders the plan which he had outlined to me in the morning. Sam Cooke and L. G. Wheeler were there, as well as Scotty, Ken and I. So was Gim Anderson, in his capacity as brigade major. No. 1 Group had had a fight crossing the Nam Mit; no details were known of it. Mike Calvert had also had a scrap at Pago, one of the villages which my scouts had visited. He had just announced his intention of going for the Gokteik on his own, and finished his message with the words, "Best wishes all." But Wingate ordered him to abandon the project and make his way independently to India.

Now let us have that whisky. There was enough for a small tot for each officer of the British columns, and we drank to our health, our success and our safe return. I shall always remember that scene, in the bushes just above the bank of the sandy Hehtin Chaung, the last reunion of a very happy band of officers, before setting out on the perilous homeward journey, which many of them did not survive.

Part Two

EMERGENCY EXIT

CHAPTER ELEVEN

FROM HEHTIN TO PYINLEBIN

27th March—30th March

"The King with half the East at heel is marched from lands of morning,
   His fighters drink the rivers up, their shafts benight the air;
And he that stands must die for naught, and home there's no re-
   turning."

A. E. HOUSMAN.

BRIGADE LED, and I resumed my old position as tail column except for the Burrif headquarters, to whom had been allotted the difficult task of obliterating our trail. Brigade left at 1 a.m., and it was close on 3 a.m. before I saw the last man in front of me move off, and gave the word to march. We had all had a good rest; and had it not been for hunger (for we had to husband our scanty ration) we should have been in very good form.

Everything depended on our reaching Inywa without our turnabout being suspected; and our route therefore avoided all tracks. Wingate's uncanny instinct for cross-country marching—his sense of watersheds, good gradients, thinner jungle and so forth—was apparent even from my place far down the long procession. But it was a slow business, with frequent halts; and, with the knowledge of the Irrawaddy stretched like a barrier between ourselves and the free country beyond, the march was anything but exhilarating. Wingate had said himself that, once over the 'Waddy, we were seven-eighths out of the wood. Meanwhile, one was aware of its sinister breadth ahead of us, a malevolent ally, however passive, of the Japanese.

But the most depressing aspect of that miserable march was the slaughter of the mules. Were this to become known to the Japanese, our intention would be clear to them. Wingate had directed that they should be led off the track and slaughtered as opportunities occurred. They could not be shot on the hill-tops, for fear of the sound carrying; but every time we descended into a *chaung* half a dozen would be led away from the track we were making, their loads and saddlery concealed in the undergrowth, and six shots would ring out. Poor Bill Smyly, who had looked after them so wisely and well all the way from the banks of the Narain Nullah in the Central Provinces, to whom they were the light of his life, who had quarrelled with half the officers in the column on their behalf, who had not lost a single beast from avoidable causes—poor Bill Smyly marched that day with a white face, slipping away every now and then to dispatch a few more, and rejoining the column with tears on his cheeks.

Soon a message came back down the line that no more were to be shot; even although the places were chosen with some care, the sound was carrying up to the head of the procession, where the Brigadier was marching. The message said that they were to be slaughtered noiselessly. We had been using pistols instead of a rifle, in the hope that the noise would be lessened. Now we tried the ghastly experiment of cutting their throats; but the first operation sickened us all so much that I said we should try it no more. We had already disposed of sixteen animals since leaving the bivouac.

The Brigadier's orders, at the conference the previous afternoon, had been as follows. We were making for Inywa, where the Shweli enters the Irrawaddy. Leaving the Hehtin Chaung at 1 a.m. on the 27th, we hoped to make Inywa at 6 p.m. on the 28th, and to begin the crossing that night. The proposed bivouac area for the night 27th-28th was the marshes of Chaungmido, where one of the other columns had reported finding water on the southward journey. If by chance the march was interrupted, the rendezvous was to be in the jungle one mile south of the village of Pyinlebin.

Once arrived at Inywa, there were to be tasks for each column. Burrif H.Q. were to help 8 Column collect boats from the lower reaches of the Shweli: 7 Column was to cross first and make a bridgehead on the west bank: Brigade Headquarters were to cross next: and 5 Column was to throw a screen all round the crossing area, to protect it while the rest of the brigade crossed. We were to be the rearguard, the place of honour; and to be the last over.

There was a very real possibility that, with the Japs lining both the Irrawaddy and the Shweli, we were already in the bag. All columns had reported their awareness of reinforcements moving up; we in No. 5 Column had learnt of it in the neighbourhood of Mogok and Myitson, and other people had similar tales. There was little one could do in the way of insurance; but two things I had already arranged. I had asked Gim Anderson and the Brigadier to make a note, in case I failed to reach India, that I recommended both Duncan and John for decoration for their sterling services; I had witnessed Gim write down their names, along with those of various N.C.O.s and men, in his notebook. Secondly, I enjoined on both Duncan and John that, in the event of their getting out alive and my failing to do so, they were to seek an audience with General Wavell in Delhi, on my behalf; and to give him my views on the feasibility of this form of warfare. I made them repeat several times over the arguments which, even should the expedition finish in disaster, seemed to me irrefutable proof that such enterprises were worth while.

Mentally and physically, it was a horrid march. At one o'clock, soon after crossing a track running north and south, the first we had seen, Hosegood, the brigade intelligence officer, came back to meet me, and to say that we were going into a midday bivouac, moving off at about three. The spot chosen was the junction between the Hintha Chaung and one of its tributaries; there was a little water in pools. Hosegood settled me down half a mile short of brigade and a little later the Burrifs came in behind me. I ordered tea to be brewed up, and told John Fraser to have his men kill a mule, and distribute it for meat. Leaving

Duncan to settle in the column, I went forward to see the Brigadier.

I found him eating some rice and raisins, and had ten minutes' talk with him; he was in good form and cheerful. I returned to the column, and had been back ten minutes when I heard some shooting on the hill above and behind me. I immediately sent out Philippe and Tommy Blow with their platoons and sent a runner to the Brigadier to say that I had done so. Colonel Wheeler came along, and said that one of his riflemen had been fired on while relieving nature a couple of hundred yards from the bivouac; he also had sent a party under Macpherson to investigate. It seemed to us that the patrol, or whatever it was, must have come along the north and south track which we had crossed shortly before we halted and either seen the smoke of our fires, or followed up our track, although a party of Burrifs had been systematically obliterating it, so far as possible.

A mounted officer came along the *chaung* from brigade with orders. Columns were to get on the move at once; brigade was already moving off. Five Column was to lay an ambush, and deal with any attempt to follow up. I asked for more details: I wasn't clear how to lay an ambush in an area which it was by no means certain the enemy would come through; but all he could say was that I was to lay an ambush: he had been given no details.

Leaving John Fraser again in charge, I went along to where I had last seen brigade, but they had gone. I saw Scotty: his column was held up by the tail of 7 Column, which was just vanishing in the wake of brigade, up the hill out of the *chaung*.

"Look here, Scotty," I said. "I'm not altogether clear what is wanted of me, but it is quite obvious you won't be away from here for nearly an hour yet. I can't help feeling the Jap is far more likely to nip round the flank and cut in on the procession than to follow up the tail. However, I'll stay here and attract as much attention as I can; and when you're clear I'll make tracks down the *chaung*, as prominently as I can, so that if the Japs have gone to bring up more men, they will follow down the *chaung* instead of up the hill. Will you explain all that to the Brigadier?

I'm sure I'm doing the wrong thing, but it seems to me the most helpful thing I can do."

Scotty agreed, and I went back to the column. Philippe and Tommy were both back, but had nothing to report; Tommy was short of one section, under Corporal McGhie, which never turned up again. Wheeler came along, and said that Macpherson was also back, having seen nothing. Since the first exchange of shots, all had been silent. He agreed that the patrol had probably done its job in locating us, and had gone off to report; somebody claimed to have heard a motor-bicycle starting up, but this was by no means certain. I told Wheeler of the message I had sent to Wingate, and asked if he agreed; he pursed his lips, and said he wasn't sure, but that as I had sent the message I had better stick to what I had said to avoid confusion.

The Burrifs couldn't get clear until Scotty's column was clear, and it wasn't until after four that the last man disappeared up the hill. I sent a couple of platoons and some animals a few hundred yards along their track, and then reversed them: the idea was to make it look as if they had bivouacked on the far side of the *chaung* for their noon halt, and then come back to resume the march. At about half-past four, I started laying my false trail.

We marched down that *chaung* in the most disgraceful fashion. Moving six abreast, and chucking down litter on the scale of a paperchase, we fairly plastered the sand with footprints; Robinson Crusoe would have had three fits and a spasm if he had seen them. We had once again the old precarious feeling of the Pinlebu Road and the approach to Tigyaing: but, as Duncan said, it was rather fun being so deliberately naughty. According to the map, the hills closed in on the *chaung* till it became a dangerous defile, about a mile and a half south of Hintha village; then they opened out for good, and the *chaung* ran away north into the flat jungle plains stretching to the Shweli. Until we were through the jaws of the defile I was thoroughly apprehensive; but we got past them without incident about six o'clock.

I had resolved, and Duncan enthusiastically approved, to make a false bivouac just before dark; and this we did on the *chaung* a mile from the village. We lit enormous fires, which felt as though they could be seen from twenty miles away; and on these we brewed our tea. The meat from a mule which the Burrifs had been slaughtering when the scare occurred had unfortunately not been distributed: we had all had to go to action stations, and except for some eager and provident Burrifs nobody had picked up any meat at all. So the food problem was acute, and I allowed only a couple of biscuits to be eaten. We certainly shouldn't be able to have a supply drop until well beyond the Irrawaddy, and whatever success attended the crossing there were obviously lean days ahead.

As soon as it was dark, we stoked up the fires in the bivouac till they looked like Jubilee Night; we tied some mules to trees well away from each other, in the hopes that they would feel lonely and bray; we used our last few explosives in setting booby traps; and in addition we pulled the pins out of grenades and weighted them down with tempting articles of kit. Then, very quietly and cautiously, in contrast to our disgraceful behaviour heretofore, we stole away five or six hundred yards down the *chaung*, and, crowded together as never before, slept an uneasy sleep until three in the morning.

Hintha village was shown on the map as being about a mile away. It seemed to me probable that it was occupied. If the enemy had us under observation at all, Hintha would be a likely place to have a post. It lay on a track junction where one track ran east and west, and another north and south—the one we had crossed just before the unlucky bivouac; and the fact that there were few tracks or villages in the area enhanced its importance. My plan was to send the column straight on down the *chaung*, while I myself took two platoons into the village to see if there were Japs there, and, if there were, to hit them. This should attract to the neighbourhood any other Japs there might be about, and distract them from following up and harassing the main body. After my conversation with Wheeler, I wasn't at all sure that I had done the right thing the previous afternoon, but I thought that a scrap at Hintha might justify it. For the platoons to take part, I selected Philippe Stibbé's and Jim Harman's commandos, and put them at the head of the column.

The plan broke down because the *chaung* proved to be blocked with prickly bamboo, and reconnaissance disclosed no alternative route to the main track into the village. This was the north and south track already mentioned, which dropped down from the hills into the *chaung* just about where we had laid the false bivouac; from this point to the village it was wide enough to take a bullock-cart. I had no alternative but to take the whole column with me so far, until the bamboo gave place to decent jungle; there I would send off the column, and go on into the village with the two platoons.

I halted more than once to probe for a gap in the bamboo, but drew a blank every time. According to the map I still had half a mile to play with before reaching the village; but the time factor was worrying me, for it was now nearing four o'clock, and by six that night we had to be at Inywa, a distance of twenty miles. I went on a little farther down the track, and suddenly saw, a hundred yards ahead of me, the sloping roofs of houses, half a mile too soon.

They say that the mind plays curious tricks in moments of crisis, and I remember distinctly that the sloping roofs at that moment reminded me of the medieval roofs of the old town of Chinon, as I saw them one moonlight night from the terrace of the ruined castle, fifteen years before. I had stumbled right into the outskirts of the village. The path forked at my feet; one branch, the less used of the two, ran along the edge of the bamboo; the other ran straight on towards the houses. Between the two was low undergrowth over which it was just possible to see: I fancy it must have been *bizat*, a thick thornless bush six or seven feet high, very common on the site of deserted villages, or on cultivation which has been allowed to fall into disuse.

The moon was still low, and where the track was flanked with trees it had been very dark: but here, where it was open, one could get a good view of the sleeping houses, moonlit on the east but with deep shadows on the west side of each. It all seemed still and peaceful; no sentries were guarding the approach; and I began to think that we had been playing our bivouac drama to an empty house. I was worried at the column being jammed together on the track behind me, with no means of getting off it should the village prove to be held. The men were very silent, fully realising how much depended on the next few minutes; the only noise came from the mules, as they shifted their feet and creaked their saddlery. I told Duncan to organise a resumed search for a way into the jungle from the track, while I went forward with Philippe Stibbé's platoon to investigate; I passed the word also for a couple of Karens to act as interpreters.

Without waiting for Philippe to complete his orders, I moved cautiously forward with Po Po Tou and Jameson. As we went, we saw over the *bizat* the reflection of a fire against one of the houses on the left. Seventy yards or so from the fork in the track, we came to a T-junction, flanked by houses, and with a small track only, between two large houses, continuing the line of that on which we were: we had obviously come on to the main east and west track.

The fire was about forty yards along to the left, in the compound of the second house. With a grenade in my right hand I walked quietly towards it. Round it, symmetrically, one on each side, sat four men. They looked so peaceful and innocent that I immediately concluded that they were Burmese; and in that tongue (of which my knowledge was limited to a few sentences) I asked, "What is the name of this village?"

The men on the far side looked up, and those on this side looked round: I was only three yards from them. They were Japs. Resisting a curious instinct which was prompting me to apologise for interrupting them, I pulled the pin out of my grenade, which had suddenly become sticky with sweat, and lobbed it —oh, so neatly—into the fire. I just caught the expression of absolute terror on their faces; they were making no attempt to move; and ran. It was a four-second grenade, and went off almost at once. I looked round when I heard it go, and they were all sprawling on the ground.

Back at the T-junction, Philippe had just arrived and was looking eager. I told him to get in at once with the bayonet and capture that end of the village. As I spoke, a man ran past me from the direction of the fire: I shot him in the side with my pistol, and he sprawled on the ground for a moment, but was up and away again in a flash.

Philippe lost no time, but as he reached the point on the track opposite the fire, light machine-guns opened up; he and his men had to go to ground, though not before they had spitted several men running out of the house beyond the fire. I called to Philippe to ask if he could get on, but he shouted back in a singularly calm voice:

"I don't think we can—it's pretty hot. I'm afraid I've been hit myself."

I told him to hand over to his platoon serjeant and to try the right flank, and they nipped into some houses on that side of the track; but by now another light machine-gun had opened up, and there were a good many bullets flying about. Duncan had come up by now, and as he arrived we heard movement from the house immediately to our left, a matter of ten yards. This was followed by two or three shots by our ears; Duncan hove a couple of grenades into it, and there were loud groans, which went on, diminuendo, to the end of the action, but no more shooting.

I was worried about the man who had run past me early on; it was obvious that he had gone to rouse other Japs at that end of the village. So I sent Peter Dorans down there with some men of column headquarters who suddenly appeared, to block that approach. Most of them came back almost immediately, and when I asked them what the hell they were playing at, they replied that Corporal Dorans had told them they were in the way; and, confiscating their grenades, had sent all of them back except two.

I went back down to the fork tracks, and got hold of Jim Harman. I told him that Philippe's platoon would keep the Japs in play from where they were, and that he was to take his platoon up the little track and catch the Japs in flank. There was still no news from the rear about any signs of a route into the jungle. I went back to Philippe and warned him what was going to happen, shouting across the same information to Serjeant Thornborrow over the way. Somewhere in the darkness we heard a motor-cyclist trying to start up his machine.

Philippe was hit in the shoulder; not badly, but he had lost a good deal of blood. I was talking to him and Corporal Litherland, who had also been hit: the two of them were at the foot of a tree on the right of the track up which we had come, just at the junction. Suddenly there was a rush of Japs up the track from the right, where Peter Dorans was, and two or three grenades came flaming through the air: the Japs have a glowing fuse on their grenades, very useful in a night action to those at whom they are thrown. One rolled to within a few yards of me, and I flung myself down behind a dark shadow which I took to be a fold in the ground; I realised only too clearly as soon as I was down that it was nothing more substantial than the shadow of a tree in the moonlight. The thing went off, and I felt a hot, sharp pain in the bone of my hip. At that moment there was a series of loud explosions: Peter, from the ditch where he was lying, had rolled half a dozen grenades among the Japs. Where I had seen them dimly in the moonlight and shadows, there was now a heap of writhing bodies, into which Peter was emptying his rifle. There was no further attack from that side.

I hopped to my feet and was overjoyed to find I was all right and able to walk. But poor Philippe had been hit again, this time in the small of the back; so had Corporal Litherland, and a third man who had been groaning and was now dead.

Philippe could still walk, and I told him to go back out of the way down the column. He walked a couple of yards, said "Blast, I've forgotten my pack," picked it up and went off. This was the last time I saw him. Litherland also, with some help, was able to walk down the track.

There came a burst of shooting and some grenades from the little track where Jim and the commandos had gone. Thornborrow and his men were firing occasional rounds when they thought they saw a target, but another effort to get forward brought more casualties. I went back to the fork to see how Jim had got on, and I found him already back.

"There was an l.m.g. there," he said, "but we've knocked it out. I've been right up to the main track, and I believe we could get the animals through that way."

Alec Macdonald was beside me, and immediately said:

"I'll have a look. Come on," and disappeared up the track. I had a feeling that, having failed on Peter Dorans' flank, the Japs would try and come in on the right, somewhere down the column; so I passed the word back to try and work a small flank guard into the jungle on that side if possible. Then I went back to the T-junction, and made arrangements to attract all the attention we could, so as to give Alec a free run. (I seemed to spend the whole action trotting up and down that seventy yards of track.)

There came another burst of fire from the little track, a mixture of l.m.g., tommy-guns and grenades. The commando platoon alone in the column had tommy-guns, which was one of the reasons I had selected them for the role. Their cheerful rattle, however, meant that the little track was no longer clear. I hurried back to the fork, and there found Denny Sharp.

"This is going to be no good," I said. "Denny, take all the animals you can find, go back to the *chaung* and see if you can get down it. We'll go on playing about here to keep their attention fixed; I'll try and join you farther down the *chaung*, but if I don't then you know the rendezvous. Keep away from Chaungmido, as we don't want to get brigade muddled up in this."

Back to the T-junction I went, and found on the right of the track the Burrif platoon. They had two or three casualties from "overs"; Jameson had one in the shoulder, and so did another splendid N.C.O., Nay Dun, whose name always made me think of a trout fly. I told John to take them back, but he must have sent them under Pam Heald, because he himself still remained with me at the end of the action.

Another casualty was Abdul the Damned. Somehow he had wandered up into the battle leading Duncan's horse: armouring being at a discount, Duncan had made him into his syce, and jolly good he had become. Abdul had a nasty wound in the shoulder and was weeping bitterly, howling like a child: the horse had also been hit in the shoulder, and could barely walk: Duncan shot it there and then.

The sound of shooting opened up where I had expected it; away back down the column, the flank attack was coming in. It was audibly beaten off, and I sent another message down the column warning them to look out for a repeat performance still farther down the line. Then a messenger arrived, and said:

"Captain Macdonald's killed, sir."

"Nonsense," I said. "How do you know?"

"Mr. Harman's back, sir. And he's badly wounded."

I went back to the fork. Jim was there, with blood streaming from a wound in his head, and his left arm held in his right hand. Alec had led the way down the track, with Jim following; then Serjeant Pester and then Pte. Fuller. They had met two l.m.g.s, new ones, which had opened up. Alec had fallen instantly, calling out, "Go on in, Jim!" Jim had been hit in the head and shoulder, Pester was unhurt, Fuller killed. Jim and Pester between them had knocked out both guns, and the track was again clear. They had had a look at Alec on the way back, and he was dead.

I reckoned we had killed a good many Japs, one way and another, but it was nearly six o'clock and would soon be light; and what I dreaded more than anything else was the possibility of being caught in daylight on the track, with the little, lithe Japs, unencumbered by packs or weariness, able to crawl under the bushes at ground level and snipe the guts out of us. There was no sign of any animals; Denny seemed to have got them back all right, but what, if any, luck he was having at the *chaung* I didn't know. At that moment somebody (I think John Fraser) came up with the news that a place had been found a couple of hundred yards back where you could squeeze through the bamboo into a stretch of disused paddy, beyond which there was open teak jungle. This decided me. At this moment came the noise of the "repeat performance" on the tail of the column which we had been expecting. There was a couple of minutes of shooting, then it too stopped.

"Well, what do we do now?" I said vaguely to John and Duncan.

"Well, you'd better make your mind up, and bloody quick too!" said Duncan affably.

"Get everybody in sight into the paddy," I said, "and don't forget Thornborrow."

The paddy was as it had been described, and in the growing light it was hard to see why we hadn't discovered it earlier. It was a stretch about a hundred yards long by forty wide, opening off the track to the westward, towards the *chaung*. And, greatest boon of all, beyond it, quite clearly in the dim daylight, one could discern that the jungle was teak—good, open teak, where you can move in any direction at any pace you like, and yet be swallowed up from view in less than a hundred yards.

"Now," I said to Duncan, "are we quite sure that everybody knows the rendezvous?"

"Absolutely," he said; and with that assurance I told Brookes the bugler to blow on his "instrument," as he always called it, the call known as "Second Dispersal," on hearing which every group in the column was trained to break off from the main body and make its way independently to the rendezvous. I waited for a moment, to reassure myself that it was being acted on; and then joined my own group as it went off confidently into the jungle on a northerly bearing.

Soon we came to the east and west track, put out stops to prevent interruption, and crossed it rapidly in one wave. We travelled about a mile, and then halted to take stock. It was now about seven o'clock.

With me were Duncan and John, the bulk of column head-quarters, Tommy Blow and his platoon, Tommy Roberts and the bulk of the support platoon, Serjeant Thornborrow and the remnants of Philippe Stibbé's platoon. Missing from column headquarters were Serjeant-major Cairns, Pepper the runner, Lance-Corporal Lee the column clerk, Foster and White the signallers and one or two others. Most of the men were accounted for somehow; Cairns had last been seen helping Denny with the animals, Foster, White and Lee were believed to have gone with the animals which carried their various bits of property, Pepper had been sent on a message. Duncan counted heads, and made us about sixty. We had two or three of Tommy Roberts's animals, which he had refrained from sending back with the others in case he was required to give mortar support. We also had one chestnut charger.

Abdul and I were the only two wounded, and Tommy Blow, who had been a member of the St. John Ambulance Brigade in civil life, was ordered by Duncan to have a look at us. There was a very small jagged hole just above my hip joint, bleeding mildly, on which he put a field dressing: it felt no worse than a kick in the football field. Abdul, on the other hand, had a really bad hole, and was in a good deal of pain. Tommy washed out the wound with sulphanilamide, of which he had a few tablets in his haversack, and put a dressing on: he also produced a sling, and made him put his arm in it. Then we pushed on: we had still nearly twenty miles to do, and eleven hours to do it in; there was no time to be lost.

We had a halt for tea sometime about midday; otherwise we marched all day. Once or twice people suggested that I should get on the charger, but I was obsessed by the idea that if I did my leg would get stiff; and anyway with a stout stick I got along very well. During the morning we got rid of all the animals except the charger, and buried their loads, leaving the mules at a place where they had water to drink and bamboo leaves to eat. The charger we kept, partly in case somebody passed out and had to be carried (everybody was pretty weak for lack of food by now) and partly because it would do for meat later. Mules are better eating than horses, but none of the support mules would do for riding, and as we had to get rid of their loads, to get rid of them as well quickened our speed across country considerably.

Early in the afternoon we found a column's track. It came in from the south-west, and headed pretty well the same direction as that in which we were going. It was fresh—not more than an hour or two old, and definitely British; so we followed it until just before dusk, when I dug my toes in and said I couldn't manage another yard. The map had proved as inaccurate this side of Hintha as it had while we were approaching the village; but we had little doubt that we were pretty well at the rendezvous, one mile south of Pyinlebin; or at all events not more than a half-mile out. During the last half-hour of daylight, we had seen some animal droppings which were still warm, and we knew we must have been gaining on whoever was making the track; so Duncan shoved on a bit, and came back with the welcome news that he had found the headquarters of the Burma Rifles, just going into bivouac, and had spoken to Colonel Wheeler. The Brigadier had ordered them to do just what we had been doing: to make misleading tracks off to the north-east.

I sent John Fraser to see them, to discuss what to do in the morning if there were still no signs of the brigade, and then tried to settle down for some sleep. Almost all the blankets had been lost; except for Philippe's platoon, they had all been carried on mules, and so were all with Denny Sharp. It was one of those nights of bitter cold which one occasionally gets in that otherwise warm climate, and nobody outside Philippe's platoon got much sleep. Duncan and I huddled together vainly for warmth, but tired as we were it was too cold for sleeping. We were anxious too, for John Fraser never came back: whether he had run into enemy or was just simply lost we could not tell, but when morning came, and brought no John, we were really anxious. We sent a patrol to the Burrif bivouac, but they had flitted.

Soon after seven there came the sound of firing over towards the Irrawaddy, and we girt up our loins and marched westward towards the sound of the guns. At nine o'clock we suddenly came to the edge of the jungle, and gazed out over a couple of miles of paddy to the river. Beyond it, the friendly hills of the Gangaw Range climbed steeply into the blue sky. The shooting had stopped, and the whole morning looked peaceful and Sabbatical. Two hundred yards out into the paddy was a small hovel, with one or two children playing outside it: Duncan and I went over and talked to the man and woman whom from time to time we saw moving about their morning tasks.

Duncan had a very good head for languages, and had picked up a little Burmese. He bought some rice and asked about Japs. The man seemed vaguely reassuring, but we couldn't follow all he said. At that moment, down the track by which we had come appeared a Jemadar and half a dozen Karens of the Burma Rifles headquarters. The Jemadar, San Shwe Htoo, spoke good English, and we used him to interpret; but we got nothing of interest out of the man. I told San Shwe Htoo to warn him that he and his family and anybody else who might come to visit him were to keep to their house, and not move before nightfall: we should watch from the edge of the jungle to make sure these orders were obeyed.

San Shwe Htoo had orders to patrol to the village of Maugon, about a mile to the southward, on the bank of the river; at my request he gave me a man who knew where Colonel Wheeler and the rest of Burrif H.Q. were. With him as guide and Peter Dorans as escort, I set off to see Wheeler and discover what he proposed doing. I wasn't very spry on my legs, and it took the best part of an hour to get there. I found Wheeler cheerful but worried; like myself he had expected to find brigade where we bivouacked last night, but there was no sign of them. He had sent a patrol into Pyinlebin to confirm that we were where we meant to be, and then, when he heard the firing, had done the same as myself and marched towards it.

John Fraser had joined him the night before, but had missed the track on the way back; and, after spending most of the night trying to find me, he had made his way back to the Burrifs, and marched with them this morning to their present location. He was now out with Macpherson on another effort to locate brigade headquarters, and to get orders. Wheeler and I had come to the same conclusion about the shooting that we had heard earlier: that the brigade's crossing had been opposed, and now, in all probability, had been abandoned. He promised to let me know the results of Macpherson's patrol, and I said I would stay where I was on the edge of the jungle until I heard from him further. Peter Buchanan the adjutant came back with me to see where I was, and to try his hand at getting further dope out of the man in the hovel. Wheeler asked me when I had last eaten, and when he heard the answer most nobly insisted on my accepting two squares of his last slab of chocolate.

When Peter Buchanan and I reached my bivouac, I was delighted to find Denny Sharp, Jim Harman and most of his commandos, Gerry Roberts and his platoon, Bill Edge, Pepper, Foster and White, all arrived in. They had had a longer march than we, having failed to get down the *chaung*, and having been compelled to go back up it the way we had come in, the previous evening. Once on the hill, they got away across country; but while climbing up it, two of the most precious mules of the whole string had tumbled over the cliff into the *chaung* below: one carried the wireless, and the other the ciphers. Lance-Corporal Lee had gone back down to recover the ciphers, and had not been seen since. They had heard, as they came away, the sound of explosions from the dummy bivouac, where some Nips presumably paid the price of their inquisitiveness. Otherwise they had not been interrupted. There had, however, been one more serious loss: while going through some elephant grass, their column had split in two, and the rear half had not caught them up again. Among those whom they had thus lost were Pam Heald and all the Burrifs, bar one rifleman, Maung Kyan; Bill Aird and some wounded; Serjeant-Major Cairns and the colour-serjeant; Willy Williamson and most of the support platoon; Bill Smyly and most of the Gurkhas.

Nobody had seen David Whitehead, and I was worried about him and Lance-Corporal Lee: about the others, I was pretty sure that they could look after themselves, and would turn up all right. But one piece of news they brought plunged us all into sorrow, and filled us at the same time with an admiration which will never diminish.

Philippe Stibbé had lost a great deal of blood by the time the dispersal was sounded, and had to be mounted on a pony. Bill

6. Interrogating the headman at a Kachin village.

7. Major Fergusson, Lieutenant Harman, Corporal Dorans and Captain Fraser with Kachin village headman in the background.

8. Supplying one of the Chindit columns from the air in April, 1943.

9. Sick members of a Chindit column are flown out from behind the Japanese lines on Easter Sunday, 1943, after a landing strip had been cleared in the jungle.

10. Safe behind the Chindwin.

Aird had had time to dress both his wounds; the second one looked as if it might be in the kidneys. To start with he had been with a party which had no other animals with it, and which was in a bad bit of country. Realising that he was slowing up the party, he had begged to be left behind. Those with him indignantly refused; but when, after another half-mile, his pony had been responsible for several more delays, he slipped from the saddle to the ground, and said, "Now you've jolly well got to leave me." Nor does the story end there; for a Burma rifleman, unwounded, cheerfully said he would stay with Philippe and look after him; and in spite of Philippe's vehement orders to the contrary, he did so. We believe that this was Rifleman Maung Tun, but have not been able to establish his identity beyond doubt. The Burrifs had always had a great affection for Philippe, and this noble story, with its double heroism, is the highest manifestation I have known of the comradeship between the British and Burman soldier.

At three o'clock John Fraser turned up. He and Macpherson had found brigade, and learned that the facts were as Wheeler and I had guessed them to be. Two platoons of 7 Column had got across before interruption occurred, and a fierce fire had opened on the near bank from the west side. Through glasses more Japanese had been seen along the bank, hurrying towards the crossing-place; and the bridgehead was not considered strong enough to hold them off. Jacksie Pickering had had an unpleasant time rowing a rubber boat about in the middle of the river under heavy fire; Scotty had had a bullet through his map-case as he stood on the near beach; the intelligence serjeant on brigade headquarters had been killed by a shot from the far side of the river. Reluctantly the Brigadier had called it off, and was now in bivouac near Pyinlebin, where he had not previously been: arriving late the night before, he had had to cut straight to Inywa, trusting to pick up the Burrifs and myself later.

John and Macpherson had both talked to the Brigadier, who had told them that his orders now were to split the whole brigade into small parties to make their way to India independently.

These parties should not exceed forty in strength, since that was the maximum number which could comfortably feed on the country. He was arranging a supply drop for brigade headquarters and the Burma Rifles; had he known that I was in the area and had lost my wireless, he would have included me also. As it was, he would put in an indent for me for any place or time that I might choose.

John had also seen Gim Anderson, the brigade major, who told him that most of the missing elements of my column had joined up with Ken Gilkes and 7 Column. He knew that Pam and a lot of Burrifs were there, very worried about John; also Bill Aird, Bill Smyly and Willy Williamson; Cairns and the colour-serjeant. John was, of course, out of touch with me at that moment, and had no particular hope of finding me again: but instead of joining up with 7 Column, whose exact whereabouts at that moment were unknown, he decided to go back with Macpherson to the Burrifs and attach himself to them, as his parent unit; knowing that they might by now have got into touch with me again.

Added to all this, he brought a message for me from Wheeler. We had discussed that morning the possibility of joining forces and walking out together. With the increase in my strength from 70 to 120, of which Peter Buchanan had told him, he felt that together we should be too strong to live on the country; and as neither of us had a wireless, it was a case of living on the country or not living at all. However, since hearing Wingate's orders about breaking up into small parties, he was resolved to get moving as soon as he could, and was prepared to bequeath to me his interest in the brigade supply drop. He was proposing to move at five that evening.

I thought I would have one more try at finding brigade, and, in order to see Wheeler before he left, I made an immediate move. At Wheeler's bivouac, I found him ready to start, and had five minutes with him. He was going to try and cross the Shweli at a village called Seikngu; thence he would steer north and east to the Irrawaddy; thence north and west; and he hoped eventually to reach the Chindwin somewhere north of Homalin. He gave me a note to the Brigadier to hand in if I found him; and I remember it ended:

"Hope to meet you in happier circumstances."

He asked if I could give him some money, and I had a whip round, which produced about three hundred rupees. I could have given him much more, but my method of carrying the column's money was to issue so much to every man, and it took time to collect.

Facetiously we arranged to dine together in Calcutta, and as he marched off I called out to him, "Shall we start with cocktails or sherry?"

"I prefer sherry," he answered, in a mock-prim voice.*

We had a little over an hour of daylight left, and we marched off towards the point in the woods where John had seen brigade. We failed to make it before dark by about a mile, so I halted for the night, impressing on the sentries that they must rouse us the very second they became aware of impending dawn. They did so, and we hastened to the brigade bivouac area. We found the place, with the depressions in the grass where they had been sleeping; but they had gone, and, with the usual standard of junglecraft which under the eye of the Brigadier they always attained, they had not left a vestige of a trail. Brigade had gone, and with them our chance of a supply drop. We were free to make for India.

* Note J: Lieut-.Colonel L. G. Wheeler.

CHAPTER TWELVE

FROM PYINLEBIN TO SHWELI

30th March—1st April

"But timorous mortals start and shrink
To cross that narrow sea,
And linger shivering on the brink,
And fear to launch away.
Could we but make our doubts remove . . ."

ISAAC WATTS.

WE MARCHED east, along the northern edge of the jungle. Open
land, pasture, with coarse grass on which waterbuffalo were
grazing, stretched on our left hand towards the Shweli. A couple
of miles brought us to a marshy patch, marked on the map as a
chaung. Here we watered our one remaining animal, the chestnut
charger. While we were so engaged, out of the jungle came
Serjeant Gunn and five men of Tommy Roberts's support group,
looking entirely at ease and under control. Gunn was a young
lad who had started the expedition as a lance-corporal, and had
shown himself to be so good that I had advanced him first to
corporal and then to lance-serjeant—both times replacing a man
who had failed under the more rigorous conditions of the field.

He told Tommy that he had become separated from Denny
Sharp's party ·with the rest, and had joined up with a body of
British troops with a wireless set and two or three officers, who
were setting out for India.

"But I didn't think it was a healthy sort of party, sir—not
according to my idea," he said.

"Why? What was wrong?" said Tommy.

"Well, they'd plenty of food, sir—five times as much as us,
I reckon; not that they'd give us any," said Gunn. "But what they
hadn't got was water discipline. Would you believe it, sir, they

164

had a pull at their water-bottles just whenever they felt like it, and nobody checked them. And the few that didn't, well, the others were offering them two packets of biscuits for a couple of mouthfuls of water. So I said to the lads, ' Come on, boys, this lot's doomed '; and we reckoned we'd go to India on our own. I've got a map and a compass; and I reckoned we could find a boat all right if we looked long enough."

I have often taken a chance of promoting a man out of his turn, and I have sometimes been disappointed in him; but it would take a good many disappointments to counterbalance the satisfaction which I felt when I heard this, from a lad who can't have been more than twenty-two, and who was younger than most of the men he was commanding and over whom he had such influence. The jungle is a place and an atmosphere where, quite illogically, you tend to feel safety in numbers; but here was a chap who realised that a few stout hearts will fare better by themselves than among a number who show signs of going craven.

At about eleven o'clock, we came to the village of Thetkegyin. We had to approach it across open paddy, with the usual feeling of nakedness; and when we got there we found one woman, two or three men, but no boats. They suggested we might find boats the next village along. This was Seikngu, the one which L. G. Wheeler had been going to try. Seikngu, a mile along the bank, we found deserted except for one man with goitre—sinister, unsmiling, malevolent. No, he had no boats. No, he had no rice. Yes, a party of Burman soldiers with four European officers had come through the village at four o'clock in the morning, and stolen all the rice he had.

As we talked to him, a post which I had established on the outskirts of the village brought in two young men, obviously superior and intelligent, but sullen and sour. One wore European clothes. We questioned them. No, there were no boats. No, there were no Japs. Very well, then, where were there boats? The Japs had taken them all.

At that moment, "Donnelly," who had retained the field-glasses which he had had as an officer, said:

"Excuse me, sir, but I can see at least half a dozen boats at that village opposite."

I borrowed his glasses, and sure enough, moored close under the bank were boats. I told John Fraser to tell the men to go and get them. Very reluctantly they stripped to a loincloth, and taking some bamboo poles which were lying on the bank, they began riding across the river on them in that fascinating fashion which I have so often tried and failed. At the same moment, two of my men came up and said they had found a perfectly good boat under one of the houses. Goitre was lying. If he had lied about the boats, perhaps he had lied about the rice: I ordered a search to be made. It revealed almost at once two bags of rice under one house alone. Meanwhile I watched the bamboo riders making their way across the river. They arrived at the sandbank in the middle, walked upstream, and then started across the second half. "Donnelly" watched them through his glasses. I was attending to something else when I heard him exclaim:

"Where are they going? . . . That's not the way to the boats. . . . Japs!"

Instead of walking along the bank to the place where the boats were lying, they had run nimbly up the bank, and into a large house opposite where they had come ashore. Almost immediately, fifteen or twenty Japs emerged from the doorway, and looked across the river at us. Peter Dorans lay down on the ground, and brought his sniper's rifle to his shoulder, but I stopped him. At that moment, as if summoned by telepathy, three large lorries rolled up to the village opposite and disgorged another thirty or forty Japanese soldiers. I reckoned that, as a potential crossing-place, Seikngu had slumped, and I wasn't taking any shares.

But I was all for taking Goitre, and we kidnapped him, together with the two bags of rice and two more men who entered the village just as we were leaving it. We entered the jungle, and found some stagnant water in a marsh: it wasn't more than three hundred yards from a point on the bank from which we could keep the Japs under observation. We cooked some rice and tea, and even gave Goitre some. We finished our meal at about the same time as our post reported the Japs bringing the boats round to the house where we had seen them appear from first; and then we moved.

The next few miles of jungle were exceedingly thick, and although we left the stagnant water at four in the afternoon, it was eleven next morning before we had covered the eight miles which I considered would bring us to the next point in the Shweli which I wanted to try. (Admittedly, we spent the hours of darkness sleeping: the moon didn't rise until about 3 a.m., and we were sadly in need of sleep.) At about ten, I reckoned we were within striking distance of the river, and I sent out two patrols to find it. The first, under Gerry Roberts, I sent along a track which we had stumbled on half an hour before, and which looked as if it led somewhere; the second, under Serjeant Pester, I sent on a north-easterly bearing.

Gerry was back about noon. He brought with him two frightened Burmese, whom he wanted to shoot. He had found the river by following the track, but on his way back he found these two lighting a fire on the path; and, mindful of the signal fires at Tigyaing, he had assumed that they were intended to disclose our position. Questioned, the two Burmese not only ceased to look frightened: they even laughed, and explained that there were so many wild elephants about that they were in the habit of lighting fires on the tracks to keep them away from the villages: elephants dislike the smell of burning, even when the fire has been two or three days extinct. It was such a tall story, and their manner in telling it so obviously spontaneous, that we felt it to be genuine, and acquitted them of the charge brought against them.

There was no sign of Pester's party, and I began to get anxious. Meanwhile, John was talking to the two latest prisoners, whom we had been at pains to keep separate from Goitre and his friends. He came to me with an idea which they had put forward. They each owned a boat, capable of carrying four men each. We wanted the best boats, they had them. There were no Japs in their village, but there were some in both villages on the other side. Just opposite where the track by which we were bivouacked came out on the river, there was an island which could be reached by wading. If we liked to be there soon after dark, they would meet us with their boats, and would land us on the far bank of the Shweli midway between the two Jap-held villages, one mile from each. They realised we might not trust them; and they therefore suggested that one should be held as a hostage, while the other went off and brought the two boats.

To me, the thing stank; but I couldn't see why. Even if it was fishy that they themselves should suggest the hostage business, where was the catch? We would have the hostage all right. I felt strongly that every day we delayed crossing the Shweli, the harder it would be; and I resolved to close with the offer. Soon after I had made up my mind Pester and his party returned. They had found the river, but had nothing else to report.

We waited for the rest of the afternoon, feeling very apprehensive. I could not dismiss from my mind the risks I was taking with my column. I pored for hours over the map, staring at the Irrawaddy and the Shweli, and racking my brain for a better plan. We had failed to cross at Inywa, we had failed at Thetkegyin and at Seikngu; and at the latter place we had seen with our own eyes the building up of the wall around the moat. There were motor-roads, by which troops could be brought from the large reserves round Mandalay: we had seen that process at Myitson ten days before, and one of those motor-roads ran from Myitson down the Shweli along the very bank to which we were about to cross. I tried to make up my mind whether my impatience to get the crossing done with was the impetuosity of foolishness, or the wisdom of resolution. It was while I bit on this problem that there came into my mind the lines of Montrose, which went far to crystallise the decision I had taken:

> "He either fears his fate too much
>   Or his deserts are small,
> That dares not put it to the touch,
>   To gain or lose it all."

At five o'clock, we dispatched the man entrusted with the task of collecting the boats; to send an escort with him would have been impossible, without news reaching the Japs when they arrived in the village; while to escort him only as far as the outskirts of the village would have done no good, and would merely have shown the man that we did not trust him. Before he left, he talked to his colleague, with John Fraser as chaperon, and arranged that we should leave our present location as soon as it got dark, and meet him at the head of the island.

At half-past six we released Goitre and his two friends, paying him for the rice we had taken, and which had been enough to allow of a distribution to each man of the equivalent of two tea-cups full. My total strength at this moment was a hundred and twenty, including nine officers.

At seven we started to move. The relief was tremendous; the waiting had been intolerable. Silently we marched for half a mile along the track, and tiptoed down the bank on to the sand: I was leading with Tommy Roberts, Duncan and John bringing up the rear. I had not realised how far we would have to march up the island, and I had ordered a rear position to be manned and held on the river bank opposite the island, in case we were caught out in the middle of the river. John was the only interpreter we had, since Maung Kyan could not speak English; so that I could not ask my guide how much farther we had to go. After half a mile, I told Tommy to lead on, and I turned back myself to bring on John, Duncan and the rearguard.

When I got back to the head of the column again, I found that the crossing had already begun. The boats were there, all right, but they were much smaller than we had hoped—mere dugout canoes. Two men with their packs were the most that could be carried, and even that freight was precarious. The night was pitch black, and the water swirled most horribly past: I had had no idea the current was so strong. The sandbank on which we were, at the extreme north end of the island, was steep to, and the scour of the water close under it very powerful.

Tommy Roberts and several of his support men had already

crossed; Denny Sharp had constituted himself the embarkation officer, and was directing the men how to sit in the bottom of the boat, with their packs on the floor in front of them. It was a nervous business, for the boat rolled with the slightest movement, and the freeboard was negligible. The boatmen handled them superbly, but the moment when the bow was allowed to pay out from the bank, by letting the stream flow inshore of it, was a moment of terror every time; for the boat heeled, water sometimes came over the gunwale, and unless the passengers sat still, the worst would happen. I watched the process several times: the whispered instructions by Denny, the men settling into the boat, the hands anxiously gripping the gunwale, the rifle between the legs, the gingerly paying out of the bow, the swirl of the black water between the bow and the bank, the immediate heavy list, the sudden jerky roll as the men tried to compensate it, and then the disappearance of the boat downstream into the dark before the boatman's frenzied paddling took effect.

Each trip took ten minutes, each boat two men. I worked out the sum, and reckoned that we should all be across by 3 a.m. barring accidents. I took Peter Dorans, and went across on the next boat, enjoying it not at all. The worst of the stream was at the embarking point; the boatmen paddled furiously across the river, allowing the current to help him all it would by keeping the canoe at an angle; and soon we were in slack water. He had asked John in Burmese to explain to the troops that they should get out and wade once they were in shallow water; and we still appeared to be in mid-river when he anchored the boat with his paddle, and motioned us over the side. However, it proved to be not more than two feet deep, and we soon found ourselves on dry sand, among fifteen or twenty wet and waiting soldiers.

"Why the hell are you hanging about here?" I asked.

"Captain Roberts is trying to find a way off the sand," someone answered, also in a whisper. "This isn't the far bank at all, it's another sandbank."

I went up the bank to look for Tommy, and found him with disturbing news. He had been nearly half a mile up the sandbank, to find a place where one could wade ashore, but there was none. It was desperately deep, and the current as bad here as where we had embarked. He was certain of treachery, and so was I. These boatmen had marooned us on an island in the middle of the river, just as the captain, described in Maurois' *Disraeli*, had marooned a shipload of Jews whom he was deporting, in the middle of the English Channel, on a sandbank which was covered at high water. I went back to the northern end, where I had come ashore, and sent a man across with an urgent message for John Fraser to come and interpret.

When John had learned what was wrong, he got hold of the next boatman returning, and asked him to show us the way across. He stripped and plunged off the northern end of the sandbank, followed by Tommy and another man. We waited for ten minutes, and then the boatman came back. Somewhere out there in the blackness, presumably Tommy had got ashore.

"All right," I said. "Let him go on with the ferrying. I'll go over."

I took with me Denny Sharp, who had handed over his embarkation duties to Duncan, Peter Dorans and two more men; it was not until I reached the other side that I found that Abdul—wounded, weak, weeping Abdul—had attached himself to me and crossed as well.

There is no word for it but "nightmare." The roaring of the waters, the blackness of the night, the occasional sucking of a quicksand were bad enough, but the current was devilish. At its deepest, I suppose it was about four feet six or a little more: I am over six foot one, and it was more than breast high on me. The current must have been four to five knots. It sought to scoop the feet from under you and at the same time thrust powerfully at your chest. The only method of progress was to lean against the current, to attempt to keep an intermittent footing, to maintain your angle against the stream, and kick off the ground whenever your feet touched it. If once you lost your vertical position, you knew as a black certainty that you would disappear down the stream for ever. It was not until almost within reach of the bank that the river shallowed to a couple of feet; and even then it was all one could do to make one's way upstream against it. Although the crossing cannot have been more than seventy or eighty yards, one finished at least forty yards farther downstream than the point of the sandbank.

Tommy's voice hailed me from the bank as I arrived, breathless and exhausted, bidding me work my way upstream. Five yards brought one to a place where one could clamber up the bank with the help of a branch of a tree which hung low over the river. The bank itself was about ten feet high. I scrambled up, and found myself on the road.

When I had got my breath back, I began making calculations. The crossing was feasible, but some of the smaller men would find it difficult. The boats would not finish ferrying on to the sandbank until 3 a.m. and it would be light before six. It might be possible to divert the boats after that hour to bringing over the smaller men, but the vast majority must wade it. I told Denny Sharp that, as soon as he felt strong enough to do so, he must go back over, and order everybody to start, bar the very small men, whom we would bring over in the boats later. He went; and a few minutes later a long line of men began to arrive. We directed them upstream, as Tommy had done for me, and hauled the weaker ones up the bank at the one place where it was possible. As they arrived, we sorted them out into platoons, and posted them on the road two or three hundred yards either side of the crossing place, in case of interruption by enemy patrols.

Several times one heard cries for help, as some unlucky chap lost his footing and went off helplessly down-stream; I fear that it happened to four or five in all. In the inky blackness there was nothing one could do to help. Some parties tried to hold hands all the way over, but it was impossible to maintain one's grip. Once during the night, the solitary charger arrived under the bank; how it had got there heaven knows, and I never found out; we tried desperately to get it up the bank, but failed; and at last with a sort of whimper it gave up the struggle, lay down in the water and in an instant had disappeared downstream.

About half the column was across when, a mile or so to the northward, we saw the headlights of three lorries approaching. It seemed as though they were coming along the river-bank. I sent a runner to Tommy, but Tommy had already seen them; so had the people on the sandbank, and the crossing ceased. The stops on the road were ready to engage them, and some men had the pins out of their grenades, when we saw the lorries halt, and their lights illumine the shrubs by the roadside, while they backed and went forward again in the act of turning round. Then to our boundless relief we saw them going off again the way they had come.

Somebody came across about three in the morning with the catastrophic news that the boats had gone; the accident we had been dreading all night had happened, and a nervous man had capsized the boat, which had gone off downstream. He himself had managed to reach the sandbank, but of the boat and boatman there was no sign. The other boatman had to be forcibly restrained from going off to look for him, of which the effect was to reduce the number of passengers each trip, since he had to be escorted on the return journey. When at last he had delivered the ultimate man on to the sandbank, he gave us the slip; and now at four in the morning we were left without boats. Big men and little men alike must cross to the bank, or stay where they were.

Some willingly, if not happily, came across at once, and joined us; but some turned back and some would not start at all. Several officers went back again to persuade them to try, but what with hunger and cold and several hours of waiting on that grim sand-bank, and hearing the cries of the occasional lost man, their nerve had been undermined. Everybody was weak from lack of food, and morale depends more on food than on anything else. I sent across a message to say that I could give them only fifteen minutes more, and then I was setting out due east. John Fraser made a last attempt to rally them, and got them all started, but unfortunately he himself lost his footing, and was swept away downstream, choking and helpless. Luckily for him, the moon was now up, and it was possible to see him; and he was rescued, though not without much difficulty. But for the others, this was the last straw, and they turned back to the sandbank.

I had to make the decision. Another hour and a quarter remained till dawn, when the Japanese patrols would renew their vigilance. I could stay and wait till dawn, take a chance on being interrupted, and search up and downstream, for more boats. There was no bamboo, or other material suitable for the quick manufacture of a raft. There was no rope. The likelihood of being able to do anything more at dawn than I could do now was remote. If I stayed, I would fling away the chances of those who had put their trust in Providence and come out safely, for the sake of those who had not had the faith to do so. The wounded were all across, and some of the Gurkhas, the smallest men of all. The salvation of those who remained on the sandbank was in their own hands.

I made the decision to come away. I have it on my conscience for as long as I live; but I stand by that decision and believe it to have been the correct one. Those who may think otherwise may well be right. Some of my officers volunteered to stay, but I refused them permission to do so.

We marched for an hour, and then, in a bamboo thicket high on the hill, we risked a fire. We were paralysed with cold, and had nothing dry but our weapons, ammunition and such other articles as we had been able to hold above our heads. We brewed some tea, and had an hour's sleep; during which time two men from the sandbank joined us. They had screwed up their courage, and done it, but they had failed to induce any one else to share their venture. They had had some difficulty in finding our track, but had eventually done so.

Before pushing on, we counted heads. Our strength was reduced to nine officers and sixty-five men; in other words, forty-six men had either been drowned or left on the sandbank. Of these the latter were certainly the vast majority.

It is a matter of fact that those who had crossed and were with the column included all the best men, and the men whose behaviour throughout the expedition had been the most praiseworthy. It does not absolve me from my responsibility for the others to say so, but it was and is a comfort to me that among those whom I thus abandoned were few to whom our debt, and the debt of their nation, was outstanding. There were two or three whom I particularly regretted, and of these one was almost certainly drowned, and two were especially small in stature. There were two more who, had they got out, would have had to face charges at a court-martial.

Nevertheless, the crossing of the Shweli River will haunt me all my life; and to my mind the decision which fell to me there was as cruel as any which could fall on the shoulders of a junior commander.*

* Note K: Crossing of the Shweli River.

CHAPTER THIRTEEN

FROM SHWELI TO ZIBYUGIN

1st April to 4th April

"He is gone on the mountain,
　　He is lost to the forest,
Like a summer-dried fountain,
　　When our need was the sorest.
The font, reappearing,
　　From the raindrops shall borrow,
But to us comes no cheering,
　　To Duncan no morrow!
Fleet foot on the correi,
　　Sage counsel in cumber,
Red hand in the foray,
　　How sound is thy slumber!"

SIR WALTER SCOTT—Coronach.

TWO OR THREE days' march east of the Shweli are the Kodaung Hill Tracts, inhabited by Kachins, who are traditionally friendly to the British. Once there I hoped our troubles would be over. We should be able to get rice and to rest, our two prime needs. For this was the 1st of April, and we had only had nine days' rations for the last three weeks, apart from three cupfuls of rice per man and a share in one bullock and one mule. It was this lamentable weakness which was really responsible for the pitiful tragedy of the early morning, and it was now that I began to be compelled to halt more frequently than the usual once an hour. If one tried longer spells, the men just toppled over. Even before the Shweli, I had lost two men from collapse, for whom we could do nothing.

But all the same, and in spite of the tragedy of the sandbank, which we all strove to efface from our minds (but I could not), our spirits were rising with the prospect of reaching the Kodaung

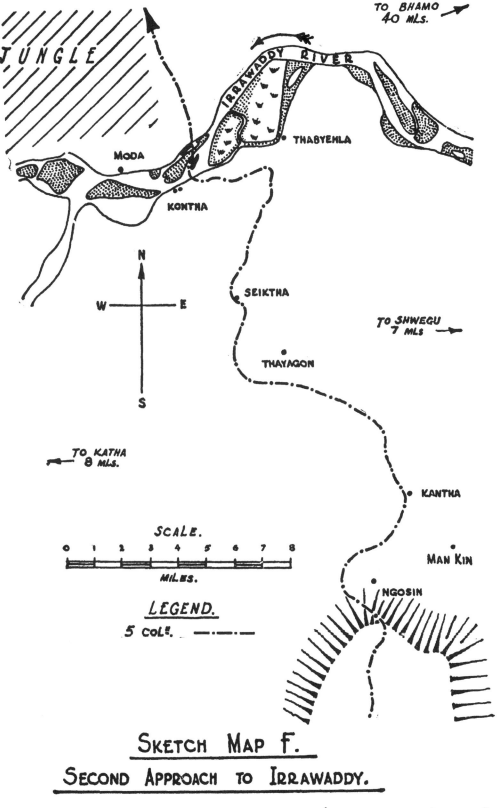

TO BHAMO
40 MLS.

JUNGLE

IRRAWADDY RIVER

MODA

THABYEHLA

KONTHA

N

W — E

S

SEIKTHA

TO SHWEGU
7 MLS

THAYAGON

TO KATHA
8 MLS.

KANTHA

MAN KIN

SCALE.

0 1 2 3 4 5 6 7 8

MILES.

NGOSIN

LEGEND.

5 COL? ——— · ———

SKETCH MAP F.

SECOND APPROACH TO IRRAWADDY.

(ACTUAL SCALE 4 MLS TO 1 INCH)

B.C.

M

Hill Tracts. John had little knowledge of Kachins outside the army, but he began to regale us with tales of their hospitality, of their feasts of pork, of their rice beer, until we had to beg him to stop. The first village marked on the map was not Kachin, to judge from its name; but the next, some thirty miles farther on, indubitably was; and we planned our route cheerfully, and calculated when we ought to get there.

All the same, I have to confess that during this period of the march I felt very low. My leg was painful, the splinter of grenade being hard up against the bone, just above the joint of the right hip, where it scraped the bone at every step; while at halts the muscles ached intolerably. The Shweli business I could not get out of my mind; and if it had not been for Duncan and John jollying me along I should have been in poor case. For two or three days I was a passenger, and it was not until the events of the 3rd and 4th of April that I managed to pull myself together.

We had hoped to make the village of Kundaw that evening, but darkness caught us about a mile short of it. We had been taking things fairly easily. At dusk, a tempting bivouac area disclosed itself, and we halted. Tactically, it was anything but suitable, for it was right on the track; but our experience of Japanese was that they were even less keen on moving at night than we were. On our right hand was a cool, splashing stream, in which, had we been in Scotland, one could have bet on the certainty of guddling trout. It seemed an age since we had so shivered from cold and wet that we had had to light a fire; we were now sticky with sweat and gritty with dust.

I slumped on to a convenient log, and gloomed round me at my depleted column. Peter Dorans and Gilmartin, Alec Macdonald's old batman, were listlessly making a fire with Maung Kyan and Abdul, who was now perpetually either weeping or about to weep. Tommy Blow had had a look at his arm (L. G. Wheeler had given us some more sulphanilamide, which, with some Elastoplast of Tommy's own, was all we had in the way of medicaments) but had wisely decided to leave it alone. He had made the same decision about Jim's arm: like Abdul's, it had been properly dressed by Bill Aird five days before, and since we had nothing new to put on it, no useful purpose could be served by looking at it. His head was another matter: the bullet had scored along its side, and the blood had congealed in his hair, so Tommy did some gentle washing. My needs were met by Elastoplast.

Duncan came up to urge me to have a wash, but I shook him off like a naughty child. I argued weakly for five minutes, until he took me by the arm and, ignoring my protests, walked me down to the stream. He knew perfectly well what was on my mind, and set out to exorcise it while, having given in to his importunity, I slowly dragged off my clothes and sat down in the water. He stood over me like a mother, and then briskly washed himself, talking cheerfully the whole time, and gradually making me smile and eventually laugh. By the time we got back to our log, I was recovered and joining in the speculations about our route to the hills. He insisted on opening the precious tin of cheese which we still had from our last supply drop. Duncan and I had messed together all along, splitting a packet of biscuits or a lump of raisins, and keeping a careful and mutually libellous check on each other. I know well that he insisted on opening that tin of cheese for my sake only. It was the last food we had; and his strength of mind was such that he would have kept it intact for another day or two, I am certain, had it not been for me. It was a two-ounce tin, and we had an ounce each.

We talked for a bit after our tea and cheese, about the future and the immediate past. We discussed the campaign and lamented having had to hang about so long in the Shweli-Irrawaddy triangle. There is nothing so pleasant as being wise after the event when one has had no share in the responsibility for major decisions, and we indulged this common British vice most comfortably that evening. Then we turned to speculation about what the other columns would be doing. We had heard what sounded like a supply drop during our march that day, and it had seemed to be on our side of the Shweli. Presumably somebody else with a wireless set had succeeded in crossing. It wouldn't be the Burrifs,

who had none; and we had always fancied that everybody else
would be trying to cross the Irrawaddy. Our chief hope was that
our Kodaung-ward pitch would not be queered by too many
people on it: I fear this was not a very generous point of view.

Where ultimately to head for was another subject for discussion. At the moment we had been heading south-east, a most
depressing direction, since every step was taking us farther from
home. The Kodaung Hill Tracts, for food, rest and sanctuary,
was definitely our immediate objective. But thereafter it was
difficult to choose. We might make for China, from whose
frontiers we were only about a hundred miles; but we had no
idea where the Japs were, where the Chinese were, or how far
into China the Japs held. Fort Hertz was four hundred miles,
and we had no maps to take us there. The last we had heard
about that neighbourhood, the Japs had been pushing for it, and
it would be too bad if we got there only to find it no longer in
British hands. A third possibility was to push up the east side
of the Irrawaddy to the approximate latitude of Myitkyina, and
thence across to the Hukawng Valley; but again we had no maps
and we knew nothing of the route or the enemy dispositions
along it.

Fourthly, we might cross the Irrawaddy between Bhamo and
Katha, and so up into the Kachin Hills, across the railway, and
out by the Uyu Valley to the Chindwin.

As we talked, there came out of the darkness a sudden hail in
Burmese, from along the track towards Kundaw. We hastily
roused Maung Kyan to answer in the same language, and hustled
his boots on to him to run along the track and see who had called
us; but there was no reply, and he failed to find anybody. It was
obviously a villager, we thought, who had taken fright and run
away. It disturbed us little, and soon we went to bed.

I have already said that Philippe Stibbé's platoon, now commanded by Serjeant Thornborrow, was the only one with its
blankets; their two blanket mules had been lost early on, and
they had put their blankets, on a scale of one per two men, on
top of their packs. These blankets were light ones, made somehow

double; and Serjeant Thornborrow had nobly torn his in two, and given me half. It was about three feet by two feet, and sufficed to put over Duncan's face and mine as we slept, to keep off mosquitoes and allow one to get some sleep. Mosquitoes had just started to get vicious. For warmth, a blanket was not necessary until about four in the morning, when one used to wake up chilled and stiff; but as an aid to sleep, our utter physical weariness was more to the point than a blanket.

It was that evening when I remember Duncan saying, "Well, this may be hell, but I wouldn't have missed even this part of the trip." Physically immensely strong, he appeared to be weathering the hardships better than most people, but his great virtue was his absolute failure to be cast down. We used to swap quotations, too, though I fear he did not get much benefit out of his Latin and Greek, having to translate them for me before I could acknowledge their appropriateness. Like myself, he had a passion for the Middle East, and he had learned some Flecker (whom he had never read) from me by word of mouth. I had written other things down for him, at his request, in the big red notebook which he always carried, and into which he transcribed every signal dispatched or received. How he got through all the work he did, and still had leisure to sit and chat, I cannot conceive. In addition to being adjutant, with a jealous eye on everything that was happening in the column (and woe betide the shirker), he was also intelligence officer, referred to on every occasion when we wanted to recall something heard long since at Imphal; he also, until I appointed Bill Edge whole-time cipher officer, did almost all the considerable amount of enciphering and deciphering which had to be done, with the help of Jimmy 'Orton.

I had come to the conclusion that to keep "Donnelly" as a private soldier was a waste of time. An officer by instinct, experience and training, he could not be usefully employed as he was; and although we had a high proportion of officers—nine out of seventy-four—three were wounded, and another would in any case be handy. So I promoted him serjeant; and it is a tribute to the spirit of the men of the column as much as to himself when I say that this interesting appointment was universally popular. One manifestation of this was when two men came up and said shyly:

"Excuse me, sir, but we just want to say 'ow all of us in the column is delighted at Mr. Donnelly being made a serjeant."

Long afterwards he told me that in spite of every protest on his part, all the troops had insisted on calling him " Mr." throughout his week as a private soldier.

Confident that we had shaken off the Japs, and that it was now plain sailing to the Kodaung Hill Tracts, I sent John off, at his own suggestion, with only Maung Kyan as escort, to precede us into the village and order rice. The column left ten minutes later. We were moving easily along the track, when we met John Fraser head on, walking very fast.

"Japs in the village," he said. "Walked right in and saw a sentry leaning up against the wall. I don't think he saw us."

My first instinct was to attack: we had seventy men, and they were unlikely to have so many, and we had to have food soon or start losing men. But I was dissuaded, and without much difficulty, on account of our physical weakness, and also because, having lost contact, we wanted our presence in the area to remain unknown as long as possible. So we hastily left the track, and went across country, determined that we should enter no village until we reached Kachin territory. It meant another five-and-twenty miles, but if we took it easily we should all get there.

All the same, this was a sad blow. It meant that the Japs had troops east of the Shweli after all; where they had come from, and with what object, we could not tell. But the map showed a small dotted track from Kundaw to Kunchaung on the Shweli, and it was probable that these had come from Myitson and Mandalay. There would in that case be a limit to the distance east that we should find them; and during that long, weary, hungry day we gradually raised our spirits with such reasoning. Even the discovery of some elephant droppings on the track, usually a sure sign of a Jap patrol, did not unduly depress us. We slept that night on a little hill just south of the track, in a clump of bamboo. There had been nothing whatever to eat that day, and I had smoked my last two cigarettes, made from a little bagful of long-hoarded stubs.

On the morning of the 3rd we left at six, all of us feeling very weak. I made a feeble joke about eating Judy the dog, quite prepared to be taken seriously; and got a mixture of answers: one school of thought was horrified as if I had suggested cannibalism; the other maintaining, truthfully, that she was too thin. We had marched for less than an hour when we came upon a couple of man-made objects, stuck on poles beside the track: one was an open basket made of a few strands of bamboo, with a bamboo stick lying in it like a pestle, and the other a bamboo tray with little models on it. Maung Kyan chattered like a monkey at the sight of them; and John said they marked the outskirts of a Kachin village. They were to become familiar to us afterwards, for every Kachin habitation has them, to ward off *nats* or spirits.

Mindful of yesterday, and not unmindful of the elephant droppings, I approached the village tactically, leaving a platoon to watch the track by which we had come, and taking a small escort with me, with grenades ready in their hands. John was obliged to accompany me, as the only person who spoke both English and Burmese. There was no doubt whatever about our welcome; they were delighted to see us. Few had seen British before, but they knew at once what we were, and greeted us with joy. Mingled with their pleasure, however, was an urgent note of warning: Japs had been there the previous evening, two hundred of them, and had ordered a meal for to-day. They were expected back at any moment to collect it. Would they sell it to us? They would.

Hastily I set sentries on the other entrances to the village. I did not expect the Japs would be back so early as seven o'clock, but it was as well to ensure that we got plenty of notice. They brought us the rice and some pork, about two cupfuls of rice and a gobbet of pork, the size of a golfball, for each man. They told us that these Japs had come from the east, indeed from the very villages we had it in mind to go for, and had told them that there might be British stragglers about. We were asking about routes and dispositions, when two Kachins and one of my sentries came running and pointing over their shoulders. It never even occurred to me to stand and fight; we had food and information, we only lacked a guide; and we got out of that village—well, not running, but only just not.

As soon as I dared, I called a halt and we sat down to cook our scarcely-won food. Smoke curled into the air peacefully, as the rice boiled, with the pork lumps embedded in it, and then the tea. When we had finished, John Fraser said to me:

"Do you realise how far we are from the village?"

"I don't know," I said. "About three-quarters of a mile?"

"About five hundred yards," said John. "I didn't realise it when I was hungry, but I do now."

I think he was about right; it certainly seemed much nearer than it had. I ordered an instant move, and we went north and then east, until we found ourselves in some thick bushes near a small *chaung*. There we settled down for the day.

We had got enough food for two meals, and a little information, but we wanted much more of both. We had learned that the village, which was not shown on the map, was called Zibyugin; that the Japs were in Pumpri and Lonpu: but it was essential to know more than that before we pushed on. We wanted information on which to decide, not only our immediate future, but our whole future policy: whether to go east or north, to China or Fort Hertz or Myitkyina or Bhamo. As we left the village, I had waved a fistful of money to pay for the food, and put it down obviously by a house; at the same time I had shouted "Guide! Guide!" in what I hoped was understandable Burmese. There was every hope that the Japs would not discover that we had been in the village at all, although unfortunately one of the sentries had failed to rejoin us. There was a good chance that the Kachins would have shuffled him into hiding.

John, Duncan and I discussed for an hour what our best course was to be, and we came to the conclusion that we must get more information, and if possible more food, from the village. If their reports about the country farther east were favourable, then we could pass from village to village all through the Kachin country, with no worries about food, and with continuous information about enemy movements and dispositions. We agreed that it was more than likely that the Japs would not have tumbled to our presence in the neighbourhood, and that they were unlikely to come into the village so early in the morning unless they were going to move on elsewhere. We thought that a patrol should go into the village, and that one o'clock would be the best time for it. Duncan volunteered to go, and to my grief I let him.

We had some tea about half-past twelve, and then Duncan got up and slowly prepared for the patrol. He had chosen to accompany him Maung Kyan, Gilmartin, who had brooded inconsolably since Alec's death, and one of the commando platoon, Stevenson. Duncan left behind his maps, but took his pack: he had always disapproved of people leaving their packs behind when they went on patrol, and had had this conviction strengthened by my adventure with Jameson a few nights before. I watched, lying on my back but propped up on my elbows. At last he was ready.

"Well, I'm off," he said. "If I get into trouble, I'll fire my rifle. So long!"

"Good luck," I said; and off he went.

The hands of my watch seemed to turn desperately slowly during the next hour. They showed two o'clock when Pepper, who was sentry, burst through the bushes.

"I just heard two shots, sir," he said.

I leaped to my feet and listened; so did John. There was a moment's silence, and then with terrible distinctness we heard three more. We stood a long time, but heard nothing.

Ages later I said to John, "They might have been killing a couple of pigs."

"It's possible," he said; "but do you really think so?"

It was at five o'clock that Maung Kyan and Stevenson got back. They had been wandering round in circles. I talked to Stevenson, and John to Maung Kyan.

The patrol had gone into the village, and advanced cautiously to the first house. All was quiet. Duncan climbed the steps and disappeared into the building. He had come out again almost immediately with a Kachin who by agitated gesture was urging silence on them all. At that moment a Burmese, probably a Jap guide, came round the corner, and seeing the patrol began shouting. Duncan and the others ran for the jungle, and reached a *chaung* on the fringe of it. There he faced the village, from which the Japs were running towards them, and threw himself on to the ground in a firing position.

"You run on back," he said. "I'll cover you and join you."

Gilmartin flung himself down beside Duncan, and that was the last they saw.

I waited till dawn next morning, and then marched miserably away to the north-west. I had stopped being a passenger and become the column commander again. As I marched, there came into my head the lines at the beginning of this chapter.

CHAPTER FOURTEEN

FROM ZIBYUGIN TO IRRAWADDY

4th April to 9th April

"Though much is taken, much abides; and though
We are not now that strength which in old time
Moved earth and heaven, that which we are, we are . . .
Made weak by time and fate, but strong in will
To strive, to seek, to find, and not to yield."

TENNYSON—*Ulysses.*

I HAD LOST many friends already in the war, but Duncan was the first to have fallen so near me, and the only one to have gone to his death at my instance. The lucky meeting on the *maidan* at Saugor had led him to his death (for I was sure it was death)* at Zibyugin; and I felt the responsibility acutely, far more than if, for instance, he had been killed in our own battalion of the regiment. We had learned so much of each other's homes and families, that I felt an almost criminal responsibility towards his. Other members of the expedition would have been on it anyhow; the presence of him and of Peter Dorans only was directly due to me.

His was far more than a family loss, for he had a brilliant future before him. His entry into Australian politics was certain, and his career both at Oxford and at home in Adelaide had already been remarkable. He combined in his character all that was best in his Australian upbringing and his pure Highland descent. He had the physique, the confidence, the matter-of-factness of the Australian, and the vision, the gentleness, the inspiration of the Highlander. All the way back to India, I seemed to see his broad shoulders, his powerful arm slashing at the jungle, his bush hat tilted back on his head; and at the halts to hear his talk, the

* Note L: Lieut. D. C. Menzies.

187

infectious laugh which wrinkled his face, the absurd bamboo pipe which he had made with his *kukri*. And in moments of stress, I seemed almost aware of the old, sage counsel.

It was a cheerless march, that of the 4th of April. In the absence of further information, I had decided to make for the Irrawaddy, somewhere between Katha and Shwegu; the reasoning which led to this conclusion is too long and involved to recall. There was a track shown on the map running north to Man Pin. To get on to it meant travelling not only cross-country, but across the grain of the country, a weary climb into and out of steep, deep *chaungs*. The map was unreliable, and we were still weak and weary. Yesterday's food was gone, and we were back on milkless, sugarless tea. Early in the afternoon we found the track. Since the map was made, it had burgeoned into a motorable road; and I did not fancy using it by daylight. We dozed until six, and although there was no moon marched along it in the dark.

During the day, while we were lying up, I made the welcome discovery that Tommy Blow and Gerry Roberts each had a small stock of malted milk tablets which Bill Aird had given them some time ago. They were the manufacture of a Calcutta firm of chemists and were about half an inch across and an eighth of an inch deep. We counted them, and found there were enough to provide two a man. I issued one all round before starting out; and although it may have been auto-suggestion I personally seemed to derive benefit from it. The rest we kept against a possibly even rainer day—hard though it was to imagine one.

The road ran for the most part along the heights, and the jungle on either side was thin; so the brilliant starlight to some extent compensated for the lack of moon. It soon became apparent that the motor-road did not follow the track marked on the map to Man Pin, but ran along a different water-shed, and would soon drop into the Irrawaddy basin at a village called Ngosin. I intended to leave the road shortly before Ngosin, and bypass it, leaving it on my east hand; but at about three in the morning two scouts who were leading a hundred yards ahead reported a fire burning on the right of the road, at the far end of an open

SEE MAP ON PAGE 177

space. I was apprehensive of fires after Hintha, and judged it wise to sleep.

Dawn showed that the fire was an innocent jungle-fire, and not of Jap origin. At that time of the year, there is much jungle burning, just as it is the season of heather-burning at home. A mile beyond it, however, we saw the marks on the surface of the road, where a lorry had been turned round; they looked relatively fresh, and only Japs use lorries in Burma to-day.

We continued down the road until I reckoned us to be within a mile of Ngosin, and here we found a small stream by the road side: we filled waterbottles, and climbed out of the road up to some scrub in the next dip, where we made tea. It was on this day that the craving for sugar became really intense; it had been growing for some time, but from now on it became almost tangible. Looking back on one's mental condition, I think it bordered on madness. Everybody had hallucinations about sugar, differing only according to their background. Mine were based on memories, fifteen years old, of a *patisserie* in Tours, where I had spent two summer holidays from Eton, learning French in a "family." Every afternoon, when I was feeling rich enough, I used to bicycle down to Massie's, on the right-hand side of the Rue Nationale, and have chocolate to drink, and cakes to eat. One would equip oneself with a plate and a curious implement, like a pair of scissors, and wander along the glass shelves, helping oneself to whichever cakes took one's fancy. It was the memory of one particular type that came back to torment me now; a concoction of coffee cream, coated with chocolate, and so rich that a couple of them made one unwilling, and three would have made one unable, to bicycle home again.

This craving for sugar was really agony, and I cannot convey its intensity. It dimmed even the craving for solid food, and that was cruel enough. We had found large, round, heavy green fruit, about the size of a croquet ball, which looked edible, though Maung Kyan shook his head when it was shown to him. Opened, it displayed an orange-coloured substance, rather stringy, with pips like a melon. We had tried boiling it, but it remained hard, and when one chewed it, the taste was bitter, and somehow reminded one of a tennis ball. I don't think anybody persevered with it.

Grass, of a thick, asparagus-like type, we also tried, boiling it in water; but it gave one no satisfaction at all, and could not be swallowed. There were some red berries too, which looked poisonous, and on tasting them one immediately decided that they must be so: however quickly one spat them out, the inside of one's mouth felt shrivelled and hard, like the skin of a walnut. None of the familiar edible plants were in evidence, and Maung Kyan was as helpless as the rest of us. We found some ginger, but that can hardly be eaten neat, and I fancy it has no nutritive value whatever. Bamboo shoots we sought in vain: there was no bamboo.

From our hill, we looked across a seemingly endless expanse of open country: endless in that it stretched east and west as far as the eye could see, but beyond it, across a mile or so, was dry-looking jungle which at any rate was potential cover. We sheered away westward to a point where the crossing of the open looked narrowest, and descended cautiously to the low ground, having already discovered by a patrol where a motor-road, shown on the map as a track, ran along the bottom of the hill. We scuttled across it like rabbits on the avenue of an English country park, carefully obliterating our footprints. It took me half an hour to decide where to cross the open, which we eventually did near a watchman's hut on the corner of some paddy.

Soon we found ourselves in dry, dusty grass, about breast high, with occasional lumps of low trees. It was now near noon, and the heat was intense; I had to grant a halt every twenty minutes or half an hour, owing to the weakness of the men. To the south, we could see the hills from which we had emerged that morning; they looked friendly and hospitable compared to the country we were in now. As we watched, we saw to our dismay first one, then two, three and four columns of smoke shoot up into the sky from behind us, all on or near the route by which we had come. In our then mood, we concluded that these must be signal fires; they may well have been so, such was the volume of smoke; but at that time and in that temper no other conclusion was possible than that they were what we feared. We started to our feet again, and hurried on.

Some of the men were giving me great anxiety; they had to be helped along by their comrades, and were frequently fainting. I still insisted that nobody should part with his rifle, or grenades, although that extra ten or twelve pounds was pain and grief; but before we ever set out for India, I had sworn that I would leave behind anybody who lost his arms. I allowed the packs to be lightened a bit that morning, not that there was much left in them that we could dump.*

A gleam of hope was roused in us about one o'clock by the sight of a couple of cows, and I sent three of the men to stalk and shoot them. Unfortunately in their eagerness, they did clumsily; and we, the watchers, to our sorrow, saw the beasts put their heads in the air, and take to their heels. The disconsolate hunters came back, to be roundly cursed by the others.

We were so obviously at our lowest ebb that I resolved we could avoid no more villages, but must go in and get food. For some time now, I had deliberately avoided anything which might lead to a fight, and this for several reasons. First, it was the Brigadier's orders to get out as many men as possible, to preserve as much experience as might be; and he had ordered that no deliberate attacks should be made. I had borne this in mind, but had told the men that if we did encounter Japs, we should take avoiding action if possible, but if not would "fly at their throats." Secondly, it had been my concern as far as possible to avoid disclosing our presence in any area other than Kachin: Kachins could be trusted to keep their mouths shut, but in Shan and Burmese areas there would always be informers. Lastly, the men were in such a pitiful physical condition that they could barely stumble along, let alone fight. Every man was supporting himself on a stick, and we looked more like a collection of Damascus beggars than a fighting force. I had already lost three men from no other cause.

*See Note M.

However, five miles ahead of us was the village of Kantha. It looked remote; it was several miles from its nearest neighbour, and was on the way to nowhere in particular. It was impossible for the Japs to have garrisons everywhere, even though we had found them in the last six villages we had seen or passed; and it was now a question of sink or swim—get food, even if it had to be fought for, or die. The alternative of giving oneself up (I have only just realised this) never occurred to anybody; or, if it did, nobody put it into words. I honestly believe it never crossed anybody's mind, even at our worst and weakest, although the desire for food, food, food was the dominating devil that possessed us all.

It was at five-thirty in the evening that we approached Kantha. I had a short conference to give orders; but I found I was hardly able to speak, and my officers, listless and glass-eyed, seemed incredibly slow in the uptake. I snapped at them for being so damnably stupid, and had to repeat my orders several times. When I had finished, John rebuked me—oh, so respectfully!—and said that their apparent stupidity, and my difficulty in articulating, were both due to lack of sugar; he said they had had the same experience in the Chaukkan Pass in 1942. I recalled the officers and apologised before we went any farther.

John and I and column headquarters went for the middle of the village, and other platoons round the flank. We moved forward, inspired by the thought of the prize that awaited us in the shape of food. But the village was deserted: I doubt if it had been lived in for twenty years, and even the site of the old plantations yielded no vegetables or edible roots.

People remained unmoved by this cruel disappointment. Apathy was strong everywhere. We settled down in bivouac for the night, as if nothing had happened; and slept as best we could for the visions of chocolate *éclairs* and birthday cakes which haunted our dreams.

The fiasco at Kantha was the turning point in our fortunes. It seemed as though this were the last and fiercest invitation of the devil to "curse God and die"; and that having failed he abandoned us to find our way out of our travails without adding to the hindrances already in our path. From then on our luck turned; and, more curious still, from this ill-defined point in the straggling jungles south of the Irrawaddy, we found ourselves taking illogical decisions which turned out amazingly to be the right ones.

To say that these inexplicable promptings were the hand of God would be presumptuous. I can only say that time and again, from now on, I found myself making up my mind, for no apparent reason, which led us in the right direction. We called them "hunches," John and I: and we had an undisputed agreement that a "hunch" on the part of either of us was accepted. Nor did either of us ever have any doubt as to what was or was not a "hunch" within the meaning of the act. We had such luck, from now on, as made it seem that "somebody was keeping goal for us," as John put it; and more than once it seemed to me that sage counsel, strangely familiar, was being offered to me.

Throughout all the expedition, I had had John and Duncan always in my confidence, in case I should meet with an accident. I do not mean to imply that my column had been run by a Soviet. But these two knew everything which I knew; and although I often failed to take their advice, I always welcomed it. From now on, I leaned more on John than before. Our expedition had ceased to be a military operation so much as a journey through a hostile country which he knew and I did not; of which he spoke the language, and I barely understood a few phrases. I had always made it my care that the men should be kept in the know as far as was compatible with the needs of security. Bad news John and I kept to ourselves, although we would pass on to the men enough to ensure that they were cautious or silent beyond normal, if the circumstances demanded it. They would not have had confidence in unadulterated good news. I felt in any case that now, when it was a question simply of getting them out, with no military success at stake, I was commanding them principally for their direct benefit; and it seemed to me that they had a right to know how their interests were being looked after.

B.C.   N

For all that, I was determined that there should be no nonsense about discipline. I was haunted by what Gunn had told me of the party from which he had severed himself, and took care that the men should hear it. I had in mind what I had read of Captain Scott on his last expedition: how in his tiny tent, shared by three officers and two ratings, he nightly drew a line to represent the boundary between quarter-deck and lower-deck, which all were bound to observe. In like manner I still preserved such state as was possible: officers ate separate from their men, and I could be approached only through the proper channel, either through John as second-in-command, or through Tommy Blow, now acting as adjutant. We might be in poor case, but we were still soldiers.

The column at this stage, and indeed ever since we had set out for India, can be best described as a despotic socialism. Nobody fared better than anybody else; and offences against the community were to be treated severely. I had warned all ranks that I would shoot them for any theft of rations among themselves, or for any act against the local population which might inflame it against us, such as pillaging or theft or offences against women. I had told them that I would pass judgment and carry out sentence myself, so that any illegality would lie at my door only. On two occasions I administered punishments not recognised in the army, for offences against the community; and public opinion on both occasions (I made it my business to learn) approved. Both men concerned were good men who bore no ill-will and pulled their weight as well, and in one case better, than the average. One of them did not finally get out; the other did, and I have met him most amicably several times since. I want to make it crystal clear that, except for such occasional lapses, the spirit, discipline, cheerfulness, courage, unselfishness and comradeship of the men were epic; and I shall be proud of my association with them for ever.

I have made that digression here because, as I have said, the fruitless raid on Kantha was the turning-point of our journey. The morning of the 6th I issued the last malted milk tablet, and we marched off. At about half-past eight we came to a fork in

the track which we were following. John insisted that we should
take the left track; I insisted on the right. The more he pro-
tested, the more certain I became that he was correct; but the
more obstinate I became in following the track I had chosen.

This was the first "hunch." Although we were not aware of
it until that evening, when we saw their tracks, a Japanese patrol
came along the track which we had spurned. It would have met
us head on had we persisted. How it failed to see our footprints
turning off, I do not know: the track was dusty and the footprints
must have been obvious even to the Japs, who are notoriously bad
at woodcraft.

Even more important, the "wrong" track led us to a *chaung*
running through paddy; and there, grazing peacefully, were
three placid water-buffalo.

This time I took no chance. I sent Tommy Roberts and Peter
Dorans, the two best shots in the column, to stalk them, and all
three fell dead.

The shots seemed to awaken the world, but we cared not at all.
Packs were dumped near the *chaung*, and gangs of cutters-up were
organised. Whittingham, of the commandos, was a butcher in
civil life, and he took command of one buffalo; Tommy Roberts
another, and the third was left where it fell, as a reserve. *Dahs*
and *kukris* were very blunt, and the skinning alone took an age.
The workers had to be frequently relieved, all but Tommy, whose
mind was stronger than his body, and who spurned relief; and
the chunks of meat, as they were cut off, were carried to the fires
which we had got going by the *chaung*, spitted on sticks and put
on to roast. Our hunger was too savage, however, to wait for it
to cook; and we gnawed raw lumps of flesh with a horrid eagerness, while the blood ran down our beards, and congealed on our
chins. We cannot have been a pretty sight, and everyone was
laughing rather oddly. Vultures were overhead, and I remember
one man saying, "Bad luck, old cock, we've kidded you this time."

From nine till five we cooked and ate almost without inter-
mission, except that sometimes we would fall asleep, and then
wake up to eat again. As the first delight in roasted meat died

down, men took to boiling it and drinking the delicious juices which resulted. Everybody took the chance also of bathing in the stream; there was a deep hole under the far bank where there was nearly four feet of water. I had not seen the men stripped for a couple of weeks, and the change in their condition was quite horrible. Even when Bill Aird had warned me, about the 20th of March, of their physical decline, they had looked bluff and hearty, with broad muscular chests and arms. Now they had no chest muscles at all, their arms and legs were strings and spindles, their skin seemed so brittle that the ribs looked like bursting through it, and they had cavities instead of stomachs. We were all in the same condition. I had no idea that men could have pined away so far, and still kept going.

We cut up the other buffalo, and cooked it. It was approaching darkness when, our packs and pockets stuffed with hunks of roast meat, and our teeth and gums aching almost intolerably, we set out again. It was when we came to the forked track, and saw the footprints of the Japanese patrol, that we realised that we had had a double salvation. Now we could have fought if necessary; there was a new spirit in us all. For myself, I felt as if I had awakened from a foul dream.

At that night's bivouac, I think I disposed of ten gobbets of meat with my cup of tea, and slept a sleep from which neither mosquitoes, nor lice, nor the dignified and not unnatural protests of my digestion could arouse me.

The new day, when it dawned, seemed full of promise, and there was meat for breakfast. There was a main road ahead, and on it wheel tracks; we crossed it cautiously, but half a mile ahead we came to an insuperable marsh, of the type which we had last seen near Metkalet, only this time too soft to make causeways. After several fruitless attempts to cross, I halted the column, and sent out reconnaissance patrols in both directions, with orders to be back in three-quarters of an hour. Both returned without having discovered a crossing-place.

I allowed the two patrols a short rest, and set off with the whole column to the westward. We reached a bluff which marked the limit of where the patrol had reached, and descended it to the edge of the marsh to see if we could travel along at its base keeping an eye open for hard ground. Of a sudden, we heard voices; and I stuffed the column into hiding while John Fraser, Maung Kyan and I watched. A party of boys appeared; they had been out fishing, or were going out fishing, and seeing only three of us, they were quite unfrightened and friendly. They knew of no Japs nearer than Ngosin, they said, although motor patrols had lately been using the road we had just crossed, which was the usual route the Japs used between Katha, in the west, and Shwegu and Bhamo in the east. Yes, they could lead us across the marshes; where did we want to go? Wherever we could buy food. Would Seiktha do? Very well, if there were food there and no Japs.

They gathered up their fishing-baskets, and I brought the column out of its hiding-place, which made the boys open their eyes considerably. We followed them by an exceedingly intricate path, which we could never have found for ourselves; our meeting them in that remote spot, where only fishermen would go, had been another stroke of luck. They led us across tiny spits of hard grass, between wicked, bubbling bogs; we crossed quagmires on tree-trunks, the boys running across nimbly in their bare feet, while we crawled on our bellies, or sat astride and swung our-selves along on our hands. At one place, there came the inevitable splash and somebody fell in, being hauled out with difficulty owing to his weakness and the weight of his pack. At another, one man collapsed: we waited for him to recover, but he was so weak he could not even stand up when supported. We made the boys note where he was, so that they could bring back help to him, and travelled on, feeling like murderers.

At last, about three in the afternoon we came to the village of Seiktha. I left the column outside, and went in with John, Maung Kyan, Peter Dorans and one section as escort. It was a big, clean village, with good houses, and a mere behind it with one or two dugouts on it. According to the map it was not more than four miles from the Irrawaddy.

The inhabitants at first refused to admit that they had any

foodstuffs; but at last a very forceful woman appeared, who seemed to be the headman's wife. She told the others not to talk nonsense, and asked us how much rice we wanted. She then produced two kerosene tins of what, as a Scotsman, I should call "taiblet," what the Englishman, in his innocence, would call "fudge," and what the Burman, who ought to know, calls *chantaga*. There was enough to give each man the equivalent of two slabs (had it been chocolate); and the immediate result was astonishing, like a modern Pentecost. The string of our tongues was loosed, and we spake plain. Such was the fact; it is for the nutritionist to make the deduction.

We left Seiktha after an hour, with seven days' worth of rice, and the *chantaga*: I had issued the latter to each man personally, making him eat a little there and then, and put the rest away. In addition to the food, we had a lad of about twenty as a guide; he wore on his head a topee, and round his middle a belt with a Boy Scout emblem, and the inscription "Be Prepared."

A mile out of Seiktha, we sat down in a wood, and cooked a magnificent meal of rice and meat; even the Irrawaddy, still between us and home, seemed less of an obstacle than before. Corporal Pike, a broad-shouldered, thickset Devonian in the commando platoon, pressed me to forecast the date of our crossing of the Chindwin. I declined to commit myself, but John Fraser produced a "Captain's number," giving the 26th of April.

Pike had made himself responsible for the well-being of Jim Harman, and looked after him day and night. Jim was making no complaint, but he was looking even more drawn than most people, and was obviously suffering a good deal. Pike cooked for him, carried most of the contents of his pack in his own, and eased him along in a jolly Devonshire fashion like an indulgent Nanny. Yet he found time also to do his proper job as an N.C.O. as well, and woe betide the shirker in the commando platoon if the rough eye of Pike should fall on him, or the even rougher tongue wrap itself around him.

Boy Scout had been told by the Lady of the Manor of Seiktha to take us to Thabyehla and introduce us to somebody there who

knew all about boats. We had feared that the process of con-
fiscation of boats, which we knew was in progress along the
Irrawaddy, would by now have extended to this area. But the
Japs, although they had flung their net wide, were badly off for
means of communication, and it was possible that the events of
Zibyugin were still unknown in this neighbourhood; for Zibyugin was 35 to 40 miles away. We were assured that there were
still plenty of boats if one knew where to look for them; and the
Burmans were no more keen that their boats should be con-
fiscated than we were. Still, we had already learned that a good
number had been collected and taken to Kontha, some three miles
downstream, where a ferry had been organised for the use of the
Japs, who crossed at that point to Moda on the north bank, and
thence marched to Katha.

Thabyehla, where we had been led to expect boats, was up a
backwater from the main stream of the Irrawaddy, and about
three miles from where we had settled down to sleep, this night
of the 7-8th April. Boy Scout seemed nervous but willing, and
the plan which he and John concocted between them was that we
should march at first light to within a mile of Thabyehla, and
that he should then go on into the village to fix up the boats.
They should meet us somewhere on the Irrawaddy at nightfall.

Next morning, therefore, we set out for Thabyehla, across a
rather dismal country of meres and odd clumps of trees. By the
first mere we came to, we found a small hut, and in it a fisherman
with a face like a gnome. He would certainly have run away had
he had warning of our coming; but as it was he consented to come
with us, and walked in front with Boy Scout, hopping and skip-
ping like a child, although he must have been full forty. At last
their pace grew slower, and they themselves seemed more anxious;
till they halted and suggested that we should wait for them where
we were. We agreed; Thabyehla seemed to be not very far ahead;
and we showed them the point on the track where our stops would
await them. It was then about seven in the morning, and they
thought their business would not take them more than two hours
to arrange.

Two hours meant nine o'clock; I would give them another hour for luck, which meant ten; and I resolved not to expect them before eleven. We were in a very small copse, and not at all a safe-feeling area. By noon I was in a fever of impatience. Had they just given us the slip? Had they gone to report to the Japs deliberately? Or had they been snapped up by a Jap patrol? We got extremely jumpy as the afternoon wore on. One instinct bade me clear out quickly, for fear of treachery; another said that if we did clear out, they wouldn't be able to find us again if they were playing fair, and had merely been delayed. I had given Master Boy Scout a fair sum of money, to do some bribery with if it should be necessary: doubtless he had merely pouched it.

At five in the afternoon there seemed no object in waiting longer, and I pulled out, and moved back on the way we had come. I sent a patrol on ahead to stalk the fisherman's hut, in case he had returned there; but the silly asses muffed it, and just before they had their cordon round the hut, he darted out like a minnow, and vanished into the jungle. There was no vice in the man: he was merely terrified. Of Boy Scout there was no sign.

John and Maung Kyan went to sleep that night in the hut, in case the fisherman should sneak back to the house in the darkness. They found his supper half cooked and ate it, fish and rice and thin Burmese tea. The column slept a little way off the track; and the column commander thought deep into the night.

For some days, my officers had been suggesting that we should split up into smaller parties. We were a considerable force to sneak across the river in one. Our attempt so far had failed, and we had shown ourselves about the place, and had been seen by more Burmans than was healthy. I now resolved to divide into three parties, but before doing so I thought I would have one more try at enlisting the help of the Lady of Seiktha. So next morning, when John walked in to report that the fisherman had been absent without leave all night, I sent him back the two miles to Seiktha with a small escort. He returned in a little over an hour to say that the temper of Seiktha had changed for the worse; that the Japs had been inquiring for us, that the Lady of the Manor had refused further help, and had not even descended from her house to talk to him; and that Boy Scout was not a native of the village, but had merely been passing through it at the same time as we. Or so she said.

All this was unrelievedly bad news, and I felt that the time had come for the split. I had put it off as long as possible, but I felt that we were once again being hunted, and that this time we would do better in three parties than in one. I gave a good deal of thought to the composition of the parties. Tommy Roberts still had a fair number of his men with him, and Tommy Blow a few; the commandos were fairly complete; Gerry Roberts had the makings of a platoon also. We had three sets of maps, more or less complete, leading to the Chindwin.

I therefore made up three parties. My own consisted of John Fraser, Tommy Blow and Jim Harman, with the commandos and the remains of column headquarters: total strength, four officers and twenty men. Tommy Roberts had his support men, plus one or two to make up numbers. Bill Edge, who was an old friend of his, asked to go with him, and made up his strength to two officers and twenty-one men. The third and last party I put under Denny Sharp; it consisted of Gerry Roberts and most of his platoon, total two officers and twenty-two men.

The orders which I gave to Tommy and Denny were simple enough, and consisted chiefly of a summary of what little I knew about the enemy. Once over the Irrawaddy, I advised them to continue north until they reached Latitude 24° 45'; which seemed to me to offer the best line to follow westward. To turn west earlier meant worse going and more Japs; while that latitude would bring them to the railway at a point where the valley was narrowest, and the friendly territory of the Kachins widest. I told them to avoid scrapping so far as they could, since it would mean stirring up the mud, not only for each other, but also for other columns or parties which might be coming out the same way; quite apart from drawing reprisals on to the local inhabitants. If, however, one did meet the enemy, I told them, then one must fight them with resolution—"go for their throats" was the phrase I used. Denny and Tommy then wrote down a word-list at John Fraser's dictation, enough to cover simple needs in villages.

Tommy had seen an old fishing boat on the back of the mere behind the fisherman's hut, and near it an old bullock-cart. He proposed to put the one on the other, and wheel it to the Irra-waddy. Denny wanted to come with me as far as the river, and share my luck there if I had any. I proposed to march boldly to the river in daylight, straight away, to see if there were any sign of boats. Either John or I had had a "hunch."

Tommy hated hanging about as much as I did, and with the prospect of doing something he became positively jubilant. He got hold of his party, harangued them briskly, and then all together we marched back to the fisherman's hut. There I shook hands with Tommy, and wished him luck. He was full of con-fidence and very cheerful; before I had gone a hundred yards I looked back and saw him organising a party to haul the boat out of the water, and sending some more men to fetch the bullock-cart. That was the last time I ever saw him.

Leaving the Thabyehla track, which was by now all too familiar, a little farther ahead, I turned north, for no particular reason, and almost immediately found a boy of ten or twelve years old. I asked him if he had seen any boats on the Irrawaddy and he immediately answered that he had seen some only yester-day, and would take us to them. Putting himself at the head of the column, he marched us a mile, and into a small group of wattle huts almost on the bank. This proved to be a colony of fishermen, of which the patriarch, when he saw us, became instantly terrified, and rushed the whole party into a clump of bamboos before he would consent to talk to us. When he heard our desires, he said that he had a couple of boats which would take ten men at a time, and that he would ferry us across that evening after dark, But we must promise to make no noise, and to build no fires, because a Jap policeman had been along that

morning on a bicycle, warning locals to prepare food for a large
Jap patrol coming that way either to-day or to-morrow.

So began another long wait. I tried in vain to keep my mind
on Trollope's *Ayala's Angel*, the only survivor of several books I
had brought with me, which I was reading for the third time;
but the sense of insecurity was strong on me that day, and I found
it hard to concentrate. Halfway through the afternoon, our new
friends came and moved us a couple of hundred yards deeper into
the bamboo, and went away again. Gradually we realised that
they had deserted us; and this was confirmed by two lads of
sixteen or seventeen, who came to see us about an hour before
dark. They said that all the people in the colony had run away.
They however were willing to help us, and we showed them the
three hundred rupees (about £25) which we proposed to give them
for seeing us across. We had already mooted to them the idea of
going after Tommy, and helping him over as well; but the most
they would promise was that if he turned up and they saw him,
they would help him: to go and look for him was more than they
were prepared to do.

At seven, one of the two boys, who had remained with us
while the other fetched the boats, ushered us out of our hiding
place and led us on to the bank. There was no moon these nights
but the starlight was flawless and beautiful. For the first time
since Tigyaing, the Irrawaddy was at our feet: it looked very
broad and black. The current at the foot of the bank was swift
and noisy, for we were on the outside of a great sweeping bend,
and looking north-east we seemed to be on an ocean beach rather
than on the bank of a river.

I was to go first. I led the small party of column headquarters
down the bank, and into the boat. It was at once obvious that the
boys had overestimated the number of passengers who could get
aboard at once, just as the men on the Shweli had done: our
heavy packs upset their calculations. We actually shoved off
before we realised how grossly overloaded we were, and pushed
back hastily, with water pouring over the gunwales, to the bank.

With some difficulty we baled out the boat and started again, this time with only seven men. Once more we got in, dark and silent. I was reminded of the flight of King James II from London. There was whispering, tension, urgency. Again we shoved off over the inky waters, and the boy, with the friend he had recruited, paddled madly.

We had not gone thirty yards before I became aware that the boat was filling. I fancy she had been lying in the sun for some time past, and that her seams had not taken up. I whispered orders to bale, very carefully, for we had no more than three inches of freeboard, and it felt perilous. Peter Dorans beside me used the aluminium *dekchi*, a relic of my sail with John Bankes the previous October, which he had carried with him all the way, and used for our rice and tea. I bailed manfully with my hat. Soon we were in smooth water, and at last the boy leapt out of the boat and steadied her, while one by one we stepped overboard into two feet of water, and waded on to hard sand. I repressed a passing thought that perhaps once again the worst of the crossing lay before us. The boat turned, and disappeared into the darkness, but the second boat appeared almost immediately afterwards, and her passengers also came ashore.

I spread out the men for four hundred yards up and down the beach, so that the next flight to come across could be heard coming in, and collected into one spot. Away across the sand, on what appeared to be the bank proper, there was a large fire: this I determined to avoid, in case it belonged to one of the gangs of river-watchers who, our friends of the afternoon had told us, were stationed up and down the river on the watch for such clandestine crossings as we were ourselves engaged in performing.

In twenty minutes' time, the creak of oars signalled the arrival of the next two boatloads, which completed my party, and included the first two men of Denny's. I had already told Denny that I was going to push on as soon as I was complete; and so, pointing out the fire to the two men of his party, and showing them the direction in which I was going, I started off along the sandbank upstream. It was half an hour of heavy marching on sand which, away from the water's edge, was soft and clinging, before we saw a steep bank hanging above us, and high, friendly jungle trees beyond it. A small lagoon separated us from the bank, and it took another ten minutes to find a way across it and scramble up on hands and knees. The jungle at the top was thick and full of a stiff thorny undergrowth; but at last we found a game track which took us far enough in to allay our nervousness about lighting fires. We lit one, cooked, ate, and, deeply grateful, slept.

CHAPTER FIFTEEN

FROM IRRAWADDY TO MEZA

10th April to 16th April

" God of all long desirous roaming,
Our hearts are sick of fruitless homing,
And crying after lost desire,
Hearten us onwards! as with fire
Consuming dreams of other bliss
The best Thou givest, giving this
Sufficient thing—to travel still
Over the plain, beyond the hill,
Unhesitating through the shade,
Amid the silence unafraid."

RUPERT BROOKE—*Song of the Pilgrims.*

AS AT HINTHA, with the coming of daylight the jungle looked less formidable, and—another similarity—we found almost immediately a long and narrow patch of disused paddy, leading past the thick, outer defences of the forest, into better going. Two incidents during the first fifteen minutes' marching cheered us up (and we were cheerful enough already, with the 'Waddy behind us). First, out of the undergrowth darted Judy the dog, whose figure already bore evidence that she had given up banting; she looked at us quizzically, nodded, practically said "O.K.," and vanished back into the trees before we could put a note in the little satchel which she still wore round her neck. She had by now become firmly attached to Gerry Roberts, so we knew that Denny was across complete, and on the move in the same general direction as ourselves.

The other incident has often been publicised by journalists and others, but as it happened to us I claim the right to repeat it. We suddenly heard the unmistakable sound of a British soldier whistling, and out of the jungle emerged the jaunty figure of

Private Pierce. Private Pierce had been one of the two men who changed his mind about remaining on the Shweli sandbank, and had caught us up after we left. Now, allotted to Tommy Roberts's party, he had left his waterbottle behind at the fisherman's hut, and had gone back a few hundred yards to retrieve it. Having done so, he had failed to find Tommy again; but, knowing the intention was to cross the Irrawaddy, he had walked in broad daylight to the riverbank, and then along it until he found a man with a boat. This chap invited him to supper which, having no previous engagement, he accepted; and was then put across the river. All directions were much the same to him, so he decided to make for the fire which I had been at such pains to avoid. Here he found another fisherman, who also invited him, not only to supper, but to spend the night. This also he accepted, and left next morning at dawn with his pack and pockets full of dried fish, tobacco and *chantaga*; plus a cooking-pot and a neat knitted bag to carry it in.

I feel there must be a moral to this story, but I cannot think what it is. But, as I said at the time, with luck like Private Pierce's no wonder he was whistling.

The next two days led us through jungle which was the thickest I have ever seen. Had we had animals with us, it would have taken us three times as long to negotiate. My course lay a little bit west of north, to avoid a village with the Burmese-sounding name of Kodaunggyi, and to hit as our first port of call any one of several villages with a Kachin name, some thirty miles to the northward. On the second day, we heard voices ahead of us, and found an old fisherman with two small children fishing in a tiny *chaung*, and we made our midday halt there. He was a simple old boy, and very chatty. Like many of the more remote people we met, away from the areas directly dominated by the Japs, he showed no surprise at seeing us; and although the children clung to him at first, they soon grew bolder and flirted with the men. He belonged to Kodaunggyi, which he said was occasionally visited by patrols, more often recently than heretofore; but he had left there three days ago, and it had been clear then.

We lay and marvelled at his primitive and laborious method of fishing. He would build two dams across the *chaung*, which at this late season was not running; and then laboriously scoop the water out of the pool thus formed. When it was practically dry, he would grub for the fish with his hands, and there you were. It was a simple method, certainly, and one calling for more patience and less skill than the type of fishing I favour myself.

We bought his complete catch from him; they were small and bony, and more suited for *ngapi*, a concoction of rotten fish, for which they were intended, than for eating fresh; but they made a welcome change. John also bought his dah off him for two rupees, and has it still.

It was in the forenoon of the 13th that we came at last to the country of the Kachins. We can never forget the names of the villages which gave us such loyal, general and courageous help; [We tried to do something for them after the war; but all that happened was that the Kachins, like the Karens, were abandoned by the British, when the sum of their desires was to be kept under British protection. This is a lamentable page in our history.] We came into that country ragged, sick, weary and wholly unimpressive; yet we were received, sheltered, fed, led and hidden with all the devotion of Highlanders after Culloden.

We met two Kachins on a track leading south, who told us that they were but newly returned from leading a party of twenty-four British soldiers with a dog—obviously Denny Sharp's lot. They told us that we could not go wrong if we followed the track we were on; and sure enough, an hour later it brought us to Hpatwat. Already we were far up the side of the hills, and could see away behind us that revolting river, the River Irrawaddy. The Kachin headman was old, with mutton-chop whiskers. Denny's party, which must have struck better jungle than we, had reached him last night, and had slept in the village. I can think of nothing which could indicate more surely the instinctive trust that one had in the Kachins than this: that a party of British on the run, who had learned to distrust the very name of villages, and who had no interpreter with them to speak the language, should nevertheless immediately feel safe enough to sleep confidently in the first Kachin village they reached.

The old headman bustled about to give us a meal, even though he had served forty-eight meals to strangers in the previous few hours. We had an excellent luncheon of rice, with a sauce to go with it of ginger, tamarind, chilli and *peing-u*, a sort of grey potato which tastes like a cross between chestnut and yam. Reluctantly at last we hoisted ourselves to our feet, and continued up the hill. We reached Shiamdebang in the evening, and heard that Denny had passed through about noon. Here they begged us to stay the night, and we yielded with no more hesitation than would have been considered well-bred in Belgravia. All of us were accommodated under roofs, John, myself, Peter Dorans and Maung Kyan sleeping in the headman's house, and listening politely to his conversation, of which I understood not one word. The success of the evening was John's first lesson in Chingpaw, the Kachin language, which afforded satisfaction to him and amusement to our hosts.

John Fraser, whose patience has limits, used to go quite frenzied if anybody interrupted him while he was interrogating. He allowed me to listen in, because he couldn't jolly well help it; but he wouldn't allow anybody else within earshot. His attitude was that of the C.O. on manœuvres, who found himself surrounded by generals when he was about to give out his orders; to whom he is reputed to have said, "All those senior to me, will you please very kindly give me air; and all those junior to me, PUSH OFF!"

Before dark, there arrived the son of the headman of Hpatwat, a tall, well-built and good-looking youth of about eighteen. He had been to Myitkyina High School in the time of the British, and although he had no English was obviously educated. As proof of his loyalty, he produced from a pocket-book his gun licence, issued in Myitkyina and signed by a British official—in 1925, when I reckoned he might have been one year old. He also stayed the night; he had heard from his father that we had come through Hpatwat, and had hurried after us to see us and pay his respects.

At Shimadebang also we heard that a party of four men had been through, marching briskly northward along the crest. They had bought some rice, but refused the services of guides. It was quite unprofitable speculating who they might be, but they sounded happy enough. We heard a couple of shots next morning, which might or might not be from them: even if it were, there was not necessarily anything sinister about it, since they might easily represent a crack at a jungle-fowl. They might even have come from a Kachin.

From Shiamdebang, you could see across the valley through which the railway runs—our next obstacle. There was a good deal of flat to be traversed before reaching the next line of hills, and more peace among Kachins. Our friends advised us to descend to the village of Saga, who would certainly give us guides across; Denny had apparently gone another way, of which they disapproved. So to Saga we descended, arriving a little before nine o'clock, and receiving the same rapturous greeting as elsewhere.

I was aiming at keeping my stock of rice at five days. This was not too heavy to carry, and it was enough to tide us over any period when, owing to a superfluity of Japs, we might have to avoid villages. Saga agreed to supply us, and had already produced the traditional mat on to which to pour the rice from the baskets in which it was kept, when a curious figure, wearing a hat of the Gurkha type, rushed into the village from the direction of the railway, announcing the arrival of a Jap patrol. At Tigyaing, this news had been the signal for an instant dispersal; at Saga, in a few seconds, although the women and children had disappeared, every man and boy was armed: some with daggers, some with long and powerful swords with edges razor-sharp, and not a few with British service rifles.

"Shall you fight, or shall you fly?" was the gist of their questions.

"How many?" I said.

"Fifty!" said the gentleman in the Gurkha hat.

"Fly!" said I; and we were bundled off into a thick clump of bamboos five hundred yards away from the village. Here again, we could have done a very nice little ambush on the Japs; but had we not been able to ensure that every one was killed without exception, we should have brought retribution on the village, and rendered far more difficult the journey of those coming behind us. Through the village of Saga eventually came the bulk of Scotty's column, and several smaller parties; and I was more glad than ever that I had not stirred up the mud.

All day long we lay and smoked and ate in that bamboo clump. The Kachins brought us cooked rice and tobacco, at the same time that they were feeding the Japs, in the village; and thought the whole affair a huge joke. They kept bringing us bulletins every few minutes. "The Japs have asked for rice." "The Japs are cooking." "They are eating their rice, and have asked for guides up the hill to Shiamdebang."

"But they will see our tracks," I said; but the Kachins only laughed the more. "We sent men in bare feet to blot them out," they said.

Among the questions which the Japs asked was whether the villagers had seen any British or American soldiers. The Kachins had expressed intense surprise at such a very odd question, but promised to let them know in Mohnyin, the big town on the railway, if they should ever hear of such an unlikely thing.

Soon after the Japs had left for Shiamdebang, the Kachins brought in Bill Edge, with two British and two Gurkha soldiers who, like himself, had been with Tommy Roberts. How Bill had avoided the Japs we could not make out; he too had come through Shiamdebang, but had seen nothing until he walked into some Kachins, who brought him safely to us.

Bill was very tired. His wound was not bothering him much now, but he had covered a long distance in the last couple of days. The attempt to drag the boat to the river on a bullock cart, which had been Tommy's plan when we last saw him, had failed: boat and bullock-cart had proved too heavy, and too slow. They had therefore marched to the river, which they seemed to have hit downstream of our crossing. They had found two dugout canoes, and Tommy had detailed Bill and the two British for the larger,

and the Gurkhas for the smaller. Bill was then to bring both
back across for the next party.

The Gurkhas, like all their kind hopeless in anything to do
with watermanship, had immediately lost both their paddles and
shot away downstream. The other dugout had sunk a hundred
yards from the north bank; and although Bill and his two men
had managed to struggle ashore, they had lost the boat. (I was
glad to see, however, that they had still retained their arms.) Bill
did not know what on earth to do; he knew that Tommy would
be waiting for him on the far bank, but had no means of getting
in touch with him. He waited till after dawn, and then, seeing
no sign of life across the river, had set out for India with his two
men, a compass, but no map.

The Gurkhas had caught him up the following day. They
claimed to have gone a long way down river, passing two villages,
of which they had seen the lights. (These must have been the Jap
ferry at Moda-Kontha). Their canoe had then drifted ashore, on
to the north bank, and they too had set out for India, having no
compass, let alone map.

Bill said that Serjeant Gunn and some men had also crossed
somewhere, and I immediately concluded that this was the party
we had heard of heading north along the top of the range. I was
hoping particularly that Gunn would make it, as he had done so
well throughout the campaign; but this was the last heard of
him, and no further news has ever been heard of Tommy.

When the Japs went, I asked our Kachin friends whether they
would give me guides to the railway, but they strongly advised
waiting until the evening, when they said they would take us
across. Before dusk fell, the guides who had taken the Japs to
Shiamdebang came back, boasting of the lies they had told. One
of them was the original man in the Gurkha hat. It seemed that
he had once been cook to a British official in Myitkyina, and he
gave us a long list of all the English dishes he knew how to cook.

A little before it was wholly dark, we set out, moving through
bamboo, and admiring the deft *dah*-work of our guides; an up-
ward flick of the wrist would sever two or three strands of bamboo

which would take a British hedger six strokes of a billhook. They had evidently sent an advanced guard on ahead, because, after many bird-whistles and mysteries, a man came towards us out of the shadows. There followed a long discussion; it seemed that they suspected the Shan dwellers in the plains of watching the track-junctions. Kachins and Shans have always been at feud, and although the Shans are no match for the Kachins at fighting, the Kachins have a deep respect for their cunning, and are always imputing to them vile and treacherous doings. Actually the Shans are a very pleasant people, but, possessing less spirit than the Kachins, are always seeking protection against them; while another result of their peaceable temperament is their anxiety to keep in with the top dog. When I say Shans, I mean really Shan-Kadus, the folk, of mixed blood, who dwell between the Irrawaddy and the Chindwin. Generally speaking, the only Burmese in Upper Burma live along the railway and on the Irrawaddy itself.

Two hours' marching brought us to a village not marked on the map, where everybody was three-parts drunk. They were Kachins living on the edge of the plain, and they gave us an uproarious welcome which might have been heard in Mohnyin. Kachins are no pleasanter drunk than anybody else, and there was a particularly obnoxious boy of about fifteen who would put his arm round my shoulder, and, having ascertained the limits of my knowledge of Burmese, repeated in a sleepy, drunken voice: "English good; Japanese no good; English good; Japanese no good. Japanese—pouph!" and he would smite off the head of an imaginary Japanese with the hand that wasn't round my neck.

Luckily—or unluckily, as they told us several times over—there was no more liquor left, and we made our excuses to push on, despite many pressing invitations to stay as long as we liked and go Jap-hunting. Then the whole village tried to accompany us, but we managed to reduce the contingent to three, two of whom mercifully fell asleep at the first halt.

For some nights past we had had a moon, and it was due to set about half-past one in the morning. In its light we marched along a motor-road, which we could sense was running parallel to the railway. This was an intelligence plum, for at that time it was not known that such a road existed. After four or five miles, we turned up a branch road, and followed it for nearly the same distance. I now began to get uneasy; the guides were obviously losing confidence, and from what I had been able to follow from my study of the map before we started and the route we had taken, I was pretty sure that we were on the track leading to Kadu railway station. I confided my fears to John, who was just behind me; and he confessed that the same bogy had been worrying him. We consulted the guides, who said they were sure they were all right, but not in tones which carried conviction. The moon had gone, and I could see lights ahead—not enough to indicate a village, but ample for a sentry post. At that moment we heard a baby cry, and it couldn't have fussed the guides more if it had been a torrent of Japanese.

"Kadu Station!" they said, and we turned on our heels and came back two or three hundred yards down the road.

Very quietly and cautiously, we pushed into the jungle on the south side of the road. We proposed to thrust along parallel to the railway, but far enough from it to be unheard by any patrols, until we had put half a mile between ourselves and the station. Our guides had told us that it was patrolled two or three times a night, and this seemed probable enough. The jungle was in-describably thick, and in the pitch dark it was impossible to see: we must have taken nearly an hour to do the half mile. We decided at last to close in to the railway, and did so until we could see the darker shadow of an embankment looming against the stars. I had just made it out when, far up the line to the north, I heard the "Choof! Choof! Choof!" of a train.

We had plenty of time to get ready for it, dodging back into the trees. Nearer and nearer it came, very slowly, and making heavy weather of its wood fuel, till it came between us and the stars, black and round-chested like a pouter pigeon. Majestically it went past, high on the embankment, spouting sparks into the air, unconscious of us peering up from the thickets below.

We crossed the line, and four or five hundred yards beyond it felt safe enough to sleep. At dawn we roused, and pushed on westward, until our guides suddenly stopped, and announced that this was their limit. We stood on a track running through teak, with no very clear idea where to go, and tried to persuade them to take us on at least until we could find more guides. But the dawn to them was apparently the same as midnight to Cinderella: it marked their *ne plus ultra*. As we stood pleading with them, there came past a young man on a bicycle, who, when hailed, stopped and talked with us. The track on which we were standing, he said, led to a mixed village, half Kachin and half Burmese: he could not conscientiously advise us to go there, since the Burmese were really most untrustworthy. He was a Kachin, then? Yes, he was. Would he give us a lead from there? Yes, he would; but first he must go and park his bicycle. We said good-bye to our friends from Saga, who, in spite of their sudden stickiness and their failure by the railway, had done us extremely well; and they scuttled off as fast as they could.

An old man then appeared from the direction in which our new friend had bicycled away. He announced himself as the headman of the mixed village, and said what pain and grief it was to him to have Burmese in his village: they were always going off to the Japs to tell them things that didn't really concern them. He was a nice old man, though garrulous, and we suspected that he wasn't over right in the head. He led us up a steep hill, to a point where another track came in from the right, and there he sat himself down and said that we should wait for our guide.

In a few minutes he came. He had changed his clothes for a more workmanlike dress than he had been wearing when he had been on his bicycle, and he immediately started off up the steep track on which we had halted. Kachins have no idea of contours, and always make their tracks straight up and down, as the crow flies; it was therefore not long before, exhausted, I called a special halt. It was at a place where the track, curling up the side of a mountain, commanded a splendid view across the valley; and as I gazed across it, the reverse of the view which I had had the previous morning, and thanked my stars that yet another obstacle, the railway, was behind us, he came up and stood beside me.

"Railway," he said, pointing. "Mohnyin up left."

"Hallo," I said. "Do you speak English?"

"Small," he answered. "Lance-Naik, Signals, 3rd Battalion Burma Rifles."

I called John, who quickly pieced his story together, while I looked at him with a new interest. He was a handsome, neat fellow, aged twenty-two or twenty-three, with an intelligent face. John was talking to him, and mentioning the names of various officers of whom I had heard him talk. He turned to me finally, with an account of the Lance-Naik's adventures since he had been with the Burma Rifles.

He had been wounded in the leg in the last campaign, and had been left behind. He had managed to make his way to his own home, where he had been living in peace ever since. We tried to persuade him to come along with us, promising him his back pay, his lance-naik's stripe, and various other inducements. When we rose to continue the march, he was obviously considering it.

At the next halt, another fifteen hundred feet up the hill, he told us that we were nearing Pinmadi, which, although Kachin, was very much under the thumb of the Japanese. Again we put to him the points in favour of coming back to India with us.

After some uncertainty, he agreed that he would come; but he was worried about his family and his livestock. We offered him two hundred rupees, and suggested he should take the money down to his family, and rejoin us that night or the following morning. His face cleared; he took the money and slipped off down the hill with the easy stride of all his race. When he had gone, we realised that we had forgotten to ask his name.

We renewed our climb to Pinmadi, where we arrived about nine in the morning. We were all tired, and particularly Bill Edge and his party, who had been marching without a halt since the previous morning. But the atmosphere of Pinmadi was not at all the same as we had found in other Kachin villages. They first tried to hustle us on; and when that failed they shepherded us nervously down the hill into a thick bamboo clump where there was some water in a kind of grotto. Here, with poor grace, they brought us food. They were obviously ill at ease. Their headman had been summoned to Mohnyin by the Japs the day before, and it looked as though they guessed that this summons was in connection with us.

So unpleasant was their reception that I moved on as soon as we had had our meal, and their relief at seeing us go was undisguised. Natmauk was shown on the map as being only a few miles on; but the journey there involved a deep descent, squandering most of the three thousand feet we had already climbed that morning, and then a steep climb back on the same level.

What the map did not show, however, was that Natmauk had moved on to another hill. All villages in Burma, but especially those of the Kachins, are peripatetic, and flit every few years. Grateful as we were to the sanctuary afforded by the hills, this and one or two other little matters made them a sore trial. I have already mentioned the distressing habit of the Kachins of making their tracks straight up and down the hill face. That was one. Next, being a warlike race, they site their villages on the topmost peaks, to afford them all round defence; with the result that water is a long carry. To them, this does not matter: their women folk nip down and up again in no time, with all the water they need; but nipping in the Kachin Hills is a bad game for Europeans. Again, fallen trees across the path mean nothing to their infernal agility, and they never bother either to clear them or to make a detour round them. What with fallen trees and steep paths, my hip, which had been dormant for some days, woke up and gave me Hades.

The Kachins have always been left in peace by us, and except for occasional high-spirited naughtinesses, chiefly taking the form of Burmese-baiting or Shan-teasing, have given surprisingly little trouble for so warlike a race. Very few government tracks have been made in their territories, and some of their villages, even in this area near the railway, had not been visited by Europeans. In some areas, missionaries have been active and had some successes; but their normal religion is *nat*-worship, and in every village we saw the baskets of offerings, and other symbols such as we had first seen at Zibyugin.

We had been told that the Japs had never yet sent patrols into this area, and as we sweated up the hills everybody in turn thought of a joke and tried it on me. People broke out of their place in the line, and sweated breathless up the track to tell it to me. At the halts, somebody would come up from the tail, sit down beside me, and crack it. There was no getting away from the darn joke:

"No wonder the Japs don't send patrols into these hills."

That march of the 15th April was definitely a shocker. For the last two miles, we had a guide, a man whom we had found fishing at the bottom of the hill. He would run on ahead of us like a gazelle, and wait for us every half-mile or so, puzzled at our slowness and shortness of breath. At long and weary last we reached the top, about five in the afternoon; and found ourselves looking across at Pinmadi, which we had left at ten in the morning, and which appeared to be still almost within mortar range. It was not until one looked down into the intervening space, and saw the nobbly hills and leaping streams, that one felt any sense of achievement at all. And in one's weariness, it came as a shock to realise that this was without doubt the most beautiful country one had ever seen.

Weary as I was, the weariest man was Bill Edge. Jim Harman, too, was looking very ill. Abdul's tears had been dry some days, but he was helpless at looking after himself, and had gone a greenish colour. He had been devoted to Duncan, who used to talk to him in Urdu about his home and family, and without him was like a lost soul. Some of the men had stomach trouble, and I was particularly anxious about White the signaller. He and Foster had taken to being infantrymen with great and praiseworthy enthusiasm, but rice did not agree with White, and we were at pains to buy chickens and eggs for him. At times, I was worried about Jim, Abdul and White, and wondered whether they could stick the journey. If any of them had to be left, the decision must be made soon; for whereas they would have a good chance in the Kachin Hills, where secrets are known to everybody but never leave the hills, the Shans are inveterate gossips, and their secrets are common knowledge among the Japs.

The village of Natmauk stands on one of two high rounded knolls, joined together by a saddle a hundred feet below them. It is very small, consisting of only three large houses. But the atmosphere was true Kachin, and the hospitality unbounded; while the headman assured us that sentries were unnecessary, since he would certainly receive word of any movement by the Japs. So we slept a glorious sleep, and had a late start in the morning, well-laden with the stock Kachin haversack ration of *htamin* or cooked rice, tightly and neatly packed in a banana leaf.

We reached Kumsai at four in the afternoon of the 16th. Some idea of the speed at which the Kachin can travel through his own hills can be gathered from this: we heard at 4 p.m. that a Jap patrol in pursuit of us had reached Pinmadi at 11 a.m. that morning. In other words a runner covered in five hours a distance which had taken us fifteen.

There was no sign of our Lance-Naik, and we debated which of several things must have happened. Either he had had no intention of joining us, which we were loth to believe of him; or he had been caught by the Japs; or he had found a Jap patrol between us and him, and had been unable or unwilling to dodge round it. On the whole, we thought the latter the most likely; and although we never gave up hope of him until we finally left the Kachin Hills, from now on we no longer expected him.*

We built up our rice to five days' worth at Kumsai, and spent the night at Kaungra, two miles on, where we were again hospitably entertained. Again, John and I, Maung Kyan and Peter slept with the headman. We had heard rumours of British in the hills south of us; and while we sat at supper, a runner came in to say that twenty-four British were at a village five miles to the south-west. This, we knew, must be Denny Sharp.

On the 17th, we had gone only three miles when we came into Pakaw. This was by far the largest village that we had seen

* Note N: The Adventure of the Unknown Lance-Naik.

in the hills, and the most prosperous. We found them fully apprised of our coming, and a sumptuous and unsolicited breakfast was almost ready for us, including a large porker. The headman was away, but his son was present to do the honours, and while breakfast was cooking, John and I sat in his new house, which was beautifully built of fine teak, and most imposing. As we sat, we saw, coming up a long path slowly from the south—a path so steep that our hearts bled for them—a party of British troops, which we knew at once must be Denny's.

We had a great reunion, and all ranks mingled to swap adventures. They had had a clean run across the railway, although like us they had nearly walked into a Jap post about two stations down the line from Kadu. Otherwise they had had no scares, and Denny, splendid fellow that he was, obviously had the whole business under control. They had had breakfast, and were for pushing on; we discussed the onward route, for we were now only six miles from the edge of the Kachin country, and would soon be emerging into the unfriendly and more nervous world. I said that I would try and catch them up at the midday halt.

I talked to his men, and found them cheerful enough. Serjeant Rothwell was in the middle of a bad go of malaria, but characteristically made light of it. There was a general wish to merge both parties, but both from the point of view of foraging, and from confusing the issue of any troops trying to intercept us, I preferred to remain separate. Interception seemed a possibility, since the Japs were evidently aware of our having crossed the railway, and might easily send warning round by the motor-roads, if not by wireless, to the Upper Chaunggyi Valley, through which we must shortly go.

After Denny had moved off westward, and just before the meal was served, John was buttonholed by a ragged-looking man and engaged in earnest conversation. This was a Chinaman, married to a Burmese in Pinlebu, where he had been a rice-merchant. Fleeing hither and thither before the Japs, he had fetched up in Pakaw, where he had been living for some months. He was anxious to work his passage to India, and said he would do anything or everything for us if only we would take him with us. I had no objection, and he rushed off to collect his scanty belongings.

It was half-past ten before we left Pakaw, and moved off down the track with guides to the Meza River. Here the Meza is a rocky stream, which has descended prematurely from the heights where it rises, and already among the hills has achieved very nearly the level at which it flows through the plains. Consequently it runs for many miles in a deep gorge far below the hills that surround it, straight as a die due south. The gorge is so clear cut and so indomitably straight among those tangled hills, that I fancy it must owe its origin to some geological fault. Even when flying over it, the eye is attracted afar off by its deep rift, as sharp and straight as a sword-cut. It marks the unadmitted frontier between the Kachin country and the Shan-Kadu, running through the middle of an uninhabited No-Man's-Land some sixteen miles across. Twenty miles farther south it debouches into a valley a mile or two wide, a smiling, prosperous, agricultural valley wherein the peaceful Shans live a life rather apprehensive of the wild men of the hills: this is the beginning of the Meza Valley proper.

Downhill walking on Kachin gradients is as tiresome as the long pull up; and two or three miles short of the Meza ford I called a halt. The guides, who were armed with British service rifles, began to paint a dismal picture of the Shan-Kadus in the Upper Chaunggyi Valley. They peopled every village for us with spies, and garrisoned most of them with Japanese. Their advice was to give it a miss altogether, and to go instead by the forest track that leads over the Taungthonlon. But a journey at five thousand feet without blankets had little appeal for me; it was raining most nights now, earnest of the monsoon not far ahead, and I was more afraid of a collapse in health than of anything else. For some days past all ranks had been taking suppressive tablets, to ward off malaria; but the supply was very limited: as it was we were taking only three tablets a week instead of the statutory one a day; and even at that rate they would barely see out the month of April. If the suppressive treatment is stopped, the suppressed malaria breaks out with increased virulence, and the last state of the drug-taker is worse than the first. It was imperative, therefore, that we should travel by the quickest practicable route.

Our guides produced a story that, a few days before, a British force some seventy strong, and consisting mostly of Burmans, had travelled north by the Meza to the Taungthonlon, taking with them two Japanese prisoners. This we thought must be Wheeler's party, although how on earth they had got here we could not conceive. Peter Buchanan had a previous acquaintance with that area, and it seemed quite likely that the party he was with would make for it. The main Japanese garrisons, they told us, were at Mansi (where they had been reported on our way in seven weeks before) and at Nanantun. They enjoined us to give these two places a wide berth; but the burthen of all their advice was not to let ourselves be seen by Shan-Kadus.

It was noon when we reached the Meza, and there was no sign of Denny's party. We stopped to brew up a cup of tea, and gave the guides a couple of grenades with which to catch fish. These we cooked and ate with them, in a farewell meal, and had a bathe in the icy water before tackling the hill; bathable streams had been scarce for some days past; indeed, that was the first proper bath for most of us since the feast of St. Bullock ten days before.

We took leave of the Kachins with real sorrow. They and their kinsfolk had shielded us from danger and given us a mental relief of which we had been sorely in need. They had taken us into their keeping without hope of reward, when the hand of every man was against us. They had fed us and given us rest, and put new heart into us for the dangers ahead. To these last two, we gave a present of some ammunition, and watched them enviously, as they began jogging up the trail back to their hill fastness. As for us, we hitched our packs on our shoulders, crossed the river, and started up the gradient of the government track, itself a symbol that we had left our sanctuary.

CHAPTER SIXTEEN

FROM MEZA TO CHINDWIN:

16th April—24th April

"After long storms and tempests sad assay
    Which hardly I endured heretofore:
    In dread of death and dangerous dismay
    With which my silly bark was tossed sore:
I do at length descry the happy shore
    In which I hope ere long for to arrive:
    Fair soil it seems from far and fraught with store
    Of all that dear and dainty is alive.
Most happy he that can at last achieve
    The joyous safety of so sweet a rest . . ."
                              SPENSER—*Sonnet LXIII.*

OUR LATE GUIDES had warned us that we should find only one stream in the next ten miles, and that we discovered at the top of the climb, about four miles from the Meza. Half a dozen fires, of which the ashes were still warm, proclaimed that Denny's party had had their midday halt there. We filled up our bottles, and pushed on; and when night fell we were still in no-man's-land. I deliberately halted early; because a bare half-mile ahead of us I could see the pass between two round hills beyond which, I knew, the track dropped down into the valley where our enemies were. For the last time, I thought, we would build large and generous fires, secure in the knowledge that they could not be seen.

There was still no sign of Denny, and I concluded that he had got tired of waiting for us during our rather leisurely march, and had given us up. We saw the traces of his night's bivouac next morning, soon after the pass. Normally one carefully obliterated such *vestigia*; but Denny was evidently, like us, celebrating for the last time the freedom from worry which we had enjoyed in the hills.

On the west side of the pass, the jungle was less dense, and consisted of teak instead of bamboo. I had planned to avoid the first village, and was confirmed in my intention by seeing pinned on a tree a notice in Burmese, which John made out to be:

"Nobody allowed in Nanhkin without a pass."

It reminded me of a wisecrack of Cairns, my serjeant-major, when we found a village one evening in the Lower Meza Valley, with a notice on the stockade to say, "Nobody allowed in this village after six." "Too bad," said Cairns, "after we've come all this way." I wondered where Cairns was now, but considered that he was as likely to get himself out of Burma, together with whoever was with him, as any man in the expedition.

Having no pass, we left the track to the south, proposing to leave Nanhkin on our starboard hand. We descended to a small *chaung* where we cooked some breakfast. Some men were careless about smoke, allowing themselves to use wet wood instead of dry, after once being warned; they forfeited their breakfast. Luckily, Peter was skilful at firemaking, and never embarrassed me by allowing smoke to show.

Shway Sike, our newly acquired Chinaman, was turning out a treasure. An adept at cooking, his chief virtue was as a maker of cigarettes. We had laid in a large stock of Burmese tobacco and our only shortage was paper in which to roll it. I still had a few pages of John Fraser's notebook, but was soon to be reduced to smoking *Ayala's Angel*, a World's Classic from the Oxford University Press, printed on paper admirably suited to the purpose. I was a little distressed at the thought of what Sir Humphrey Milford and Mr. John Johnson, printer to the University, would have to say if they knew to what use it was being put.

Peter Dorans had a good deal of trouble in getting his tongue round "Shway Sike." In the end, he made up his mind that the name was really "Forsyth," and "Forsyth" he became. The language difficulty was serious, since Forsyth spoke only Chinese and Burmese, Maung Kyan spoke only Burmese, Bill Edge's two

Gurkhas spoke only Gurkhali and Urdu; John Fraser spoke Burmese and Urdu, and Tommy Blow Urdu: nobody spoke Gurkhali or Chinese. So whenever there were orders to be transmitted to the Gurkhas, John or Tommy had to be called, while John was the only intermediary for Maung Kyan and Forsyth.

Peter, like so many Jocks, had it firmly in his head that any Oriental who really tried could understand a mixture of Urdu and Arabic. Once I heard him say:

"Forsyth, tak' the Major's *piyala* awa' doon tae the *pani* and we'll make him some *char*. *Iggeri*, now."*

Long pause, during which Forsyth looks at him disdainfully.

"Forsyth, I'm tellin' ye, now." Then to John Fraser in despair: "Sir, Forsyth is no' pullin' his weight—he'll no' dae a bluidy thing I tell him."

Relations between Forsyth and Maung Kyan, on the one hand, and Peter on the other became really strained, Peter being convinced that they could understand him perfectly well and were just being Bolshy, and the other two regarding Peter as a harmless madman. Forsyth had brought some private goodies with him from Pakaw, which he shared with Maung Kyan, and Peter was convinced that this constituted grounds for shooting him. However, in the end they made it up and became good friends.

After breakfast, we had to force our way through *bizat* bushes, of which the dry particles got down our necks and rubbed irritatingly against the skin. We came at last to some paddy, where we walked head-on into about twenty natives, who lifted up their *longyis* and ran like the wind. Our presence in the valley was already divulged. In the jungle just beyond the paddy, we heard the sound of wood being chopped, and stalked it. The choppers were two brothers, who readily consented to be our guides. They remained with us until noon next day, and turned out to be first-class men, especially the elder, who was extremely intelligent. From them we learned that the Kachin intelligence was out of date, and that except for occasional patrols, they were little

* *Piyala*=cup (Urdu); *Pani*=water (Urdu); *Char*=tea (Urdu); *Iggeri*=hurry (Arabic).

B.C.   P bothered nowadays with Japs in the valley. The garrison at Mansi had been greatly reduced lately, and he thought the bulk had gone to Indaw. This was likely enough, since they had probably joined the concentration designed to hedge in our expedition.

Although we did not know it till after the Chindwin, Denny Sharp had bumped a patrol that very hour, two miles north of us. He had gone right-handed round Nanhkin, and come back on to the track beyond it. One of his men had collapsed from exhaustion, and they were giving him half an hour's rest to see if he would recover. It was during this period that the Japs came up the path, and bumped their sentry. The sentry had shot the leading Jap, and was then killed himself. In the exchange that followed, one more Jap had been shot, and Denny's party then withdrew. The sick man had been hit during the fighting, and was unable to walk.*

That night was the first I remember when I definitely lost my sleep through the machinations of lice. They had been gaining on us all for some time past, but it was from now on that sleep began to be a serious problem. In addition to the lice, the mosquitoes were intensifying their offensive: they co-ordinated their dive-bombing with the tunnelling activities of their disreputable allies. Between them, they made sleep by night almost impossible, despite one's weariness; while by day the flies were almost as bad. Peter used to sleep, of nights, in the ashes of the fire, partly for warmth and partly because he hoped the mosquitoes would dislike the smell of cinders. That night on the Hmawbon Taung it came on to rain heavily in the small hours of the morning, and we brewed up some tea on what until a moment before had been Peter's bed.

We paid off our guides at noon on the 19th, somewhere south of Hmawbon. The country was easy walking, thick only near the *chaungs*. We met people twice, who ran away both times before we could persuade them to stop: this led us to think that there must be Japs about, but very possibly it was mere nervousness.

* Note O: Skirmish near Nanhkin.

An hour before dark, we reached the banks of the Chaunggyi, and were settling down for the night when a fishing party of one old man, one middle-aged man and several women walked into us. We had heard their voices as they came along the bank, and had taken steps to ensure that they did not avoid us.

The old boy turned out to be the headman of a nearby village, but the other man was the more useful of the two, since he was an ex-employee of the Bombay Burmah Trading Corporation, and most intelligent, as well as loyal. He stayed to discuss with us our onward route, while the headman went off to get us rice and tea.

For our tea was getting low now, and we had to lay in a stock of the Burmese variety. Tea had been our solace all through the lean days, and I repeat that without it we should have been far worse off, and would indubitably have lost more men. I could hardly bear to drink mine, it seemed so quickly done; at first it was too hot to drink, and then, unlike Maurice Baring's February day, "too cold too soon." One was always reluctant to drink the last two mouthfuls, well knowing one would get no more for a long while to come. The blissful prospect of second and third and fourth cups, in India, seemed very far away. I could never make up my mind whether I wanted my cup of tea prepared as soon as I got in, before my rice; or to sip it before going to sleep, after my rice. This was worse than the nursery problem of whether to have mince-pie or plum pudding. There was neither enough tea nor enough water for both.

Meanwhile, we talked topography with our friend of the B.B.T.C. Immediately beyond the river was the Zibyutaungdan escarpment, constituting a real obstacle. The only routes up it known to me were, from south to north: that via Namza, which Mike had used: this was too far south. That via Hwemaukkan, which the Japs used regularly. That via the "Secret Track," which it seemed certain the Japs would be watching. That via Payindaung which was marked on the map, but of which I knew nothing: it took off from the plain about two miles south of where we were. And finally the Chaunggyi itself, not properly a route up the escarpment, so much as a way through it.

Our friend, who had only lived in these parts since the evacuation, had never heard of the Payindaung route, and advised that via the Chaunggyi. The Hwemaukkan one was definitely not advisable, since it was used by the Japs two or three times a week, and rice from the neighbourhood in which we were was constantly being taken there in convoys. I knew that many refugees had used the Chaunggyi route in 1942, but it seemed to me such a desperate defile. Once committed to it, one could not leave it; the contours on the map showed that the sides were vertical, and it would be an easy matter, once the Japs knew we had started down it, to warn the garrisons at the western end. It would take at least two days to negotiate; the distance as the crow flies was not great, but it twisted up and down, doubled back on itself, almost tied knots in itself, in its course through the range.

The headman, when he came back with the rice, potatoes, tobacco, and tea which we proposed to buy, advised against the Chaunggyi. It was very rough, he said, and one had to cross the stream many, many times. On the other hand, he said that the Payindaung track had not been used for many years, if indeed it existed now at all. However, he dared say that it could be found, and in his view we should have a difficult job to dodge the garrisons at the far end of the Chaunggyi.

He had a little gossip for us. Tonmakeng and Tonbawdi were now both strongly garrisoned, and patrols went regularly from there to the Uyu. He estimated the Tonmakeng force at five hundred; they had been there in strength ever since we passed through in February. There had been a battle a few days before at a place called Le-u, near Sinlamaung, between British and Japs, but he did not know the outcome.

I decided that night that, although we knew little about the possibilities of the Payindaung track, it was preferable on balance to risking the defile of the Chaunggyi. Too many people had seen us during the day for the Japs not to know about us, and they were almost certain to warn the Uyu garrisons to watch the gorge, if they were not watching it already. I had a certain personal fear, also, that the Chaunggyi might entail scrambling over boulders, which neither I nor the other wounded were likely to enjoy. I went to sleep with my mind made up to go via Payindaung.

Next morning, the 20th, we had our packs on our backs, ready to move, when John claimed to have a "hunch" that we should go by the Chaunggyi. I gave in immediately, and within two hours we were in the gorge.

The Chaunggyi, or Great Stream, gorge is inexpressibly beautiful. At times the walls press in close to the stream; at others, they slope gently down, covered with low forest and vegetation. At the entrance to the gorge, we had seen the broken and rusting skeletons of many motor-cars and lorries which had been driven up from Rangoon and the south during the evacuation to this, the last point to which it was possible to motor. Many were embedded in the sand, where their desperate drivers had tried the experiment of driving through the gorge; the waters of the last monsoon had bowled them over and over, and twisted them into fantastic shapes. There they were, a monument of the relentless pursuit of the year before, and of the beastliness of warfare. But in the peace and beauty of the Chaunggyi it was almost possible to forget the war, and to forget even the fact that we were hunted men, who had ventured themselves into a trap which the hunters might at that very moment be closing. High up on the hillsides were little waterfalls, "like a downward smoke, slow-dropping veils of thinnest lawn"; birds and butterflies were innumerable. Upper Burma abounds in beautiful valleys, but the Chaunggyi is something all its own: it is Sick Heart River as Lew Frizel hoped to find it.

None of us were ornithologists, and we had long since made up our own names for those birds of which the songs were most often in our ears. There was the bird with the steadily rising and quickening note, it seemed to us, of panic: this was the Windy Beggar bird. There was a bird whose song wandered aimlessly out of tune all round the scale, the Lost Property bird. There was another who whistled briskly right down the scale like a falling bomb: he was the Tall Story bird. We, the officers of No. 5

Column, claim that, as nomenclature, these are more appropriate in every case than half a yard of Latin.

We picked a point on the map which we hoped to reach that first evening. We would have made it, too, had it not been for an incident which added further to our vocabulary. We had seen on the sand the prints of an elephant going down to water, and beside them a curious track which we could not identify. Elephants usually suggested Japs, and we moved thereafter, with some caution. Soon we heard the unmistakable sound of an elephant moving fast through bamboo, on the same side of the stream as we, and two or three hundred yards ahead. I sent Peter and Forsyth ahead to investigate, and it was nearly half an hour before we, moving more cautiously, caught up with them. They were coming back towards us.

"Well, Peter," I said. "Did you see it? And was there anybody with it?"

"No, sir," he said, "it was just a *lonely* elephant."

The incident had lost us half an hour, but gained us a useful expression; for, whenever afterwards we were working out our estimated time of arrival at any particular place, we always allowed an hour for "lonely elephants."

The track beside the hoof-prints was made by the broken chain which the elephant was dragging.

Although at times the path ran along the bank, for the most part it disappeared into the stream, and we walked on the sand. The river, of course, took the outside bend at every corner, which meant splashing across to the sand on the other side: I suppose we were wading for about a quarter of the time. It was no more than knee deep, unlike many of the streams we had had to cross elsewhere, and which used to wring from Duncan and me that verse from the ballad of Sir Patrick Spens:

> "Laith, laith were our guid Scots Lords
>   To wet their cork-heel'd shoon;
> But lang ere a' the play was played
>   They wat their hats aboon."

We emerged from the Chaunggyi in the late afternoon of the 21st, at a deserted village. We caught and kidnapped an elderly man, who by his conversation made it quite clear that he thought we were Japs. The night was spent in the ruined houses, and, from what we heard from him, we judged it best to cut across to the south; for he, deducing from our talk that we wanted to find the nearest Japanese, gave us the minutest instructions how to find them two miles farther on. John teased him unmercifully. He would ask him straight out, " What do you think of the Japanese ?"

" Splendid people, splendid people," said the poor old man, fervently.

" And the British ?" persisted John.

" Shocking cads, shocking cads; the most awful bounders," he said. But the catechism went on so long, that he began to be a little uneasy as to whether he was or was not saying the right thing. We detained him only so long as we needed him, and exchanged him in his own village for two younger men, to whom he imparted his misconception. They led us across country, avoiding the nearest Japs by a couple of miles, on to the Nam Kadin and thence upstream to the village of Manawngpawng.

Here we fell in with a young man working in his garden, who, when tackled by the guides, gave us a searching look, and then joined us. He was of medium size with an intelligent face, and, stripped to the waist as he was, he displayed a physique remarkable even among his well-built race. He led us across a long footbridge and then over a shoulder of the hill to Manawngpawng, where we halted for a midday meal. Manawngpawng, like so many villages on a main Japanese route, was deserted, but the former neatness of the houses and industry of the gardens were apparent even in their desolation. At the halt, our friend managed to find one of the natives of the village, who was sneaking back to his garden to collect some vegetables. He told us that a Japanese force of about 200 had gone through towards the west the previous day, coming up from the Hwemaukkan track to the south, and turning off at the Manawngpawng Rest House, just beyond the village. Had we got on to the Payindaung track, as had been our original intention, we should almost certainly have met this party.

Our new guide took John aside, and told him that, although the men we had brought with us were under the impression that we were Japs, he was an old employee of one of the British firms, and was not to be taken in. He asked us to take a note of his name, and report it to the Calcutta branch of his firm as having helped us, with a view to getting his job back after the war. He confirmed that Tonmakeng was strongly held, that there was a smaller garrison at Tonbawdi, and a stronger one at Nawngpuawng, on the Uyu, with outposts at several villages around. Only last week, at Namset, they had shot three Shan-Kadus on suspicion of giving information to the British. He gave us advice about our onward route, counselling us to avoid various tracks which the Japs were in the habit of using. He thought we should be safe enough following in the wake of the force which had gone by yesterday, because they usually used a different route for the return journey.

I asked John to sound him as to his willingness to take us on to the Chindwin; he was obviously an able fellow, and to have a Shan to ask questions for us, and to precede us into villages, would be an enormous help. But, although he did not refuse point-blank, he was most unwilling to come, since the Japs were apt, in these parts nearer the Chindwin, to shoot out of hand anybody away from his village who was unable to give a satisfactory reason for his absence. "Is your journey really necessary?" was the test question, the answer to which was a matter of life or death.

He took us as far as the rest house to put us on the road; and there we found the unmistakable tracks of the Japs ahead of us. They had evidently had elephants and ponies with them in some number; and we found also on the track cigarette cartons of, apparently, an English make, marked "Pirate," with a picture of the well-deck of a pirate ship. These were doubtless the fruits of plunder from Rangoon or Singapore.

The guides we had brought from the mouth of the Chaunggyi

we did not dismiss till that night; we wanted to ensure that they did not get back to their village until at least a day had elapsed. An hour before dusk we let them go; and soon afterwards we came to the main track from Nawng-puaung to Sinlamaung, the same track, only some eight miles farther north, as that on which Bill Smyly and Macpherson had had their posts while we were at Tonmakeng. We slept in bamboo half a mile beyond it until early morning.

The next day's march was entirely without incident, but both White and another were causing me a lot of worry. Jim Harman had picked up; Abdul was almost cheerful; I was going like a steam train. Rice was getting a little low, but we had a couple of days in hand. We were having a halt in a *chaung* when two men ran into us, moving down it from north to south; they were going to Tonmakeng, from where, they had heard, the Japanese had moved to Sinlamaung the previous day. This news was confirmed in a small village that evening—a mere hamlet of three houses, which gave us the welcome news that twenty-two British had passed through earlier in the day. (This revised figure was the first inkling we had had of Denny Sharp's clash near Nanhkin.) They had picked up a guide from there to Tonbawdi, from which the Japs had also gone.

The only man in the village was a cheerful little body, who said he could provide no rice, but produced instead three fat ducks and some duck's eggs, which did nicely for the sick.

For the first time in the campaign feet were becoming a major worry. It was not so much that our boots were falling to pieces, and that many men were now marching in tattered rubber shoes. The two days of splashing through the Chaunggyi had, despite every precaution, brought on many cases of footrot, and it was a matter of time whether the affected feet lasted out. We had nothing to put on them, and they were already in the painful state where the sufferer could hardly bear them to be touched. One got them wet not less than six times a day, wading across streams; earlier on one had thought nothing of it, but now every stream was a definite set-back.

We were coming to the edge of our last map. The next sheet had been lacking from one of the three sets, and I had accepted the deficiency for my party, since it was more than offset by my having the one and only interpreter. John now sat down and produced from memory a remarkably accurate version of the twenty miles of country between the edge of our last sheet, and the Chindwin beyond Myene. I was intending to cross at the bottom of the Myene valley, where we remembered having seen boats just after our original crossing.

For now we were near enough to the Chindwin to be thinking about such things. It was a month since we had lost our wireless set at Hintha, and since then we had not an atom of knowledge as to what was going on in the outside world. For all we knew, the British might have withdrawn from the Chindwin; we were pretty certain, at all events, that they had not crossed it. Homalin we knew to be occupied, and we imagined that a close watch was being kept on the river by the Japs. Without a map, and without, so far, any local information, I intended the Myene valley as our objective, unless or until we picked up news to make me change my mind.

Between us and the Chindwin there stretched a broad patch of five miles of paddy; beyond it twenty miles of jungle; and then seven miles of the Myene valley, lengthwise with our route. Of these, the five-mile width of paddy must obviously be crossed at night, the more so since on both the east and the west sides of it were main patrol tracks. This paddy was formed by the confluence of the two valleys in which lay Metkalet and Tonmakeng; the hills between them sank in plain, all of which was cultivated.

One's instinct, now that one was so close to safety, was to hurry, hurry, hurry. We were not doing so badly, having marched a hundred miles in the last six days; but I was obsessed with the fear that in our eagerness to get out we would do something foolish, and throw away all that our patience had gained.

For two nights we marched by moonlight, and lay up by day. We heard of various Jap patrols, but they had always just gone past. On the morning of the 24th, we were nine miles short of

Myene, and on that same track which we had left for our goose-chase to Metkalet. We reached Myene about half-past nine in the morning, and found the villagers surly and suspicious. The reason was not far to seek. They had been bullied by the Japs for allowing us to have a supply drop there (not that they could have done much to prevent it); and since then they had been visited by British and Japanese patrols alternately. Their simple minds could not grasp why the British and Japs did not settle which side held Myene, and they were in the mood to say, "A plague o' both your houses."

We bought rice there and at another village farther down the valley; for we still did not know how far we were from territory controlled by the British; and even if it were dominated by patrols, we did not expect that they would be sufficiently flush with food to feed us. In one village we heard of a strong Jap patrol just south of the Myene valley, watching its mouth. I still had in mind a vision of the boats we had seen there on the way in; and I had left two rubber boats hidden opposite Hwematte: both these possible crossing places seemed to be covered by this irritating patrol. To be pipped at the post was now my one dread.

We accordingly engaged guides to take us to a village about two miles north of the mouth of the valley, and, instead of halting for the heat of the day, as my practice had been for the last month, we continued to march. Four of the men, including White, were now very sick and weak; they had the greatest difficulty in stumbling along, and were utterly unable to carry their packs; so I pressed coolies into service.

One of our guides (who bore an absurd resemblance to a cousin of mine in the Wavy Navy) was very garrulous; I was in a bad temper, and shut him up with a roar. For two miles he sulked, and then at a halt he ventured to John Fraser that just across the river there were British soldiers, with lashings of rations, which had been brought over the hills by coolie. Why he hadn't said this before, I couldn't think; but as soon as John told me, I got the column to its feet and we marched at a pace which would not have shamed a rifle regiment.

We halted for fifteen minutes at the little village of Sahpe, which was a bare five hundred yards from the bank of the river. The headman told us that a British patrol had left there only half an hour before to return across the river; they had taken the only available boats, except one small one. He added that there was a British camp somewhere just across the river and about a mile downstream, with a *Thakin Gyi*, or Big Fella, in command. I sent Tommy Blow across, with Maung Kyan, in case Burmese was needed, and two British soldiers, to say that Major Fergusson, with four officers, twenty-five other ranks and a Chinaman, had arrived; and that the rest of the party would cross as soon as more boats were available.

I moved the requisite mile downstream. Then I climbed the bank, and stood looking at the Chindwin. Inevitably my mind travelled over the many days and many miles since I had last seen it. It flowed unchanged, except that its level had sunk a little; still it reminded me of the quiet Thames above Bourne End, and a few punts or white-painted motor-cruisers would not have seemed out of place. A Shan, rather fussed, rushed up to me where I stood, with a piece of paper in his hand. It read something like this:

"Bill has heard of a party of British moving to Dokthida. It looks as if they are heading straight for the Japs. I'm off to try and catch them."

This was presumably for the *Thakin Gyi*, and I promised I would give it him. Probably it referred to one of our own parties; perhaps to Denny's. Two small boats were coming across, and I told off the first eight men to stop making tea, and get ready: they showed no unwillingness to do so. They scrambled into the boats with their packs, and pushed off.

Another Shan came up, and said that a Jap patrol was on the same bank as we, two miles downstream. This was about the Myene valley mouth, and was probably the same as that which we had heard of already. They were apparently stationary, and it sounded as if they did not know of our presence. The next two boatloads filled up and went across, and I told Peter I thought we had time for another cup of tea.

At last the only two people left on the east bank were Peter and I. We stood, concealed in the bushes, watching the boats reaching the far side of the river. It was then that he told me something which I cannot forget. The day after I was wounded, Duncan had apparently been in doubt as to whether I could keep going. He had said to Peter, "If we have to leave the major, so as to get the rest out, are you game to come back with me and fetch him?"

Yet, after all, it was he who was "lost to the forest," and I who now stood on the bank of the Chindwin, waiting for the boat to fetch me to safety.

The boat came back; and Peter and I stepped into it, and were paddled across.

EPILOGUE

THE next few days seemed like a dream; and to this moment they still have something of that quality. The trouble I had with the Assamese sentry on the west side of the Chindwin, because I didn't know the password; the kindness of Colonel Murray and his officers; the difficulty he had in persuading his Headquarters that I was not, as had been reported, dead; the news they gave us of the arrival of Denny Sharp's party six hours, and of Mike Calvert's six days, earlier; the simple Thanksgiving Service which I held in default of a padre at the top of the hill above the Chindwin, on Easter morning, the day after we crossed; the drive from roadhead to Tamu in an ambulance; the remorseless burning of our clothes by a disdainful Field Hygiene Section; dinner with Jack Dalrymple, who had given me luncheon three months before, and his general; the drive to Imphal in a staff-car, and the warmth of our reception there; the refusal of the men to be parted from their rice, and their insistence on cooking some every few hours, to the astonishment of all beholders; the arrival of Orde Wingate four days after me; his reproaches because, not being dead, as he had heard, I had wasted the obituary notice which he had been composing all the way back (I should have liked to have seen it); my failure to recognise the men in hospital with their beards off; the brazen fashion in which Judy produced a litter of puppies at Imphal soon after her arrival there; all this is of the stuff of dreams. I weighed myself, and found that I had lost three out of my usual twelve stone.

I reached Imphal with John Fraser on the 26th of April, the

day that he had forecast as that on which we would cross the Chindwin: he had proved two days too pessimistic in his guess. We found that Sam Cooke and Scotty were still in wireless touch with Imphal: they were just north of the Irrawaddy, some twenty-five miles east of where I had crossed. They had found a possible landing-ground, and the day after I arrived at Imphal a Dakota landed and took off seventeen sick and wounded, among them Sam Cooke himself, whose jungle-sores would otherwise have overwhelmed him. (The pilot's name must be remembered: Michael Vlasto.) I wrote out for Scotty an account of my journey from that area onwards, which was flown in to him to help him choose his route: he followed mine as far as Saga, and found the testimonials which I had written to my various hosts. On the way, he was unfortunately ambushed, and David Rowland, with other good fellows, killed. David Hastings was missing from some days earlier.

Of 7 Column, nothing was heard for many weeks, until they turned up in China, with Ken Gilkes himself, Jacksie Pickering and Erik Petersen; the last named was a Free Dane who had been wounded in the head at Baw, and whom I never expected, from what I saw of him at the Hehtin Chaung, ever to reach safety. Pam Heald was also with him; but of all the other men of 5 Column who had joined him, only Cairns and fifteen reached China. They had acted as his rearguard all the way, and had lost eleven killed in four actions.

Others of mine who had joined 7 Column had been so weak that they had formed a party of their own, with the weaker members of 7 Column under Rex Walker; Bill Aird had stuck to them, and nothing more is known of them or him.

Two men reached China on their own, the survivors of a party of seven; the Colour-Serjeant reached Fort Hertz with a party of three; Lance-Corporal "Sailor" Thompson got there by himself, the only survivor of five.

Bill Smyly reached Fort Hertz in July with five Gurkhas, including Naik Jhuriman Rai, he who had killed his five men at Kyaik-in on the 6th of March. Bill had had malaria and dysentery all the way, but had been nursed with the greatest devotion by his five men and the Kachins.

Willy Williamson reached Fort Hertz in a small party led by George Astell, shortly after Peter Buchanan with Macpherson and Toye and the Headquarters of the Burma Rifles. This party had not as we had surmised gone to the Taungthonlon; no such party ever reached India, and we never discovered the source of the Kachins' story.

Almost all the Burrifs of No. 5 Column were taken prisoner, but Nay Dun got out in spite of his wound, and Aung Pe escaped in the following December. He had seen Philippe Stibbé in hospital but believed that the Rifleman who stayed to look after him had been shot by the Japs. Many months later still, several others escaped, including Ba Than the subedar and Nelson the groom. Billy, Po Po Tou, Jameson, Robert and Pa Haw are still missing.

John Kerr was announced on the wireless by the Japanese as being a prisoner, about the middle of April, 1943. David Whitehead is also thought to be a prisoner, but nothing more has been heard of Tommy Roberts or Bill Aird.

Out of the thirty men in my party, one, Private Owen, died of cerebral malaria at Imphal, a week after we crossed the Chindwin.

Gim Anderson and John Jeffries got out with the Brigadier, and George Borrow with Scotty. Many other fellows also got out who have not been mentioned in this book.*

John Fraser was awarded the Military Cross; and a special case was made for Duncan Menzies, so that he got one also, in spite of the recommendation not having been initiated until after his death. Serjeant Pester and Corporal Dorans received the D.C.M.; Serjeant-Major Cairns and Serjeant Thornborrow the M.M.; and Serjeant Rothwell the B.E.M. Denny Sharp, Jim Harman, Lance-Corporal Foster, and Signalman White were all mentioned in despatches. "Donnelly" on my strong recommendation was restored to the rank of Captain. As for "Forsyth,"

---

* See Note P.

he received the important appointment of Wine Waiter (Class III) in the Officers' Mess of the Burma Rifles.

The following year, 1944, we had our revenge; and among those who came with me were John Fraser, Jim Harman, Bill Smyly, George Astell, Chit Khin, Peter Dorans and San Shwe Htoo.

. . . .

What did we accomplish? Not much that was tangible. What there was became distorted in the glare of publicity soon after our return. We blew up bits of a railway, which did not take long to repair; we gathered some useful intelligence; we distracted the Japanese from some minor operations, and possibly from some bigger ones; we killed a few hundreds of an enemy which numbers eighty millions; we proved that it was feasible to maintain a force by supply dropping alone.

But we amassed experience on which a future has already begun to build. The very fact that our weary parties trudged out all round the clock, from Mike Calvert (that incomparable fighting man, on whom Wingate's spiritual cloak has fallen) far down the Chindwin, through Peter Buchanan at Fort Hertz, to Ken Gilkes in China, amassed for us a wealth of knowledge which has since been put to good account. Wingate went home and to the States; he captured the imagination of Mr. Churchill and of President Roosevelt; and it was thanks to them that in 1944 his force entered Burma, not with forlorn parties as in 1943, but with the best backing that the ingenuity of man could devise. Every brigade except one was flown in, constituting an operation that the world admired and applauded; and it was just my luck that mine was the one which had still to walk. It was a great campaign; and surely posterity will not grudge to the memory of the great leader and military genius, who fashioned us, the honour that should be his if his teaching and spirit survive.

Perhaps in these pages he may appear as something of an ogre. He was, indeed, a fearsome man to cross ; he had only one standard, and that was perfection. He seemed almost to rejoice in making enemies, and in erecting additional barriers through which to break. By some, chiefly journalists, he has been idealised; by others, chiefly professional rivals, he has been decried. His was a complex character, but two things are sure. First, he was a military genius of a grandeur and stature seen not more than once or twice in a century. Secondly, no other officer I have heard of could have dreamed the dream, planned the plan, obtained, trained, inspired and led the force. There are men who shine at planning, or at training, or at leading: here was a man who excelled at all three, and whose vision at the council-table matched his genius in the field.

While his spirit must be crystallised, his ideas must be fertilised; not put in a glass case, but grown, and crossed with other seedlings of comparable merit. His was not a static mind that evolved a thought and placed it reverently in a *Hortus Siccus*; he was for ever growing, and grafting, and crossing, and always far from satisfied. It is not his teaching of 1942, or 1943, or 1944 that has the ultimate merit. It is for us who had the benefit of his vast mind to pursue the ideas which he threw off whither he would have pursued them. His was a voice in the mist, calling back to us the discoveries which he was making, and urging us to follow him. Now he is gone farther into the mist than we can probe; yet, to keep faith with him, we must follow, spurning the pedestrian ways of commonplace thought, and trying to see the path along which he would have led us had he still been within hail. Such is our duty and the honour which we owe him.

And posterity must honour not only him, but all those, many of them with names not widely remembered, who like him sacrificed their life or their liberty to make possible the future in which he believed.

APPENDIX A

Major Bernard E. Fergusson, The Black Watch, Column Commander.

Captain John C. Fraser, Burma Rifles, Second-in-Command, and Commander, Detachment Burma Rifles.

Lieut. Duncan C. Menzies, The Black Watch, Column Adjutant.

Captain Alec I. Macdonald, The King's Regiment, Administrative Officer.

Captain Tommy C. Roberts, The King's Regiment, Commander, Support Group.

Captain Bill S. Aird, R.A.M.C., Medical Officer.

Flight-Lieut. Denny J. T. Sharp, Royal Air Force.

Lieut. John M. Kerr, Welch Regiment, Platoon Commander.

Lieut. Philippe G. Stibbé, Royal Sussex Regiment, Platoon Commander.

Lieut. Gerry Roberts, Welch Regiment, Platoon Commander.

Lieut. Tommy Blow, 14th Punjabis, Indian Army, Attached Officer, subsequently Platoon Commander.

Lieut. Bill Edge, South Wales Borderers, Cipher Officer.

Lieut. Willy Williamson, The King's Regiment, Commander, Machine-Gun Section, Support Group.

Lieut. Jim B. Harman, Gloster Regiment, Commander, Commando Platoon.

Lieut. David Whitehead, Royal Engineers, Commando Platoon.

Lieut. P.A.M. (Pam) Heald, Burma Rifles, Second-in-Command, Detachment Burma Rifles.

2nd Lieut. Bill Smyly, 3/2nd Gurkha Rifles, Animal Transport Officer.

Subedar Ba Than, Burma Rifles.

Jemadar Aung Pe, Burma Rifles.

Company Serjeant-Major J. Cairns, King's Own Scottish Borders, attached The King's Regiment.

Lieut. J. A. C. Carbonell, Cameron Highlanders, Air Base.

APPENDIX B

Commander: Brigadier O. C. Wingate, D.S.O., late Royal Artillery.

Brigade Major: Major G. M. Anderson, Highland Light Infantry.

Staff Captain: Capt. H. J. Lord, Border Regiment.

No. 1 Group

Commander: Lieut.-Colonel Alexander, 3/2nd Gurkha Rifles.

Adjutant: Capt. Birtwhistle, 3/2nd Gurkha Rifles.

No. 1 Column: Major G. Dunlop, M.C., Royal Scots.

No. 2 Column: Major A. Emmett, 3/2nd Gurkha Rifles.

No. 3 Column: Major J. M. Calvert, Royal Engineers.

No. 4 Column: Major R. B. G. Bromhead, Royal Berkshire Regiment.

No. 2 Group

Commander: Lieut.-Colonel S. A. Cooke, The Lincolnshire Regiment, attached the King's Regiment.

Adjutant: Capt. D. Hastings, The King's Regiment.

No. 5 Column: Major B. E. Fergusson, The Black Watch.

No. 7 Column: Major K. D. Gilkes, The King's Regiment.

No. 8 Column: Major W. P. Scott, The King's Regiment.

2nd Bn. The Burma Rifles

Commander: Lieut.-Colonel L. G. Wheeler, Burma Rifles.

Adjutant: Capt. P. C. Buchanan, Burma Rifles.

NOTES

THESE NOTES comprise information which became known to us only after the campaign was over. The reader who wishes his knowledge throughout the narrative to be exactly the same as ours was, and neither more nor less, should not read the notes until he has finished the book.

Note A—Chapter III, Page 42.—Lieut. G. H. Borrow.
Lieutenant George Borrow, The Royal Sussex Regiment, attached The King's Liverpool Regiment, came out of Burma with No. 8 Column, and was awarded the Military Cross for his gallantry in the campaign. He had jaundice when the Brigade entered Burma, but refused to be left behind; and although he suffered from constant ill-health the whole time, he set such a magnificent example as to inspire everybody who saw him, by the way in which he endured the hardships, intensified in his case by physical weakness. He collapsed just after crossing the Chindwin on the way out.

He became A.D.C. to General Wingate for the campaign of 1944, and was killed with him in the fatal aircrash of 24th March.

Note B—Chapter V, page 76—The Loss of the Mail.
Brigadier Wingate appreciated that it would take the Japs three days to translate and make deductions from the captured mail-bags. Long after the campaign, we had information that this forecast was almost exactly right. Within three days they knew the composition of the brigade and the numbers of the columns. How much later they pieced together other details I do not know; but it was in January, 1944, that I had the pleasure of seeing a captured document with the names of all the column commanders in Japanese characters. Mine looked rather pretty.

Note C—Chapter VI, page 84.—Milestone 20, Road Bramauk-Indaw.
This old dream was realised at midnight on the 26th-27th March, 1944, by a column which I sent there for that specific purpose. The site proved not to be quite as good as the map led one to believe; the bank between the road and the river was not so steep as I had thought, and the road could not be clearly seen from the lip of the hill.

The battle group of the column reached M.S. 20 on the evening of the 23rd, and while the column commander was carrying out his reconnaissance a convoy of sixteen vehicles went past. The column remained in position all the 24th and 25th; but saw nothing more tempting than single cars or lorries, which went through each evening at about 7 p.m.

On the afternoon of the 26th I wirelessed them to say that they must come away next morning, whether or not they had caught anything. That night, nothing came past at all until midnight, when a convoy of six lorry-loads of troops came into the trap. The ambush was sprung; all the lorries but one were knocked out, and in the subsequent fighting about thirty Japanese were killed, for the loss of one officer and four other ranks on our side. The enemy made no further attempt to use the road for at least a month; and when I flew over it on the 25th April, the wrecked lorries were still lying in the middle of the road.

Note D—Chapter VIII, page 101.—No. 4 Column.
4 Column was forced to disperse in a short, sharp engagement on the 3rd or 4th of March. The greater part of its personnel and animals reached India in safety, towards the end of the month.

Note E—Chapter VIII, page 103.—The Missing Men of Captain Roberts's party.
These men, having lost touch with Captain Roberts in the action, went back through the jungle to where the column had been bivouacked, just off the Tatlwin road, taking with them a wounded Gurkha. They hoped to find the main body of the column still there. They waited there an hour, during which time the Gurkha died. Had they waited an hour longer, they would have been found there by Captain Roberts, who suspected that they might have gone there, and went to see.

Finally, under their two N.C.O.s, Serjeant Scott and Serjeant McNulty, they set out for the Chindwin, having two compasses but no maps. They had with them, however, the Burma rifleman missing from Lieut. Heald's section, who proved exceedingly useful at foraging and procuring guides. They followed the general line by which we had come, using the "Secret Track" over the escarpment; the Burma rifleman was killed in one brush, but the remainder reached safety early in April.

Note F—Chapter IX, pages 122 and 131.—No. 2 Column.
Major Emmett and the greater part of his column were reaching India just about the time when I saw Lieut.-Colonel Alexander.

The adventures of Captain George Carne and Lieut. Charles Bruce, both of the Burma Rifles attached to No. 1 Group, are worth recording. Charlie Bruce had been sent on ahead, before No. 2 Column got into trouble, to seize a village on the Irrawaddy, and capture all its boats. He occupied the village with six Burma riflemen, and held it for some days before he heard from local gossip what had happened to No. 2 Column.

During his stay in the village, he disarmed the local police, who had been armed by the Japs; sank with Tommy-gun fire a boatload of Japs, whom he dispatched; and made a remarkable propaganda speech. He had just said, "I can call great Air Forces from India at will," and thrown his arm in the air with an extravagant gesture, when he suddenly heard, far away behind him in the west, the droning of air-craft. He remained with his arm in the air, like Moses when he was dealing with the Amalekites; and six British bombers flew slowly over his head, in the direction of Mandalay. "What did I tell you?" said Charlie, recovering himself. From then on he was a made man.

Hearing at last that his column had been ambushed he joined up with Captain Carne. They crossed the Irrawaddy; it was they who occupied the Rest House at Yingwin when 5 Column was at Pegon. After many exciting adventures, they arrived in India, early in April. Both received the Military Cross.

Note G—Chapter IX, page 132.—No. 1 Group.

No. 1 Group Headquarters and No. 1 Column, having executed a remarkable march round Mogok and Mong Mit, and had some hard fighting, in the course of which Captain Wetherall was killed, began their return march to India. Towards the end of April they were ambushed. When last seen, Lieut.-Colonel Alexander had been severely wounded, and was being carried into shelter by Flight-Lieut. Edmunds and Lieut. De la Rue. Major Dunlop, M.C., and Lieut. Chet Khin each arrived in India at the head of separate parties. The latter was awarded the Military Cross.

Note H—Chapter X, page 134.—Supply Drop at Nam Pan.

After returning to India, we learned that the third aircraft, con-taining another four days' rations, had failed to take off owing to engine failure.

Note J—Chapter XI, page 163.—Lieut.-Colonel L. G. Wheeler, Burma Rifles.

Lieut.-Colonel Wheeler, an account of whose death will be found in Note L, was one of the best fellows who ever walked the earth, and would have made a splendid brigadier. He had been over twenty years in the Burma Army, and had built a house somewhere in the Shan States, to which he proposed eventually to retire. He had a great sense of humour, and was adored by his officers (who were all civilians from the big corporations in Burma, and not too enthusiastic by nature about Regular soldiers), and by his men. Many of the Riflemen knew him by name before ever they joined the army, since his was a name to conjure with in all the recruiting areas whence they came. He was one of those rare wits whose humour never palls, and John, Duncan and I often amused ourselves by inventing possible Wheeler comments on given situations. He was at his best that last day on which I saw him, when things were thoroughly sticky, but were having no effect whatever on his normal mood.

He received the rare distinction of a posthumous D.S.O.

Note K—Chapter XII, page 175.—Crossing of the Shweli River.

In April, 1944, when I was in Burma again within sixty miles of the Shweli, an escaped Gurkha arrived in my bivouac, who had been brought thither by friendly natives. He had been working on the railway as a member of a prisoners' of war gang; and had seized the chance of escape afforded by an air raid, which had sent all the Japanese guards to earth.

He had already said he was a member of my column, before his arrival was reported to me; and when I went to him he recognised me. He was one of those who had remained on the sandbank, and he gave an account of what happened after we left.

The Japs arrived just after first light, and fired a few rounds at the wretched men huddled on the sand, hitting one or two of them. An N.C.O. raised a white flag, consisting of a piece of parachute silk, on his rifle, on which they ceased fire, and motioned them to lay down their arms. One Jap then swam across, and collected the weapons in a heap. After a long delay, two boats were brought, and the prisoners ferried across to the bank, where British prisoners had their hands tied in front of them, and Gurkhas behind them. They were given an ample meal of rice, and asked in English where the rest of us had gone. Although they had every reason to feel bitterly towards us, and knew well that we had gone east, they all said we had gone south down the road. Three lorry-loads of Japs immediately set off in pursuit, but returned empty-handed after four hours.

The Gurkha gave a graphic description of the drowning of John Fraser, and admitted that it was that incident which took the heart out of the others. I was able to assure him, much to his surprise, that John Fraser was alive, and within a few miles of him at that moment.

Note L—Chapter XIV, page 187.—Lieut. D. C. Menzies.

On the 4th of April, the day after Duncan failed to return from his patrol, the Burma Rifle headquarters, about 100 strong, reached

Zibyugin and attacked it. The small number of Japanese in the village withdrew, and Jemadar Lader (now Captain Lader, B.G.M.) penetrated into the village. Here he found Duncan and Gilmartin, both dressed in Japanese clothes, with their beards shaved, and tied to trees. Gilmartin was dead, and Duncan dying. Both had been shot, when the Burrif attack came in. Duncan was still conscious, and told Colonel Wheeler and Peter Buchanan about the movements of No. 5 Column, and described how the bulk of the Japanese had left the village, presumably in search of my party.

He gave Wheeler his watch, to be sent to his parents if Wheeler reached India safely. Wheeler gave him some morphia but he was obviously near the end, and he died before the Burrifs left the village.

One minute after Wheeler gave him the morphia, he was himself killed by a stray bullet.

It has always seemed to me the saddest and strangest fate that Wheeler and Duncan, two of the finest men in the force, should both meet their end in this small and hitherto unknown village, unmarked on any map. They had the greatest admiration for each other, and Wheeler was much moved when he found Duncan in that condition. The news of Wheeler's own death spread through the Kachin Hills like wildfire, and he was widely mourned for the great figure and friend of the Kachins that he was.

Note M—Chapter XIV, page 191.

The total weight on the man when we first set out was about 72 lb.—half the weight of the average man, and more in proportion to a man's weight than the load carried by a mule. The Everest pack fitting alone weighed 6 lb.; seven days' rations 14 lb. Blankets and Bren guns were carried on mules. The man also carried rifle and bayonet, *dah* or *kukri*, three grenades, groundsheet, spare shirt and trousers, 4 spare pairs of socks, balaclava, jack-knife, rubber shoes, housewife, toggle-rope, canvas life-jacket, mess-tin, ration-bags, water bottle, *chagal* (canvas waterbottle) and many statutory odds and ends.

Note N—Chapter XV, page 219.—*The Adventure of the Missing Lance-Naik.*

In April, 1944, John Fraser came into my camp from a week's patrol in the hills, bringing with him the Lance-Naik. He had heard of John's presence in the area, and had come to join him. He told the following story of his adventures after leaving us on the track to Pinmadi, exactly a year before.

Less than five minutes after he had left us he had run into a patrol of twenty Japanese coming up the hill in pursuit. How they had got on to our trail so quickly he did not know. With them was a Burmese guide, who searched him and found the two hundred rupees we had given him, which he pocketed. Through the Burmese, as interpreter, they asked him our strength. He had the presence of mind to exaggerate it greatly, and the Japs apparently decided that they had insufficient men, and turned back for more. With their enhanced force, they then followed up the track to Pinmadi, and were presumably the patrol which we were told about at Kumsai the following day.

It is more than likely that the nervousness of the villagers of Pinmadi on our arrival, was due to their having seen the Jap patrol coming up the path. Only thus can I account for their un-Kachin-like reception of us.

Note O—Chapter XVI, page 226.—Skirmish near Nanhkin.
I was in the neighbourhood of Nanhkin in March, 1944, and made inquiries about the fate of the two men. The villagers whom I questioned confirmed that two Japs had been killed; they had no knowledge of any British being killed, but said they believed that two wounded British had been taken prisoner. I was unfortunately in too much of a hurry to go to Nanhkin itself, where I might have been able to get more accurate information.

Note P—Epilogue, page 240.
The reader will wonder what happened to the other officers and men mentioned by name, whose fate is not apparent from the narrative. The following arrived in India, by one route or another:—Lt. Gillow, Capt. Griffith, Capt. Herring, L/Cpl. Horton, Jemadar Lader, Lt. Pearce, F/Lt. Thompson.

Over 65 per cent of the force got out safely.

Note Q.—
When Rangoon was recaptured in May 1945, twenty-seven members of No. 5 Column were recovered, either in the jail or on the march. All those fit to walk were being moved eastward, but their Japanese escort turned them loose after a few days' marching. All had suffered appalling hardships while in jail, and many had died before they ever reached Rangoon. The officers had made shift to piece together the stories of the various inmates of the prison, and they estimated that in all a hundred and forty members of the Column had been picked up. Of these, only twenty-eight survived, the twenty-eighth being Tommy Roberts, who was found in Singapore. No. 5 Column went into Burma 318 strong; 95 got back to India; these, with the 28 survivors of captivity, make up 123 survivors in all.

Of the five missing officers, all except Bill Aird turned up. He reached the Chindwin with a party of sick and sorry, and was caught by the Japs on its bank; he died a few days later on the way to Rangoon.

I preserve as treasured possessions the letters from the other four in which they reported to me their various adventures and eventual liberation. Of the four men left with John Kerr, at Kyaik-in, two died on the spot; Corporal Dale, recovering a little, crawled away into the jungle, where he was found and murdered by Burmese within earshot of John; the fourth died on the way to Rangoon. John was put to torture to divulge my plans, but managed to hold out until it no longer mattered.

David Whitehead, in trying to join up with his platoon in the scrap at Hintha, lost touch with everybody, and set off westward on his own. He walked into a Jap patrol at ten yards range, but gave it the slip; dodged two others, and finally got across the Irrawaddy. He managed to find a guide in the Kunbaung Valley; but he proved to be a wrong 'un, who led David into an ambush and then darted away, leaving David a prisoner with seven bullet-holes in his body and five in his clothes.

Tommy Roberts did splendidly, as I expected. He found the crossing area hotching with Japs, but managed to pass over several small parties, such as Bill Edge's. He himself, after several false starts, got across himself some twenty miles farther upstream, with a corporal and six men, paddling a raft of his own making. Five days later they ran into an ambush at 10.30 a.m. They managed to get into a good position, got their packs off, and settled down to fight back. At 2 p.m., having had two men killed and four wounded, their ammunition was finished; and when, an hour later, the Japs came in with the bayonet from thirty yards, Tommy ordered his men to sit tight, and himself stood up and surrendered them. The Japs numbered two officers and thirty-four other ranks, and of these seven were killed. Tommy himself was flown to Singapore for interrogation, and finished up on the notorious Siam railway.

Phil Stibbe has told his own story in *Return Via Rangoon*, and a fine tale it is. The Burma Rifleman proved, as we thought, to be Maung Tun. He was captured through the treachery of a Burmese from Hintha, with whom he was negotiating for food, and tortured to death by the Japanese for refusing to divulge Phil's hiding-place. Phil, despairing of his return, crawled to Hintha two days later and was made prisoner; it was there that he heard the tale of Maung Tun's martyrdom. Small wonder that he wrote afterwards: "As long as I live I shall have the feeling that my life is not my own, and the memory of Maung Tun will inspire me to the end of my days."

Serjeant Gunn was among those who died in prison; Brookes the Bugler and Bill Edmunds among those who survived.

INDEX